Generating Technological Innovation

The
Executive
Bookshelf

Sloan
Management
Review

Arnoldo C. Hax (Editor), *Planning Strategies That Work*

Stuart E. Madnick (Editor), *The Strategic Use of Information Technology* (in press)

Edward B. Roberts (Editor), *Generating Technological Innovation*

Edgar H. Schein (Editor), *The Art of Managing Human Resources*

Generating Technological Innovation

Edited by

Edward B. Roberts

New York   Oxford
OXFORD UNIVERSITY PRESS
1987

Oxford University Press

Oxford New York Toronto
Delhi Bombay Calcutta Madras Karachi
Petaling Jaya Singapore Hong Kong Tokyo
Nairobi Dar es Salaam Cape Town
Melbourne Auckland

and associated companies in
Beirut Berlin Ibadan Nicosia

Published by Oxford University Press, Inc.,
200 Madison Avenue, New York, New York 10016

Oxford is a registered trademark of Oxford University Press.

Library of Congress Cataloging-in-Publication Data
Generating technological innovation.
(The Executive bookshelf)
A selection of articles from the Sloan management review.
Includes bibliographies and index. 1. Technological innovations—Management.
I. Roberts, Edward Baer. II. Sloan management review.
HD45.G39 1987   658.5'14   86-33119
ISBN 0-19-505023-1

9 8 7 6 5 4 3 2 1

Printed in the United States of America
on acid-free paper

Foreword

The Executive Bookshelf reflects the mission of the *Sloan Management Review*, which is to bridge the gap between the practicing manager and the management scholar. Based on real-world business concerns, *SMR* articles provide the practicing manager with state-of-the-art information on management theory and practice. These articles are of particular benefit to the executive who wants to stay abreast of some of the best research and analysis coming from top business schools.

This series draws together *SMR* articles that make significant contributions to the management fields they cover. Each book is edited by one of the Sloan School of Management's most respected professors in the field, and begins with the editor's introduction, which guides and broadens the reader's understanding of the subject at hand.

The great value of these collections lies in how the articles complement one another. The authors do not always agree, but each has something important to say. Consequently, when read in its entirety, each book will challenge the reader to think more carefully about specific management issues. The editors' selection of, and introduction to, the articles will help readers interpret the various perspectives that are presented.

The usefulness of this series is enhanced by the *Sloan Management Review*'s rigorous editorial standards. Articles must not only have a practical focus, but they must also be accessible to the reader. Before an article is accepted for publication, it must be reviewed and accepted by an independent referee. The combination of applicability, academic seriousness, and solid writing assures that the series is readable and authoritative. The language is nontechnical, with minimum discussion of research and methodology, and the authors are influential leaders in the field of management.

The qualities that make these books useful to managers also make them invaluable as assigned readings in academic executive development programs and in private sector management training. In addition, they are helpful to students needing practical information to complement the theoretical materials in standard textbooks.

On a broader scale, this series is an extension of the Alfred P. Sloan School of Management. As one of the leading business schools in the country, the Sloan School complements its educational programs with research intended to produce new and better solutions to management problems. The *Sloan Management Review* in general, and this series in particular, reflects this combined research and training orientation.

The *Review* has a tradition of facilitating communication between executives and academics, and this series is an exciting addition to that tradition. We hope that you share our enthusiasm and that these books help you to become increasingly challenged, informed, and successful.

Cambridge, Mass.   Abraham J. Siegel
March 1987   Dean, Alfred P. Sloan School
                          of Management
                          Massachusetts Institute of Technology

Preface

Generating Technological Innovation brings together for the first time some of the best and most influential articles that have appeared in the *Sloan Management Review*. The book is intended to provide practicing managers with a systematic range of ideas and applications in the increasingly important area of the management of technological innovation. Designed for easy reading and reference, the book should be equally valuable to specialists and nonspecialists alike.

The book goes to press at the same time as the MIT Management of Technology Program at the Sloan School of Management is about to celebrate its twenty-fifth anniversary. In 1962, when we started our effort—then called the MIT Research Program on the Management of Science and Technology and under the leadership of the late Donald G. Marquis—we saw many challenges but not many precedents that might guide us. No school of management in the 1960s had yet recognized the critical importance of learning and teaching how to manage research, development, and technology-based innovation. The research program was initiated as a result of a visionary request from James Webb, the administrator of the newly organized National Aeronautics and Space Administration. Julius Stratton, then president of MIT, and Howard Johnson, then dean of the Sloan School of Management, responded with enthusiasm and now, twenty-five years later, the program is stronger than ever.

Since the 1960s, we have seen the management of technology become universally recognized as the key element in international competitiveness in both military and commercial arenas, encompassing concerns for effective product and process design, development, and implementation. The need for thoughtful scholarship on the managerial issues involved in technology has become increasingly acknowledged and pursued by academics and far-sighted managers. The *Sloan Management Review,* founded just before our research program began, has been in an ideal position to encourage the publication and diffusion of new ideas in this emerging field, as exemplified by the articles included in this volume.

In selecting and arranging the articles, I have used my personal organizing paradigm for the critical dimensions of managing technology: staffing, structure, and strategy. These building blocks of managerial effectiveness constitute the three parts of the book. In the introductory chapter, I summarize the current state of technology management knowledge by searching for generalizations that apply to the field as a whole. The introduction also places in perspective the chapters that follow. The book's organization should permit ease of use both to practicing managers who seek alternative solutions to their current problems and to graduate students who are embarking on a career in one of the youngest and most promising fields today.

Cambridge, Mass.   E.B.R.
October 1986

Contents

Contributors

William J. Abernathy is deceased. He was the William Barclay Harding Professor of the Management of Technology at the Graduate School of Business, Harvard University. His last book was *Industrial Renaissance: Producing a Competitive Future for America,* coauthored with Alan M. Kantrow and Kim B. Clark.

Thomas J. Allen is Gordon Y Billard Fund Professor of Management at the Sloan School of Management, MIT. His professional interests include management of research and development, organizational communications, and technology transfer. He is also the author of articles on research performance and research program effectiveness.

Charles A. Berry is Marketing Director of Barr and Stroud, Ltd., a wholly owned subsidiary of Pilkington Brothers, plc. His professional interests focus on corporate development and diversification, including acquisition, corporate ventures, corporate venture capital, and corporate strategic planning.

Robert A. Burgelman is Associate Professor of Management at the Graduate School of Business, Stanford University. He is coauthor with Leonard R. Sayles of *Inside Corporate Innovation: Strategy, Structure, and Managerial Skills.*

Balaji S. Chakravarthy is Assistant Professor of Management at the Curtiss L. Carlson School of Management, the University of Minnesota. His professional interests include government initiatives, technological innovation, and the theory of adaptation.

C. Merle Crawford is Professor of Marketing at the University of Michigan, Graduate School of Business Administration. Dr. Crawford's professional interests center on marketing strategy and new product development.

Alan R. Fusfeld is Vice President and Director of the Technology Management Group of Pugh-Roberts Associates, Inc. He has written various articles in the area of technology management.

David H. Gobeli is Assistant Professor of Management at the Oregon State University College of Business. He is also Director of the Technology Management Research Program, Chairman of the Technology Transfer Committee, and Director of the Small Business Institute Program. Dr. Gobeli has six patents and has worked as a consultant with several high-technology businesses on such issues as patents, marketing strategies, strategic planning, and project management.

Robert H. Hayes is Professor of Business Administration at the Graduate School of Business Administration, Harvard University. He has consulted widely on issues of manufacturing strategy.

Mel Horwitch is Associate Professor of Management at the Sloan School of Management, MIT. His professional interests include corporate strategy, management of technology and technology strategy, energy policy, and business history.

Modesto A. Maidique is Professor of Management at the University of Miami, Florida, and Director of the Innovation and Entrepreneurship Institute. Dr. Maidique has published widely on the subjects of innovation and technology.

C. K. Prahalad is Associate Professor of Policy and Control at the University of Michigan, Graduate School of Business Administration. His teaching, research, and consulting interests lie in the area of strategic management and control in large, complex organizations. He is the coauthor of *Financial Management of Health Institutions* and *The Management of Health Care.*

James Brian Quinn is the William and Josephine Buchanan Professor of Management at the Amos Tuck School of Business Administration, Dartmouth College. He is a well-known lecturer and consultant to major U.S. and foreign corporations, the U.S. Congress, the State Department, and foreign nations. Dr. Quinn has written widely on corporate and national policy questions, particularly in the technological realm.

Edward B. Roberts is the David Sarnoff Professor of Management of Technology and Director of the MIT Management of Technology Program at the Sloan School of Management. He is also President of Pugh-Roberts Associates, Inc., and a General Partner at Zero Stage Capital Co. He is a consultant to numerous industrial corporations in the fields of strategic planning, organization design, and the management of technical innovation.

William Rudelius is Professor in the Marketing Department of the School of Management at the University of Minnesota. His current fields of interest include managerial decision making, marketing research, household energy savings, the management of technology, and marketing forecasting, planning, and strategy.

Hans J. Thamhain is Associate Professor at Worcester Polytechnic Institute, Worcester, Massachusetts. He has published widely on the subjects of program management, team building, conflict management, and leadership.

Eric A. von Hippel is Professor of Management at the Sloan School of Management, MIT. His professional interests include management of the product innovation process and examination of R&D cooperation among competing innovators.

David L. Wilemon is Professor of Marketing and Director of the Innovation Management Program at the Graduate School of Management, Syracuse University. He has published widely in the area of management.

Generating Technological Innovation

Introduction:

Managing Technological Innovation— A Search for Generalizations

Edward B. Roberts

The management of technological innovation is the organization and direction of human and capital resources toward effectively (1) creating new knowledge; (2) generating technical ideas aimed at new and enhanced products, manufacturing processes, and services; (3) developing those ideas into working prototypes; and (4) transferring them into manufacturing, distribution, and use. Technologically innovative outcomes take many forms: incremental or radical in degree; modifications of existing entities or entirely new entities; embodied in products, processes, or services; oriented toward consumer, industrial, or governmental use; based on various single or multiple technologies. Despite obvious variations in managerial issues, across these differences in intended outcomes and settings, a number of consistent generalizations emerge from over twenty years of systematic managerial research. This introduction seeks to identify those generalizations (shown below in italics), and this book aims at providing more depth, detail, and illustration of them.

The first generalization is *innovation = invention + exploitation*. The invention process covers all efforts aimed at creating new ideas and getting them to work. The exploitation process includes all stages of commercial development, application, and transfer, including the focusing of ideas or inventions toward specific objectives, evaluating those objectives, downstream transfer of research and/or development results, and the eventual broad-based utilization, dissemination, and diffusion of the technology-based outcomes.

Invention is marked by discovery or a state of new existence, usually at the lab or bench. Innovation is marked by first use, in manufacturing or in a market. This distinction is critical, because for too many years related research writings and even managerial practice have focused only on managing "creativity," with relatively too much attention devoted to the lives of great inventors or famous scientists and their radical breakthroughs. Yet most organized scientific and engineering activity, certainly within the corporation, is beyond this idea-generating stage and produces not radical breakthroughs, but rather a broad base of incremental technological advance, sometimes leading cumulatively over time to major technical change.

The next two generalizations about technological innovation are portrayed in Figure I.1, a process view of how technological innovation occurs. First, *technological innovation is a multistage process, with significant variations in the primary task as well as in the managerial issues and effective management practice occurring among these stages.* Figure I.1 presents six stages, but the precise number and their division are somewhat arbitrary. (Chapter 1, for example, also presents a six-stage innovation process, but the stages are different!) What is key is that each phase of activity is dominated by the search for answers to different managerial questions.

At the outset, for example, emphasis is on finding a motivating idea, a notion of possible direction for technical endeavor. Coming up with one or more technical and/or market goals that stimulate initiating a research, development, and/or engineering (RD&E) project is the task undertaken during stage 1. The relevant managerial question for this stage is, How do more and better targets get generated? Which people, which structures, which strategies can be employed toward more effective idea generation for these objectives? Good managerial practice at this stage frequently involves loose control, "letting many flowers bloom," fostering conflict or at least contentiousness, stimulating variety of inputs. At a later stage, the stage 5 commercial development as an alternative example, the task involves in-depth specification and manufacturing engineering of ideas that have by now already been reduced to an acceptable working prototype. The managerial issues in this stage involve coordinating a number of engineers of different disciplinary backgrounds toward achieving, within previously estimated development budget and schedule, a predefined technical output ready for manufacture in large volume, reliably, and at competitive production costs. Effective managerial practice in this stage might well involve tight control, strong financial criteria for resource use, single-minded adherence to plan, especially in regard to those resources—in many ways the opposite of what is encountered in stage 1.

The next generalization embodied in Figure I.1 is that *innovation occurs through technical efforts carried out within an internal organizational context, but involving heavy interaction with the external technological as well as market environment.* Proactive search for technical and market inputs, as well as receptivity to information sensed from external sources, are critical aspects of technology-based innovation. All studies of effective innovations have shown significant contributions of external technology and awareness of customer needs and competitor activity.

The details of Figure I.1 specify a set of key flows and decision points that occur during the process of innovating. A number of major managerial elements that are embodied in those details will be treated in the discussion that follows. Two aspects of the diagram, however, are potentially misleading and deserve immediate mention. First, for ease of presentation, all stages are shown at equidistant intervals, inappropriately suggesting perhaps the similarity of these phases from a time duration and/or resource consumption perspective. This is by no means true. In particular, stage 5, commercial development, usually takes as long as the several earlier stages combined and requires more resources than most of the other stages together. Second, for simplicity sake no feedbacks are pictured in Figure I.1 from later stages back to earlier ones. Yet, inevitably, these feedbacks exist and cause reiteration to occur among the stages. For example, involvement in the problem-solving process, stage 3, generates new insights as to alternative idea formulations, stage 2; and efforts at transfer into manufacturing as part of technology utilization, stage 6, often create new requirements for problem-solving, stage 3. Thus the real process of technological innovation involves flows back and forth over time among differing primary activities, internal and external to the dominant innovating organization, with major variations in tasks, managerial issues, and managerial answers.

Three dimensions provide a framework for synopsis of factors affecting successful innovation: staffing, structure, and strategy. These dimensions are the basis for organization of both this introductory chapter and of the entire book. For each dimension a number of managerial generalizations can be identified, supported by the research literature and the selected articles contained in this volume.

Staffing

Two primary questions arise in regard to staffing the technological organization: What kinds of people need to be involved for effective technical development? And what managerial actions can be taken to maximize their overall productivity? In regard to people requirements, as explained by Roberts and Fusfeld (1981) in Chapter 1, *a number of "critical behavioral roles," not just technical skills, must be practiced by the people involved in a technical development.* Roberts and Fusfeld identify five key roles for achieving successful innovation, although others have since added to this list (e.g., Maidique in Chapter 2 argues for six key roles).

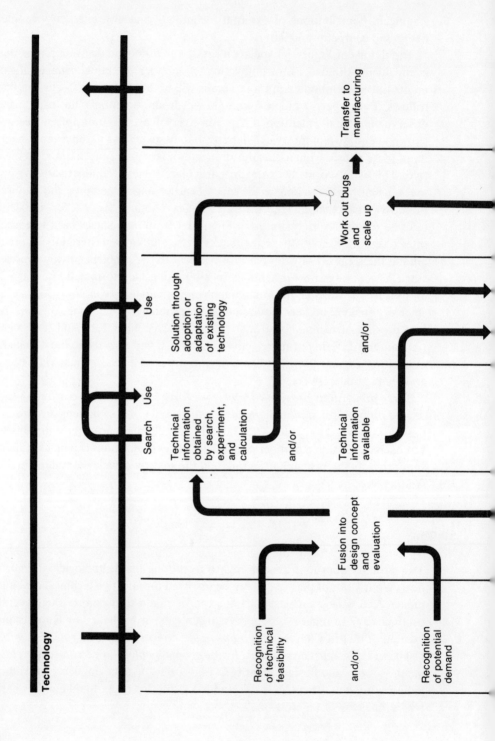

Technology

Recognition of technical feasibility

and/or

Recognition of potential demand

Fusion into design concept and evaluation

Search   Use

Technical information obtained by search, experiment, and calculation

and/or

Technical information available

Use

Solution through adoption or adaptation of existing technology

and/or

Work out bugs and scale up

Transfer to manufacturing

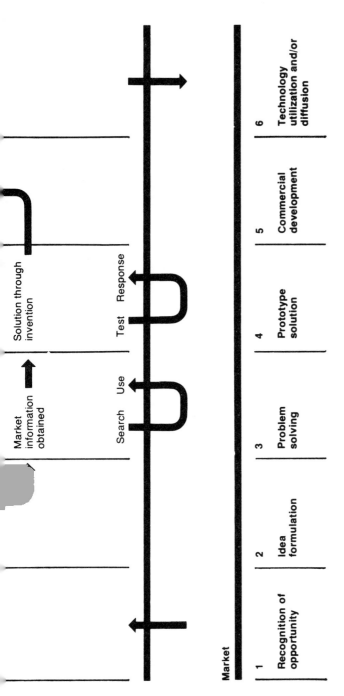

Figure I.1 The Process of Technological Innovation. (Reprinted with permission from E. B. Roberts and A. L. Frohman, "Strategies for Improving Research Utilization," *Technology Review*, March–April 1978.)

Critical Innovation Roles

First are *idea generators,* the creative contributors of new insights that both initiate projects and contribute to problem solutions throughout technical projects (Pelz and Andrews, 1976; Andrews, 1981). Ideas can be drawn from the
"market pull" of sensing real or potential customer needs or demands, or
from the "technological push" of envisioning the possible extension of technological performance of a material, component, or system. Ideas include not
just those that lead to project initiation, but also the many throughout an innovation-seeking endeavor that contribute importantly toward invention or innovation outcomes. Thus idea generators for technical projects may be scientists
or engineers, sales or marketing persons, or even managers!

But many studies have pointed out significant differences between "idea-
havers" and "idea-exploiters"—those who come up with ideas, and those who
do something with the ideas they have generated (Peters and Roberts, 1969;
Roberts and Peters, 1981). The generally low rate of energetic pursuit of
newly created RD&E ideas mandates the requirement for the second key role
in technical innovation-seeking activities, that of the *entrepreneur or product
champion.* Entrepreneurs advocate and push for change and innovation. They
take ideas, whether their own or others, and attempt to get them supported
and adopted. The entrepreneurial "role" is the same, whether carried out internally in existing organizations or "externally" in their own newly founded
companies (Roberts, 1968). But the mode of behavior and what is needed for
"internal" vs. "external" entrepreneurial success may well be different, as expanded by Maidique (1980) in Chapter 2.

A third required role in effective innovative activities is the *program manager or leader,* sometimes strangely called the "business innovator," supplying
the support functions of planning, scheduling, monitoring and control, technical supervision, and business and financial coordination relating to R&D
(Marquis and Rubin, 1966). This is the one "role" that is also usually an assigned job in the organization, the other roles being incidental to the specific
work assignment. Some of the major issues involved in effective handling of
this role/job are described in Chapter 3 (Thamhain and Wilemon, 1977).

Gatekeepers, or special communicators, are the fourth critical role identified, the link-pins who frequently bring information messages from sources
outside of a project group into that group (Allen, 1977). These human bridges
join technical, market, and manufacturing sources of information to the potential technical users of that information. Gatekeepers may bridge one technical
group to another within the same company, or may link university research activities to a corporate advanced technology center, or may tie customer concerns into a supplier's design team.

The final key role is that of the *sponsor or coach,* performed usually by a more senior person who is neither carrying out the R&D itself nor is directly and personally aggressively championing the change. The role is one of providing encouragement, psychic support, facilitation to the more junior people involved in the task implementation, often including important help in "bootlegging" the resources needed by those trying to move technological advances forward in an organization (Roberts, 1968).

These several critical roles are all needed within or in close contact with each internal working group in order for it to achieve the goals of an innovative outcome. But in addition the effective development and maintenance of a technical organization requires recognition of these differentiated roles in order to create and implement appropriate people-management processes, including recruiting, job assignment, training, performance measurement, and rewards.

Individual and Organizational Productivity

Beyond the managerial issues relating to the people and role behaviors needed for effective staffing are those that affect staff productivity. *Stages of a scientist's or engineer's career, and the composition of his/her immediate work group are primary influences upon technical productivity.* This generalization rests upon a broad foundation of research into the performance of technical people and project groups. Katz (1982) has demonstrated that technical professionals evolve through three career stages that he labels socialization, innovation, and stabilization. As with the different stages of a project cycle, *each stage of an individual's career provides a new set of managerial challenges for maximizing personal productivity.* The setting of work norms, providing task direction, and joining new employees into the internal technical communications network are managerial issues confronted during the socialization or job "break-in" stage. In contrast, maintaining the employee's earlier motivation and renewing technical skills are among the very different questions needing treatment in the stabilization or job-maturity phase.

But personal and group productivity are not just influenced by the individual's job cycle. *The nature of the immediate work group, its composition and supervision, matter greatly.* In general, what Kuhn (1963) called *"creative tensions,"* a mix of comfort-reinforcing stability and conflicting challenge, seems desirable. For example, *multidimensional diversity* among technical colleagues in a project team heightens technical performance (Pelz and Andrews, 1976). Variations in age, technical background, even personal values, correlate with enhanced group productivity. This need for internal challenge is further reflected in the findings that the *average tenure of a group's working life* significantly impacts upon its technical productivity (Katz and Allen, 1982). The long-term stable technical group apparently becomes too secure, diminishes its outside technical contacts, and decreases its performance. Supervisory intervention at the technical group or RD&E project level, however, seems able to affect this performance. For example, *technical skills of the first-level group leader,* and not human-relations skills, enhance group effectiveness (Farris, 1973). And even the stable technical team can be moved to high-performing status with proper leadership, in this case requiring strong direction and control by the project manager (Katz and Allen, 1985). The analysis presented in Chapter 3 (Thamhain and Wilemon, 1977) supports the importance of the project manager's technical expertise and reliance upon work challenge as major sources of effective technical performance.

Structure

The design of organization structures that will enhance technological innovation requires focusing on both the organization's inputs and its outputs. Effective RD&E organizations need appropriate technical and market information inputs, and their outputs need to be integrated toward mission objectives and transferred downstream toward their ultimate users.

Market Inputs

Managerial research has repeatedly demonstrated that *60 to 80 percent of successful technical innovations seem to have been initiated by activities responsive to "market pull,"* i.e., forces reflecting orientation to perceived need or demand (Utterback, 1974; Gerstenfeld, 1976; Rothwell et al., 1974). The studies less frequently indicate how technical organizations uncover these needs. As mentioned in Chapter 1, *market "gatekeepers" frequently aid the technical organization to understand better its customers' requirements, priorities, and preferences.* Organizing to gain meaningful market inputs for research and engineering use may depend upon explicit assignments of such responsibilities to cooperating marketing staff or to RD&E people themselves. *The product development cycle should be organized,* as suggested in Figure I.1, *to bring market inputs into design repeatedly* during the early product specification stage and again during prototyping through active involvement of selected customers. Depending on the company and industry, the manufacturing organization of the developing company is anywhere from one- to two-thirds of those eventual "customers." Manufacturing will (or won't!) "buy" the developed improvement in materials, components, manufacturing equipment, or overall production process for its own internal "consumption." That prospective "customer" needs at least the same degree of involvement with the design and development process as does an outside firm or individual.

Rather than seeking collaboration to provide market information to the RD&E process, many companies have substituted marketing-oriented control of RD&E. Organizational subordination of research and engineering to "product managers" (inevitably marketing or sales people) or tight budgetary control of RD&E by these units may force market-based criteria to dominate technical project selection. But this is usually accompanied by short-term quick-fix orientation, erosion of technical capability, and gradual destruction of product/process competitiveness. Analyses by Souder (1978) have demonstrated that *strong and positive relations between R&D and marketing organizations significantly improve the track record on new product introductions.* In my view this is *best achieved by welding partnerships among equals,* rather than by compliance from subordinates.

Market-research techniques have long been used to help define consumer preferences in new product designs (Urban and Hauser, 1980). These methods have been less helpful for developing industrial goods. Recently von Hippel (1986) has demonstrated that *potential industrial customers whose needs place them along the leading edge of technological demands can be used to specify detailed desired performance characteristics and features for as yet nonexisting products.* Urban has suggested that the R&D organization itself should include the staff capabilities to apply these new methodologies (1986).

Technical Inputs

For years managers have understood that professional depth in an organization was achieved by grouping people in their own area of specialization, with work assigned and performance supervised by a more accomplished person of the same specialization (Lawrence and Lorsch, 1967). This is called functional or discipline-based or specialty-oriented organization. It is the traditional organization structure of the craft guild and of the university. Multiple specialists working together interact comfortably, using the same general knowledge base, analytic skills and tools, and vocabulary. When technical people are organized in functional arrays, their natural interplay brings depth of specialized capabilities to bear on technical problems. Indeed, Marquis and Straight found that *technical groups organized in functional forms have the highest technical excellence* (1965).

But in any nontrivial technical field, the vast majority of applicable technical know-how exists outside of a performing technical organization. *For technical effectiveness even a strong functional team needs to draw upon the preexist-*

ing technical knowledge that is in the outside world, whether in the technical literature, in already developed products and processes, or in the minds of other technical professionals. For example, several studies point out that, for innovations eventually developed within a firm, about 60 percent of the sources of the initial technical ideas had outside origins (Utterback, 1974). In Chapter 4 Allen (1966) demonstrates the relative differences among channels for technical-information input to an organization, distinguishing what is readily accessed from what is used from what is used most effectively in coming up with high-rated problem solutions. His work as well as that of others (Myers and Marquis, 1969; Langrish et al., 1972) indicates the minor role played by the literature, especially in contributions to engineering and development, in contrast with personal contacts, experience, and training. At the end of his classic article, Allen suggests the possibility that *technological gatekeepers may be critical link-pins between a working technical group and outside information sources.*

One factor that inadvertently has significant effect on technical inputs to RD&E groups is the architectural layout of their work space. Early observations by Jack Morton, then vice-president of Semiconductor Research at Bell Laboratories, led to his concern for the physical separation between technical organizations that were intended to relate to each other (1971). Research at MIT by Muller-Thym in the early 1960s empirically established spatial effects on the frequency of communication among engineers and scientists in the same laboratory. These concepts have been developed by Allen (1977) into careful findings on specific design elements of RD&E architecture. The distance between two potential communicators, vertical separation, walls, and other architectural features importantly influence technology flows.

Thus far we have addressed technical inputs in support of internal invention activities, the first element of the two-step innovation process we defined initially. What about postinvention technical inputs? Clearly technological solutions already exist elsewhere, and an innovating organization might merely adapt or adopt them by a slight modification for a new purpose. An early U.S. study determined that 22 percent of key innovations had been adopted or adapted (Myers and Marquis, 1969), while comparable U.K. data indicated a 33 percent adoption rate (Langrish et al., 1972). Japanese data on license fee payments for foreign technology show a long-established pattern of heavy use of outside technology. A small study of Taiwanese innovations found adoptions to have accounted for the bulk of successes (Gerstenfeld and Wortzel, 1977). While these specific percentages no doubt have changed in recent years, *adoption or adaptation or prior outside inventions is a major source of innovation worldwide.*

One unique source of adoptions is the user. In Chapter 5 von Hippel (1977) shows that *users frequently create and implement innovations for their own use, followed by later manufacturer adoptions of those innovations for large-scale production and distribution.* von Hippel's research on scientific instruments and several areas of manufacturing equipment demonstrates that heavy percentages of new products have been user-developed.

Technical organizations need to be designed to make these sources of information accessible, whether as contributions toward internal inventions or as sources for adoption more directly as innovations. A variety of approaches are suggested, ranging from such simple considerations as ensuring that salespeople have technical skills and/or incentives, so that they bring back a customer's ideas in addition to his orders. Much more ambitious are the IBM marketing department's several "applied science centers" across the United States, established near concentrations of innovative users to learn about new software and hardware developments and transfer that technical information back into IBM's product-development groups. IBM's Cambridge operation in Technology Square, working closely with MIT's pioneering Project MAC, thus became the source of IBM's first computer time-sharing system, a field adaptation of an innovative user's development. Increasingly corporations are establishing vice-presidents of technology, with broad responsibility for both internal technology development as well as external technology acquisition. Organizational experiments to enhance both technical and market information inputs are under way across a broad front.

Output-Focused Organization

Just as the functional organization structure maximizes technical inputs, the project, program, mission or product organization is intended to integrate all inputs toward well-defined outputs. By placing all contributors toward a given objective in the same group, under a single leader, *the project organization maximizes coordination and control toward achieving output goals.* The Marquis and Straight study (1965) cited earlier supports these findings. *But project structures have a fundamental flaw* that seriously affects many technical organizations. The project form tends to remove technical people from organizational groups in which they interact with colleagues of their own scientific or engineering discipline. Furthermore, the project manager may be technically expert, but only in one of the disciplines of his subordinates, not all of them. If the project is of long duration, especially when the technology base is rapidly changing, the *technical skills of the project members may erode over time,* due to lack of stimulating technical reinforcement and supervision.

This dilemma has led to the creation of a compromise organization—the "matrix" structure—in which technical performers are supposed to maintain active membership in two organizations: their original discipline-based functional group, and the focused project group. In theory the "matrixed" person thus has two bosses, one functional and one project, each of whom will extract his appropriate "due," thereby maintaining the technical skills and performance of the individual, to some extent, while orienting his loyalty and contributions toward the project's output goals, to some extent! Indeed, *most technical "matrix" organizations are only "paper" matrices, not "real" matrices.*

If one wanted to obtain truly matrixed individuals, the factors that influence their time and attention toward competing sets of objectives would have to be roughly balanced between those objectives. Those influences include: (1) the source of performance evaluation and reward distribution; (2) the source of individual task assignments; (3) the physical location of the individual relative to the two "competing" managers; (4) the longer-term career relevance of the competing groups; and (5) the relative persuasiveness (whether based on personality or power) of the two managers. Achieving such a balance would be practicable only by dominance of the functional manager on some of these influencing dimensions, dominance of the project manager on other dimensions, and perhaps rough equivalence of the two managers on still other influences upon matrixed persons. The absence of reasonable balance in most "paper matrixed" cases leads the actual situation to its "default" condition, with the achieved results reflecting the characteristics of the dominant organization form, either functional or project but seldom both. Recent studies suggest that certain patterns of dominance among these contending influence sources achieve better performance in matrix organizations (Katz and Allen, 1985).

Output Transfers

But in addition to generating outputs, the technical organization needs to be designed to enhance output transfer downstream toward eventual customers and users. Downstream is where innovation takes place and where benefits are realized! Studies of major research laboratories, among other RD&E organizations, have indicated high degree of dissatisfaction with the extent and effectiveness of transfer of results to potential recipient groups (Roberts, 1979; Roberts and Frohman, 1978). *Three different clusters of bridging approaches were found helpful in increasing transfer—procedural, human, and organizational.* Most organizations used a variety of these approaches, often several simultaneously. Roberts' findings have been supported by recent comparative case studies of IBM (Cohen et al., 1979) and Union Carbide (Smith et al., 1984), among others.

Procedural methods include joint planning of RD&E programs by performing and expected receiving organizations (often resisted by R&D as an "invasion" of its turf); joint staffing of projects, especially pre- and posttransfer downstream; and joint project appraisal after project completion, done cautiously if at all after failures in order to avoid destructive fingerpointing.

Human bridges are the most effective transfer mechanisms, especially the upstream and downstream transfers of people. Movement of people upstream (1) brings with them information on the context of intended project use; (2) establishes direct person-to-person contacts that will be helpful in later posttransfer troubleshooting; and (3) creates the image that the project eventually being transferred has involved prior ownership and priority inputs from the receiving unit. Later movement of people downstream: (1) carries expertise for posttransfer problem solving; and (2) not unimportant, conveys the risk-reducing impression that the receiving unit will not be stuck with solving posttransfer problems by itself. Other human bridges that are widely used include rotation programs, market gatekeepers, joint problem-solving sessions, and other formal and informal meetings.

Organizational techniques for enhancing transfer are complicated to design and implement and consequently are left as last in this discussion of alternatives. "Integrators," sometimes called "transfer managers," or integrating departments are frequently appointed to tie together the sending and receiving organizations. This person or unit is given the responsibility for moving the project from the sender into operating condition in the receiver organization, either lacking authority in one or the other organization or being matrixed between both.

More ambitious organizational approaches include dedicated transfer teams, established solely for the period during which technical results are being transferred to their "customers," done especially for moving purchased process technology. The "design and demonstration organization" described by Frontini and Richardson (1984) is another type of temporary organization, set up to show project feasibility at a scale beyond pilot plant level, to help reduce resistance to later full-scale implementation. In Chapter 6 Quinn (1979) discusses the organizational issues facing the major corporation seeking to create new businesses and suggests parallels between the individual entrepreneur's approaches and the means by which a large corporation can achieve growth and change. Quinn's article anticipates the multifaceted discussion of corporate entrepreneurship in Part III of this book.

Strategy

Strategic management of technology includes both strategic planning and strategic implementation aspects at either of two levels: (1) overall, for the entire technology-dependent firm, government agency, division or product line; or

(2) more focused, for just the technology development/acquisition process/department/laboratory of the entire organization. As recently as ten years ago, neither of these levels of strategy was the subject of much serious scholarship, or even of management-consulting practice. Few researchers carefully studied the overall management of the technology-intensive company. And fewer still addressed the questions of how to incorporate technological considerations into overall business strategy.

Strategic planning focuses upon the formulation of an organization's goals and objectives, and upon developing the policies needed to achieve those objectives, including identification of the organization's primary resources and priorities. But developing corporate strategy with such a global perspective, including technological dimensions, is quite new. Indeed, the evolution of corporate strategic planning as a field of practice is divisible into three decades: the 1960s, during which multiyear budget projections became the earliest forms of financial planning, sometimes labeled "long-range planning"; the 1970s, when market growth/share matrices and market attractiveness considerations added a new dimension to strategic analysis; and the 1980s during which technology as a strategic factor became so widely acknowledged as to cause firms and even countries to realize that financial, marketing, and technological considerations needed to be integrated in overall strategy development (Roberts, 1983).

Strategic Thinking and Planning

The strategy sections of this introduction and the book both begin by discussing some elements of overall strategic thinking involving technology, proceed into aspects of technology planning and strategy development, and end with discussing some options for implementation of technology strategies. Horwitch and Prahalad (1976) provide in Chapter 7 an early set of perspectives at the overall strategic level. They differentiate the key issues of technology-oriented strategic management among three modes: the small usually single-product high-tech firm; the large multimarket multiproduct corporation; and the multiorganization even multisector societal program. For each of these, Horwitch and Prahalad find a primarily nonoverlapping set of strategic issues and priorities. More recent writing has focused upon similarities between the first two "modes," the entrepreneurial smaller firm and the successfully innovative larger corporation (Quinn, 1979; Peters and Waterman, 1982; Maidique and Hayes, 1984; Friar and Horwitch, 1985; and Roberts, 1968). Their extensive observations lead Maidique and Hayes in Chapter 8 to conclude that to be innovative the large corporation needs to manage the "paradox" of chaos versus continuity, as the innovative technical person needs to manage creative tensions

(Kuhn, 1963; Pelz and Andrews, 1976). They advocate six broad managerial approaches for overall strategic technology management. It is important to note that Horwitch/Prahalad and Maidique/Hayes offer perspectives about what makes the first more innovative overall, not methods for formulating strategic plans.

In moving from strategic thinking toward strategic planning we need principles for developing more detailed technology strategies. But what are the underpinnings of technological change, especially as it relates to the corporation, upon which overall technology strategy should be based? Three general observations seem critical here, all linked to the dynamics of technological innovation processes: (1) *characteristic patterns occur over the life cycle of a technology in the frequency of product and process innovations;* (2) *each stage of a technology has differing critical implications for innovation, including type, cost, degree of invention, and source;* and (3) *organizational efforts to generate technological innovation create resource allocation dynamics with attendant multiple consequences.* Each of these will be discussed more fully below, with suggestions of related technology-planning and strategy-development approaches.

Utterback and Abernathy (1975) demonstrated that the evolution of a technology tends to follow a three-phase pattern. *Most technologies move from an early "fluid stage," dominated by frequent product innovations, through a "transition stage," characterized by significant process innovation and the emergence of a dominant product design, into a "specific stage," featuring lower rate of and more minor product and process innovations.* Variations in this pattern occur, of course, some of which are already well understood (Utterback 1980; Utterback and Kim, 1986), but this generalization becomes one important basis for developing a company's or a product line's technology strategy.

The potential stability or predictability of such patterns of technology evolution is the rationale for attempting to use technological forecasting techniques as part of technology planning and strategy development. Most technology-forecasting methods are simple and often inadequate for the task (Roberts, 1969; Fusfeld and Spital, 1980). Indeed, despite recent "rediscovery" of technology S-curves for forecasting and planning, the intellectual development of the field more or less stopped over a decade ago (Roberts, 1964; Martino, 1972). Yet some corporations have benefited enormously from thoughtful application of technology forecasting methods to their strategic analyses. Tracy O'Rourke, the chief executive officer of Allen-Bradley, for example, cites a comprehensive technology forecast as the basis for planning his company's successful transition from electromechanical to solid-state electronic devices (1986).

Each stage of a technology is associated with different strategic implications.

The earliest stage in a technology's life cycle tends to feature frequent major product innovations, heavily contributed by small entrepreneurial organizations, often closely tied to lead user needs. The intermediate stage of a technology may include major process innovation, with continuing product variation, with increasing numbers of competitors, both large and small. The late stage of a technology features less frequent minor product and process innovations, contributed primarily by large corporations, motivated mostly by cost-reduction and quality-improvement operational objectives (Utterback and Abernathy, 1975). These key dimensions of a technology should strongly influence choices made by a firm or government agency in developing its technological strategy. A company's detailing of Crawford's "product innovation charter" (Chapter 9), or its application of project-selection principles or techniques (Baker and Pound, 1964) as part of technology planning, ought to reflect at least general consideration of the current stages of its principal technologies. In particular, the late stage of one technology usually corresponds to earlier stages of other potentially threatening technologies. Most corporations fail to anticipate or even appropriately respond to these technological threats (Cooper and Schendel, 1976).

Technology life cycles occur in an industry as a whole, thus providing an "environmental" set of influences upon a single organization's strategy. A different kind of cycle, however, is produced within a firm by its own attempts to develop and commercially exploit technology. *As a major project moves downstream through research, design, development, production engineering, and field trouble shooting, resource acquisition and allocation decisions can cause major instability in overall performance, including the rate and character of new product releases and the resulting sales and profits* (Roberts, 1978; Weil, Bergan, and Roberts, 1978). For many small firms the resulting "boom then bust" often spells disaster. Similar though less evident problems arise at the product-line level of large corporations and government agencies. Self-induced cycles of primarily discovery followed by primarily exploitation seem to have plagued the growth years of Polaroid Corporation, almost causing its bankruptcy in the late 1970s. Large-scale and realistic computer-simulation models have been developed and increasingly employed in recent years for coping with this aspect of technology and overall organizational strategy development (Cooper, 1980).

While the computer-modeling methods described above are primarily strategic support tools, the technological forecasting and project-selection techniques that were mentioned principally enhance tactical and operational aspects of technology planning and management. Other approaches to technology planning have been developed and successfully applied at both the tactical and strategic levels. For example, in Chapter 9 Crawford (1980) elaborates his concept of a "product innovation charter," prescribing five major areas for inclusion in a formal strategy statement, with each of the five subdivided into finer categories. Crawford argues for taking into account the company's target business arenas, objectives of product innovation, specific program of activities, the degree of innovation sought, and any special conditions or restrictions on the strategy.

Another most impressive technique for technology planning is "competitive product profiling," in which an organization's product line is compared to its key competitors in terms of seven technology-based measures: functional performance; acquisition cost; ease-of-use; operating cost; reliability; serviceability; and system compatibility (Fusfeld, 1978). IBM adds "availability" to this list of competitive measures, making "reliability, availability, serviceability" (RAS) a critical element of its internal technology planning. Extending this approach to analysis of manufacturing processes has been attempted, but with less success, due to relative lack of competitive data. Fusfeld (1978) has tried to overcome this limitation and bring technology planning to the level of assessment of overall organizational capability. He uses in his analytical framework the "technology planning unit," the level of generic technology in the organization as it is being applied to a particular market opportunity, and tries to evaluate relative technical strength. Further developments of technology planning approaches, especially at the strategic level are needed and can be expected during the coming decade (Porter, 1985).

Strategic Implementation

But beyond strategic planning must come strategic implementation. Tactics and operations are the means of implementation of strategy. Not much has yet been written about specific implementations of technology strategies. At the national level Johnson (1984) concludes that, relative to American firms, Japanese industry has more heavily invested in applied rather than basic research, adopting and improving on preexisting products and technologies, in already well-developed market areas. He cites government policies in regard to patents, subsidies, and tax incentives as important in both countries. In his recent survey studies while at MIT Hirota (1985) has developed strong empirical evidences on U.S.-Japanese technology strategy differences, supporting but going beyond Johnson's observations. However, recent Japanese pioneering efforts in such areas as compact-disk technology and more advanced semiconductor memories suggest that Japanese R&D strategy may be in transition toward what had been a dominant U.S. approach.

Although now of increasing interest to nontechnical industries, *the development and use of so-called venture approaches have been a unique means for im-*

plementing overall strategies seeking accelerated technology-based new business development for growth and/or diversification. These venture approaches involve larger organizations in attempts to emulate or couple with smaller entrepreneurial units. The spectrum of possible strategic and organizational alternatives includes venture capital investments, sponsored spin-offs of new product development-commercialization groups, "new style joint ventures" that feature alliances between large and small companies, internal ventures, and integrated venture strategies (Roberts, 1980). A subject of active study and industrial practice off and on since the early 1960s, venture approaches have recently been increasingly attempted by companies and countries as part of their strategies for intensifying their technological base. *They require long-term persistence for effective implementation and dramatic differences in management style and policies from traditional mainstream approaches.*

The variety of venture alternatives for entering new businesses has raised issues as to means for selecting among them. Roberts and Berry (1985) have devised a research-based matrix reflecting primarily the organization's "familiarity" with the market and technology aspects of the new business. (See Chapter 10.) The Roberts/Berry framework, supported by a field test in a large diversified U.S. firm, concludes essentially that the further the new areas is from the firm's base "familiar" business, the less resource-intense the venture approach to be taken. Among the alternatives the internal-ventures choice represents a high degree of organizational commitment to growth and/or diversification and has received broad recent attention (Fast, 1979). The problems of implementing internal ventures primarily reflect their challenge of conventional effective means of managing (Roberts and Frohman, 1972). Burgelman's process model for internal venturing, developed from an intensive field study of a large diversified U.S. firm, reaffirms and adds significantly to these findings (1984; Chapter 11 in this volume).

With the exception of its brief mention in regard to U.S. and Japanese R&D investments, the role of government policies and actions in affecting technology strategy has been ignored thus far. Yet *government regulatory activities in regard especially to health and safety have had significant positive and negative influences on technological innovation* (Capron, 1971; Allen et al., 1978; Hauptman and Roberts, 1985). But, as pointed out by Abernathy and Chakravarthy (1979) in Chapter 12, *government's strategic role has also included actions to create technologies directly as well as indirectly through market modifications* (Utterback and Murray, 1977). In a sense the variety of alternatives facing governments for influencing technological change (Figure 5 of Chapter 12) are equivalent to the corporate venture alternatives described in Figure 7 of Chapter 10.

Conclusion

In Chapter 13 Gobeli and Rudelius (1985) provide a fitting finish to the book with an integrative comparative analysis of five firms in the technology-intensive cardiac-pacemaker industry. They observe the need to examine the multiple stages of the innovation process. They reaffirm the importance of key innovation-supporting people roles. They describe the importance of market-technology linkages, effective program management, government intervention, and appropriate goal-setting, planning, and risk-taking. As illustrated in this medical-electronics example, technological innovation can provide potential for altering the competitive status of firms and nations. It can contribute to increased corporate sales and profits, as well as individual and national security and well-being. But its purposeful management is complex, involving the effective integration of people, organizational processes, and plans.

This introduction has set forth generalizations about the management of technological innovation, each supported by literature, empirical research, and practitioner experience. But each of these is also subject to debate, modification, and even rejection as we learn more. Both academics and technology managers need to join in this continuing search for clearer insights and more effective performance.

PART I

Staffing

1

Staffing the Innovative Technology-Based Organization

Edward B. Roberts

Alan R. Fusfeld

In this article, the authors identify and describe five informal but critical behavioral functions needed for effective execution of technology-based innovative projects. They observe that some individuals are capable of performing concurrently more than one of these critical functions. They also find that a person's role in the innovation process may change over the course of his or her career. The authors discuss the managerial implications of their findings, particularly with respect to manpower planning, objective setting, and performance measurement and rewards. They then illustrate how an organizational assessment can be carried out. Finally, they discuss how critical functions concepts may be appropriate in other types of organizations. *SMR.*

This article examines the technology-based innovation process in terms of certain behavioral functions. These functions are usually informal, but they are critical. They can be the key to an effective organizational base for innovation. This approach to the innovation process is similar to that taken by early industrial theorists, such as Frederick W. Taylor, who focused on the production process. However, examination of how industry has organized its innovation tasks—those tasks needed for product or process development and for responses to nonroutine demands—indicates an absence of comparable theory. Many corporations' attempts to innovate consequently suffer from ineffective management and inadequately staffed organizations. Yet, through studies conducted largely in the last fifteen years, we now know much about the activities requisite to innovation. We also know much about the characteristics of the people who perform these activities most effectively.

From *Sloan Management Review*, Spring 1981, Vol. 22, No. 3. Reprinted with permission.

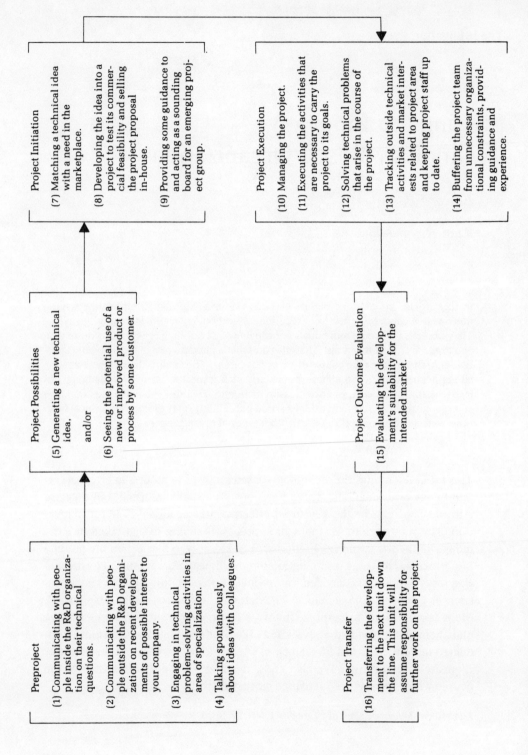

Preproject

(1) Communicating with people inside the R&D organization on their technical questions.

(2) Communicating with people outside the R&D organization on recent developments of possible interest to your company.

(3) Engaging in technical problem-solving activities in area of specialization.

(4) Talking spontaneously about ideas with colleagues.

Project Possibilities

(5) Generating a new technical idea,

and/or

(6) Seeing the potential use of a new or improved product or process by some customer.

Project Initiation

(7) Matching a technical idea with a need in the marketplace.

(8) Developing the idea into a project to test its commercial feasibility and selling the project proposal in-house.

(9) Providing some guidance to and acting as a sounding board for an emerging project group.

Project Transfer

(16) Transferring the development to the next unit down the line. This unit will assume responsibility for further work on the project.

Project Outcome Evaluation

(15) Evaluating the development's suitability for the intended market.

Project Execution

(10) Managing the project.

(11) Executing the activities that are necessary to carry the project to its goals.

(12) Solving technical problems that arise in the course of the project.

(13) Tracking outside technical activities and market interests related to project area and keeping project staff up to date.

(14) Buffering the project team from unnecessary organizational constraints, providing guidance and experience.

The Innovation Process

The major steps involved in the technology-based innovation process are shown in Figure 1.1. Although the project activities do not necessarily follow each other in a linear fashion, there is more or less clear demarcation among them. Each stage and its activities, moreover, requires a different mix of "people" skills and behaviors to be carried out effectively.

The figure portrays six stages in the typical technical innovation project. It also shows sixteen representative activities associated with innovative efforts. The six stages are identified as:

1. Preproject
2. Project possibilities
3. Project initiation
4. Project execution
5. Project outcome evaluation and
6. Project transfer

These stages often overlap and frequently recycle.[1] For example, problems or findings that are generated during project execution may cause a return to project initiation activities. Outcome evaluation can restart additional project execution efforts. And, of course, project cancellation can occur during any of these stages, thus redirecting technical endeavors back into the preproject phase.

A variety of different activities are undertaken during each of the six stages. Some of the activities, such as generating new technical ideas, arise in all innovation project stages, from preproject to project transfer. Our research studies and consulting efforts in dozens of companies and government labs, however, have shown other activities to be concentrated in specific stages, as discussed below.

Preproject. Before formal project activities are undertaken in a technical organization, considerable technical work is done, which provides a basis for later innovation efforts. Scientists, engineers, and marketing people find themselves involved in discussions that are internal and external to the organization. Ideas are discussed in rough-cut ways, and broad parameters of innovative interest are established. Technical personnel work on problem-solving efforts to advance their own areas of specialization. Our discussions with numerous indus-

---

Figure 1.1 (left)   A Multistage View of a Technical Innovation Project

trial firms in the U.S. and Europe suggest that from 30 to 60 percent of all technical effort is devoted to work outside of or prior to formal project initiation.

Project Possibilities.   Specific ideas for possible projects arise from the preproject activities. They may be technical concepts for developments that are assumed to be feasible. They may also be perceptions of possible customer interests in product or process changes. Customer-oriented perspectives may originate with technical, marketing, or managerial personnel, who develop these ideas out of their own imaginations or from direct contact with customers or competitors. Recent evidence indicates that many of these ideas enter as "proven" possibilities inasmuch as they have already been developed by the customers themselves.[2]

Project Initiation.   As ideas evolve through technical and marketing discussions and exploratory technical efforts, the innovation process moves into a more formal project initiation stage. Activities occurring during this phase include attempts to match the directions of technical work with perceived customer needs. (Of course, such customer needs may exist either in the production organization or in the product marketplace.) Inevitably, a specific project proposal is written, proposed budgets and schedules are produced, and informal pushing as well as formal presentations are undertaken in order to sell the project. A key input during this stage is the counseling and encouragement that senior technical professionals or lab and marketing management may provide to the emerging project team.

Project Execution.   When the project is approved formally, activities increase in intensity and focus. Usually, someone undertakes planning, leadership, and coordinating efforts. These efforts are related to the many continuing activities of the engineers and scientists assigned to the project. These activities include problem solving and the generation of technical ideas. Technical people make special attempts to monitor (and transfer in) the results of previous activity as well as relevant external information. Management or marketing people take a closer look at competitors and customers to be sure the project is appropriately targeted.[3] Senior people try to protect the project from being controlled too tightly or from being cut off prematurely. The project manager and other enthusiasts fight to defend their project's virtues (and budget). Unless canceled, the project continues toward completion of its objectives.

Project Outcome Evaluation.   When the technical effort seems complete, most projects undergo another intense evaluation to see how the results compare with prior expectations and current market perceptions. If successful innovation is to occur, some further implementation must take place. The interim results are transferred either to manufacturing or to further stages of development. All such later stages usually involve heavy expenditures. The project outcome evaluation can then be viewed as a way to screen projects prior to their possible transfer into these later stages.

Project Transfer.   If the project results survive this evaluation, transfer efforts take place (e.g., from central research to product department R&D, or from development to manufacturing engineering).[4] The project's details may require further technical documentation to facilitate the transfer. Key technical people may be shifted to the downstream unit to transfer their expertise and enthusiasm, since downstream staff members in the technical or marketing areas often need instruction to assure effective continuity. Within the downstream organizational unit, the cycle of stages may begin again, perhaps bypassing the earliest two stages and starting with project initiation or even project execution. This "pass down" continues until successful innovation is achieved, unless project termination occurs first.

Needed Roles

Assessment of activities involved in the several-stage innovation process, as just described, points out that the repeated direct inputs of five different work roles are critical to innovation. The five roles arise in differing degrees in each of the several steps. Furthermore, different innovation projects obviously call for variations in the required role mix at each stage. Nevertheless, all five work roles must be carried out by one or more individuals if the innovation is to pass effectively through all six steps. The five critical work functions are:

- *Idea Generating:* Analyzing or synthesizing information about markets, technologies, approaches, or procedures, from which is generated an idea for a new or improved product or service, a new technical approach or procedure, or a solution to a challenging technical problem.[5] The analysis or synthesis may be implicit or explicit; the information may be formal or informal.
- *Entrepreneuring or Championing:* Recognizing, proposing, pushing, and demonstrating a new technical idea, approach, or procedure for formal management approval.[6]
- *Project Leading:* Planning and coordinating the diverse sets of activities and people involved in moving a demonstrated idea into practice.[7]
- *Gatekeeping:* Collecting and channeling information about important

changes in the internal and external environments. Information gatekeeping can be focused on developments in the market, in manufacturing, or in the world of technology.[8]

- *Sponsoring or Coaching:* Guiding and developing less experienced personnel in their critical roles; behind-the-scenes support, protection, advocacy, and sometimes "bootlegging" of funds.[9]

Lest the reader confuse these roles as mapping one-for-one with different people, three points need emphasis: (1) some roles, e.g., idea generating, frequently need to be filled by more than one person in a project team in order for the project to be successful; (2) some individuals occasionally fill more than one of the critical functions; and (3) the roles that people play periodically change over a person's career with an organization. The latter two points will be discussed in more depth later in this article.

Critical Functions

These five critical functions represent the various roles that must be carried out for successful innovation to occur. They are critical from two points of view. First, each role is unique and demands unique skills. A deficiency in any one of the roles contributes to serious problems in the innovation effort, as we shall illustrate below. Second, each role tends to be carried out primarily by relatively few individuals, thereby making the critical role players even more unique. If any one of these individuals leaves, the problem of recruiting a replacement is very difficult. The specific qualities needed in the replacement usually depend on unstated role requirements. Most critical functions cannot be filled by new recruits to an organization.

We must add at this point that another role clearly exists in all innovative organizations, but it is not an *innovative* role. "Routine" technical problem solving must be carried out in order to advance innovative efforts. Indeed, the vast bulk of technical work is probably routine. It requires professional training and competence, to be sure, but it is nonetheless routine in character for an appropriately prepared individual. A large number of people in innovative organizations do very little critical functions work; others who are important performers of the critical functions also spend a good part of their time in routine problem-solving activity. Our estimate, supported now by data from numerous organizations, is that 70 to 80 percent of technical effort falls into this routine problem-solving category. But, the 20 to 30 percent that is unique and critical is the part we emphasize here.

Generally, the critical functions are not specified within job descriptions, since they tend to fit neither administrative nor technical hierarchies. But they represent necessary activities for R&D, such as problem definition, idea nurturing, information transfer, information integration, and program pushing. Consequently, these role behaviors are the underlying informal functions that an organization carries out as part of the innovation process. Beyond the five roles described earlier, different business environments may also demand that additional roles be performed in order to assure innovation.[10]

It is desirable for every organization to have a balanced set of abilities for carrying out these roles as needed. Unfortunately, few organizations have such a balanced set. Some organizations overemphasize one role (e.g., idea generating) and underplay another role (e.g., entrepreneuring). Technical organizations tend to assume that the necessary set of activities will somehow be performed. As a consequence, R&D labs often lack sensitivity to the existence and importance of these roles, which, for the most part, are not defined within the formal job structure. Yet, the way in which critical functions are encouraged and made a conscious part of technology management is probably an organization's single most important area of leverage for maintaining and improving effective innovation.

Impact of Role Deficiencies

Such an analytic approach to developing an innovative team has been lacking in the past. Consequently, many organizations suffer because one or more of the critical functions are not being performed adequately. Certain characteristic signs can provide evidence that a critical function is missing.

Idea generating is deficient if the organization is not thinking of new and different ways of doing things. However, when a manager complains of insufficient ideas, we commonly find the real deficiency to be that people are not aggressively entrepreneuring or championing ideas—either their own or others. Pools of unexploited ideas that seldom come to managers' attention are evidence of an entrepreneuring deficiency.[11]

Project leading is suspect if schedules are not met, activities "fall through cracks" (e.g., coordinating with a supplier), people do not have a sense of the overall goal of their work, or units that are needed to support the work back out of their commitments. Project leading is most commonly recognized by the formal appointment of a project manager. In research, as distinct from development, this formal role if often omitted.

Gatekeeping is inadequate if news of changes in the market, technology, or government legislation comes without warning. It is also inadequate if needed information is not passed along to people within the organization. If, six months after the project is completed, you suddenly realize that you have just succeeded in reinventing a competitor's wheel, your organization is deficient in needed gatekeeping! Gatekeeping is also lacking if the wheel is invented just as a regulatory agency outlaws its use.

Inadequate or inappropriate sponsoring or coaching often explains how projects are pushed into application too soon and why project managers have to spend too much time defending their work. It also explains why personnel complain that they do not know how to "navigate the bureaucracy" of their organizations.

The importance of each critical function varies with the development stage of the project. Initially, idea generation is crucial. Later, entrepreneurial skill and commitment are needed to develop the concept into a viable activity. Once the project is established, good project leadership is needed to guide its progress. Of course, the need for a critical function does not abruptly appear and disappear. Instead, the need grows and diminishes. Each function is the focus at some points, but it is of lesser importance at others. Thus, the absence of a function at a time when it is potentially important is a serious weakness, regardless of whether or not the role had been filled at an earlier, less crucial time. As a corollary, assignment of an individual to a project, at a time when the critical role that he or she provides is not needed, leads to frustration for the individual and to a less effective project team.

Frequently, we have observed that personnel changes that occur because of career development programs often remove critical functions from a project at a crucial time. Although these roles are usually performed informally, job descriptions are made in terms of technical specialties. Thus, personnel replacements are chosen on the basis of their technical qualifications rather than on their ability to fill the needs of the vacated critical roles. Consequently, the project team's innovative effectiveness is reduced, sometimes to the point of affecting the project's success.

Characteristics of the Role Players

Compilation of several thousand individual profiles of staff in R&D and engineering organizations has demonstrated patterns in the characteristics of the people who perform each innovation function.[12] These patterns are shown in Table 1.1. The table indicates which persons are predisposed to be more interested in one type of activity than another and to perform certain types of activities well. For example, a person who is comfortable with abstractions and theory might feel more suited to the idea-generating function than would someone who is very practical. In any unit of an organization, people with different characteristics can work to complement each other. For instance, a person who is effective at generating ideas can be teamed with a colleague who is good at gatekeeping and with another colleague who has good entrepreneurial abilities. Of course, each person must understand his or her own expected role in a project and must appreciate the roles of others in order for the teaming process to be successful. As will be discussed later, some people have sufficient breadth to perform well in multiple roles.

Table 1.1 underlies our conclusion that each of the several roles required for effective technical innovation presents unique challenges and must be filled with different types of people. Each type must be recruited, managed, and supported differently; offered different sets of incentives; and supervised with different types of measures and controls. However, most technical organizations seem not to have grasped this concept. The result is that all technical people tend to be recruited, hired, supervised, monitored, evaluated, and encouraged as if their principal roles were those of creative scientists, or, worse yet, of routine technical problem solvers. In fact, only a few of these people have the personal and technical qualifications for scientific inventiveness and prolific idea generating. A creative, idea-generating scientist or engineer is a special kind of professional. This person needs to be singled out, cultivated, and managed in a special way. He or she is probably innovative, technically well educated, and enjoys working on advanced problems, often as a "loner."

The technical champion or entrepreneur is a special person, too. He or she shows creativity, but it is an aggressive form of creativity that is appropriate for selling an idea or product. The entrepreneur's drives may be less rational and more emotional than those of the creative scientist; he or she is committed to achieving but is less concerned about how to do so. This person is as likely to pick up and successfully champion someone else's original idea as to push something of his or her own creation. Such an entrepreneur may well have a broad range of interests and activities. He or she must be recruited, hired, managed, and stimulated very differently from the way an idea-generating scientist is treated in the organization.

The person who effectively performs project-leading or project-managing activities is yet a different kind of person. He or she is an organized individual, is sensitive to the needs of the several different people who are being coordinated, and is an effective planner. The ability to plan is especially important if long lead time, expensive materials, and major support are involved in the project development.

The information gatekeeper is a communicative individual and is the exception to the truism that engineers do not read (especially that they do not read technical journals). Gatekeepers provide links to sources of the technical information that flows into and within a research and development organization and that can enhance new product development or process improvement. But those who do research and development need market information as well as

Table 1.1 Critical Functions in the Innovation Process

Critical Function	Personal Characteristics	Organizational Activities
Idea Generating	Expert in one or two fields. Enjoys conceptualization; comfortable with abstractions. Enjoys doing innovative work. Usually is an individual contributor. Often will work alone.	Generates new ideas and tests their feasibility. Good at problem solving. Sees new and different ways of doing things. Searches for the breakthroughs.
Entrepreneuring or Championing	Strong application interests. Possesses a wide range of interests. Less propensity to contribute to the basic knowledge of a field. Energetic and determined; puts self on the line.	Sells new ideas to others in the organization. Gets resources. Aggressive in championing his or her "cause." Takes risks.
Project Leading	Focus for decision making, information, and questions. Sensitive to the needs of others. Recognizes how to use the organizational structure to get things done. Interested in a broad range of disciplines and in how they fit together (e.g., marketing, finance).	Provides the team leadership and motivation. Plans and organizes the project. Insures that administrative requirements are met. Provides necessary coordination among team members. Sees that the project moves forward effectively. Balances the project goals with organizational needs.

Gatekeeping	Possesses a high level of technical competence. Is approachable and personable. Enjoys the face-to-face contact of helping others.	Keeps informed of related developments that occur outside the organization through journals, conferences, colleagues, other companies. Passes information on to others; finds it easy to talk to colleagues. Serves as an information resource for others in the organization (i.e., authority on who to see or on what has been done). Provides informal coordination among personnel.
Sponsoring or Coaching	Possesses experience in developing new ideas. Is a good listener and helper. Can be relatively objective. Often is a more senior person who knows the organizational ropes.	Helps develop people's talents. Provides encouragement, guidance, and acts as a sounding board for the project leader and others. Provides access to a power base within the organization—a senior person. Buffers the project team from unnecessary organizational constraints. Helps the project team to get what it needs from the other parts of the organization. Provides legitimacy and organizational confidence in the project.

technical information: What do customers seem to want? What are competitors providing? How might regulatory shifts affect the firm's present or contemplated products or processes? For answers to questions such as these, research and development organizations need people we call the "market gatekeepers." These people are engineers, scientists, or possibly marketing people with technical backgrounds who focus on market-related information sources and communicate effectively to their technical colleagues. Such individuals read trade journals, talk to vendors, go to trade shows, and are sensitive to competitive information. Without them, many research and development projects and laboratories become misdirected with respect to market trends and needs.

Finally, the sponsor or coach is, in general, a more experienced, older project leader or former entrepreneur, who has a "softer touch" than when he or she was first in the organization. As a senior person, he or she can coach and help subordinates in the organization and can speak on their behalf to top management. This activity makes it possible for ideas or programs to move forward in an effective, organized fashion. Many organizations totally ignore the sponsor role; yet our studies of industrial research and development suggest that many projects would not have been successful were it not for the subtle and often unrecognized assistance of such senior people acting in the role of sponsors. Indeed, organizations are most successful when chief engineers or laboratory directors naturally behave in a manner consistent with this sponsor role.

The significant point here is that the staffing needed for effective innovation in a technology-based organization is far broader than the typical research and development director usually has assumed. Our studies indicate that many ineffective technical organizations have failed to be innovative solely because one or more of these five quite different critical functions has been absent.

All of these roles can be fulfilled by people from multiple disciplines and departments. Obviously, technical people—scientists and engineers—might carry out any of the roles. But marketing people also generate ideas for new and improved products, act as gatekeepers for information of key importance to a project (especially about use, competition, and regulatory activities), champion the idea, sometimes sponsor projects, and sometimes even manage new projects, especially for new product development. Manufacturing people periodically fill similar critical roles, as do general management personnel.

Multiple Roles

As indicated earlier, some individuals have the skills, breadth, inclination, and job opportunity to fulfill more than one critical function in an organization. Our data collection efforts with R&D staffs show that a few clusters explain most of these cases of multiple role playing. One common combination of roles is the pairing of gatekeeping and idea generating. Idea-generating activity correlates, in general, with the frequency of person-to-person communication, especially with that which is external to the organization.[13] Moreover, the gatekeeper, who is in contact with many sources of information, can often connect synergistically these bits into a new idea. This ability seems especially true of market gatekeepers who can relate market relevance to technical opportunities.

Another role couplet is between entrepreneuring and idea generating. In studies of how new technical companies are formed, the entrepreneur who pushed company formation and growth was found in half the cases also to have been the source of the new technical idea underlying the company.[14] Furthermore, in studies of MIT faculty, 38 percent of those who had ideas that they perceived to be of commercial value also took strong entrepreneurial steps to exploit their ideas.[15] The idea-generating–entrepreneuring pair accounts for slightly less than half of all entrepreneurs.

Entrepreneuring individuals often become project leaders. This progression is thought to be a logical organizational extension of the effort of effectively "selling" the idea for the project. Some people who are strong at entrepreneuring also have the interpersonal and plan-oriented qualities needed for project leading. The responsibility for managing a project, though, is often mistakenly seen as a necessary reward for successful idea championing. This mistake arises from a lack of attention to the functional differences between the two roles. One should not necessarily assume that a good salesperson will be a good manager. If the entrepreneur can be rewarded appropriately and more directly for his or her own function, many project failures caused by ineffective project managers might be avoided. Perhaps giving the entrepreneur a prominent project role, while clearly designating a different project manager, might be an acceptable compromise.

Finally, sponsoring occasionally evolves into a takeover of any or all of the other roles, even though it should be a unique role. Senior coaching can degenerate into idea domination, project ownership, and direction from the top. This confusion of roles can become extremely harmful to the entire organization: Who will bring another idea to the boss, once he steals some junior's earlier concept? Even worse, who can intervene to stop the project, once the boss is running amok, with his new pet?

The performance of multiple roles can affect the minimum size group needed for attaining "critical mass" in an innovative effort. To achieve continuity of a project, from initial idea all the way through to successful commercialization, a project group must effectively fill all five critical roles. It must also satisfy the specific technical skill requirements for project problem solving. In a new, high-technology company, this critical mass may sometimes be ensured by as few as one or two cofounders. Similarly, an elite team—such as Cray's famed Control Data computer-design group, Kelly Johnson's "skunk works" at Lockheed, or McLean's Sidewinder missile organization in the Navy's China Lake R&D center—may concentrate in a small number of select multiple-role players the staff needed to accomplish major objectives. But, the more typical medium-to-large company had better not plan on finding Renaissance persons or superstars to fill its job requirements. Staffing assumptions should more likely rest on estimates that 70 percent of scientists and engineers will turn out to be routine problem solvers only, and that even most critical role players will be single dimensional in their unique contributions.

Career-Spanning Role Changes

We showed above how some individuals fill multiple critical roles concurrently or in different stages of the same project. Even more people are likely to contribute critically but differently at different stages of their careers. This difference over time does not reflect change of personality, although such changes do seem partly due to the dynamics of personal growth and development. The phenomenon also clearly reflects individual responses to differing organizational needs, constraints, and incentives.

For example, let's consider the hypothetical case of a bright, aggressive, young engineer who has just joined a company upon graduation. What roles can he play? Certainly, he can quickly become effective at solving routine technical problems and, hopefully, at generating novel ideas. But, even though he may know many university contacts and be familiar with the outside literature, he can't be an effective information gatekeeper, for he doesn't yet know the people inside the company with whom he might communicate. Nor can he lead project activities, since no one would trust him in that role. He can't effectively serve as entrepreneur, as he has no credibility as champion for change. And, of course, sponsoring is out of the question. During this stage of his career, the limited legitimate role options may channel the young engineer's productive energies and reinforce his tendencies toward the output of creative ideas.

Alternatively, if he wants to offer and do more than the organization will allow, this high-potential young performer may feel rebuffed and frustrated. His perception of what he can expect from the job and, perhaps more importantly, what the job will expect from him, may become set in these first few months on the job. Though he may remain with the company, he will "turn off" in disappointment from his previously enthusiastic desire to make multidimensional contributions. More likely, he will leave the company in search of a more rewarding job. He will perhaps be destined to find continuing frustration in his next one or two encounters. For many young professionals, the job environment moves too slowly from the stage where idea generating is encouraged to a time when entrepreneuring is permitted.

The engineer's role options may broaden after two or three years on the job. Though routine problem solving and idea generating are still appropriate, some information gatekeeping may now also be possible as communication ties increase within the organization. Project leading may start to be seen as legitimate behavior, particularly on small efforts.[16] The young engineer's work behavior may begin to reflect these new possibilities. Nevertheless, his attempts at entrepreneurial behavior might still be seen as premature and sponsoring as still an irrelevant consideration.

After another few years at work, the role options are still wider. Routine problem solving, continued idea generating, broad-based gatekeeping (even bridging to the market or to manufacturing), responsible project managing, and project championing may become reasonable alternatives. Even coaching a new employee becomes a possibility. Though most people tend usually to focus on one of these roles (or on a specific multiple-role combination) during this mid-career period, the next several years can strengthen all these role options.

Losing touch with a rapidly changing technology may later narrow the available role alternatives as the person continues in his or her job. Technical problem-solving effectiveness may diminish in some cases, idea generating may slow down or stop, and technical information gatekeeping may be reduced. Market or manufacturing gatekeeping, however, may continue to improve with increased experience and outside contacts. Project-managing capabilities may continue to grow as he or she tucks more projects under his or her belt. Entrepreneuring may be more important and for higher stakes. Sponsoring of juniors in the company may be more generally sought and practiced. This career phase is too often seen to be characterized by the problem of technical obsolescence, especially if the organization has a fixation on assessing engineer performance in terms of the narrow but traditional stereotypes of technical problem solving and idea generating. Channeling the engineer into a role that is more appropriate for an earlier stage in his or her career can be a source of mutual grief to both the organization and the individual. Such a role will be of little current interest and satisfaction to the more mature, broader, and now differently directed professional. An aware organization, thinking in terms of critical role differences, can instead recognize the self-selected branching in career paths that has occurred for the individual. Productive, technically trained people can carry out critical functions for their employers up to retirement if employers encourage the full diversity of vital roles.

At each stage of his or her evolving career, the individual can encounter severe conflicts between the organization's expectations and his or her personal work preferences. This conflict is especially likely if the organization is inflexible in its perception of appropriate technical roles. In contrast, if both the organization and the individual are adaptable in seeking mutually satisfying job roles, the engineer can contribute continuously and significantly to innovation. In the course of a productive career in industry, the technical professional may begin as a technical problem solver, spend several years primarily as a creative idea generator, and add technical gatekeeping to his or her repertoire while maintaining his or her earlier roles. He or she may then begin to serve as a project entrepreneur and lead projects forward. Gradually, he or she will develop greater market linking and project managing skills and eventually will assume a senior sponsoring role, maintaining a position of project, program, or organizational leadership until retirement. This fully productive career would not be possible if the engineer were pushed to the side early as a technically obsolete contributor. The perspective taken here can lead to a very different approach to career development for professionals than is usually taken by industry or government.

Managing the Critical Functions for Enhanced Innovation

To increase organizational innovation, a number of steps can be taken to facilitate a balance of time and energy among the critical functions. These steps must be addressed explicitly or organizational focus will remain on the traditionally visible functions, such as problem solving, which produce primarily near-term incremental results. Indeed, the results-oriented reward systems of most organizations reinforce this short-run focus, causing the other, more significant activities to go unrecognized and unrewarded.[17]

Implementation of the results, language, and concepts of a critical functions perspective is outlined below for the selected organizational tasks of manpower planning, job design, and selection of measurement and rewards. If managers thought in critical functions terms, other tasks, not dealt with here, would also be carried out differently. These tasks include R&D strategy, organizational development, and program management.

Manpower Planning

The critical functions concept can be applied usefully to the recruiting, job assignment, and development or training activities within an organization. In recruiting, for example, an organization needs to identify not only the specific technical or managerial requirements of a job, but also the critical function activities that the job inspires, e.g., the organization needs to ask whether the job requires that less experienced personnel be coached and developed in order to ensure the longer-run productivity of that area. If the job requires entrepreneuring, then the applicant who is more aggressive and has shown evidence of championing new ideas in the past should be preferred over the less aggressive applicant who has shown more narrowly technically oriented interests in the past.

Industry, at best, has taken a narrow view of manpower development alternatives for technical professionals. The "dual ladder" concept envisions an individual rising along either scientific or managerial steps. Attempted by many but with only limited success ever attained, the dual ladder reflects an oversimplification and distortion of the key roles needed in an R&D organization.[18] As a minimum, the critical function concept presents "multiladders" of possible organizational contribution; individuals can grow in any or all of the critical roles, while benefiting the organization. Depending on an organization's strategy and manpower needs, manpower development along each of the paths can and should be encouraged. Furthermore, there is room for individual growth and development from one function to another, as people are exposed to different managers, different environments, and jobs that require different activities.

Job Design and Objective Setting

Most job descriptions and statements of objectives emphasize problem solving and sometimes project leading. Rarely do job descriptions and objectives take into account the dimensions of a job that are essential for the performance of the other critical functions. Yet, the availability of unstructured time in a job, for example, can influence the performance of several of the innovation functions, and it needs to be designed into corresponding jobs. To stimulate idea generating, some slack time is necessary so that employees can pursue their own ideas and explore new and interesting ways of doing things. For gatekeeping to occur, slack time needs to be available for employees to communicate with colleagues and pass along information learned, both internal to and external to the organization. The coaching role also requires slack time, during which the "coach" can guide less experienced personnel.[19]

Essential activities for filling alternative roles also need to be included explicitly in a job's objectives. An important goal for a gatekeeper, for example, should be to provide useful information to colleagues. A person who has the attitudes and skills to be an effective champion or entrepreneur could be given responsibility for recognizing good new ideas. This person might have the charter to roam around the organization, talk with people about their ideas, and encourage their pursuit of these ideas. He could even pursue these ideas himself.[20]

Performance Measures and Rewards

We all tend to do those activities that will be rewarded. If personnel perceive that idea generating will not be recognized but that idea exploitation will, they may withhold their ideas from those who can exploit them. They may try to exploit ideas themselves, no matter how unequipped or uninterested they are in carrying out the exploitation activity.

For this reason, it is important to recognize the distinct contributions of each of the separate critical functions. Table 1.2 identifies some measures relevant for each function, indicating both quantity and quality dimensions. For example, an objective for a person who has the skills and information to be effective at gatekeeping could be to help a number of people during the next twelve months. At the end of that time, his or her manager could survey the people who the gatekeeper felt he or she had helped to assess the gatekeeper's effectiveness in communicating key information. In each organization, the specific measures chosen will necessarily be different.

Rewarding an individual for the performance of a critical function makes the function more manageable and open to discussion. However, what is perceived as rewarding for one function may be seen as less rewarding, neutral, or even negative for another function, because of the different personalities and needs of those filling the roles. Table 1.2 presents some rewards that seem appropriate for each function. Again, organizational and individual differences will generate variations in the rewards selected. Of course, the informal positive feedback of managers in their day-to-day contacts is a major source of motivation and recognition for any individual performing a critical innovation function, or any job for that matter.

Salary and bonus compensation are not included here, but not because they are unimportant to any of these people. Financial rewards should be employed as appropriate, but they do not seem to be linked explicitly to one innovative function more than to another.

Table 1.2 Measuring and Rewarding Critical Function Performance

Dimension of Management	Critical Function				
	Idea Generating	Entrepreneuring or Championing	Project Leading	Gatekeeping	Sponsoring or Coaching
Primary contribution of each function for appraisal of performance	Quantity and quality of ideas generated.	Ideas picked up; percent carried through.	Project technical milestones accomplished; cost/schedule constraints met.	People helped; degree of help.	Success in developing staff; extent of assistance provided.
Appropriate rewards	Opportunities to publish; recognition from professional peers through symposia, etc.	Visibility; publicity; further resources for project.	Bigger or more significant projects; material signs of organization status.	Travel budget; key "assists" acknowledged; increased autonomy and use for advice.	Increased autonomy; discretionary resources for support of others.

Performing a Critical Functions Assessment

The preceding sections demonstrate that the critical functions concept provides an important way to describe an organization's resources for effective innovation activity. To translate this concept into an applied tool, one needs to be able to assess the status of an R&D unit in terms of critical functions. Such an assessment potentially provides two important types of information: (1) inputs for management evaluations of the organization's ability to achieve goals and strategy; and (2) assistance to R&D managers and professionals in performance evaluation, career development, and more effective project performance.

Method of Approach

The methodology chosen for a critical functions assessment is contingent on the situation. From experience gained with a dozen companies and government agencies in North America, the authors have found the most flexible approach to be a series of common questionnaires, which are developed from replicated academic research techniques on innovative contributors and modified as needed for the situation. Questionnaires are supplemented by a number of structured interviews or workshops. Data are collected and organized in a framework that represents: (a) the critical functions; (b) special characteristics of the organization's situation; (c) additional critical functions required in the specific organization; and (d) the climate for innovation provided by management. The results include a measure of an organization's current and potential strengths in each critical function; an evaluation of the compatibility of the organization's R&D strategy with these strengths; and a set of personnel development plans for both management and staff that support the organization's goals. This information is valuable for both the organization and the individual.[21]

Some Actions Taken in One Firm

As a result of a critical functions analysis in a company, multiple actions are usually taken. In order to consider some of the typical steps, we draw here from the outcomes implemented in one medium-sized R&D organization. The first action was that all first-line supervisors and above, after some training, discussed with each employee the results of the employee's critical functions survey. (In other companies, employee anonymity has been preserved; data were returned only to the individual. In these companies, employees frequently have used the results to initiate discussions with their immediate supervisors regarding job fit and career development.) The purpose of the discussion was twofold: to look for differences in how the employee and his or her boss each perceived the employee's job skills; and to engage in developmental career planning. The vocabulary of the critical functions plus the tangible feedback gave the manager and the employee a meaningful, commonly shared basis for the discussion.

Several significant changes resulted from these discussions. A handful of the staff recognized the mismatch between their present jobs and skills. With the support of their managers, job modifications were made. Another type of mismatch that this process revealed was between the manager's perception of the employee's skills and the employee's own perception. Most of the time the manager was underutilizing his or her human resources.

In this particular firm, the data also prompted action to improve the performance of the project-leading function. An insufficient number of people saw themselves performing this function. Moreover, they saw themselves as lacking skills in this area. As a result of these deficiencies, upper management conducted several "coaching" sessions, worked to further clarify roles, and showed increased support for project leadership efforts.

Important changes also were made in how the technical organization recruited. The characteristic strengths behind each critical function were explicitly employed in identifying the skills necessary to do a particular job. This analysis led to a useful framework for interviewing candidates. It helped determine how the candidates might fit into and grow within the present organization. Upper management also became conscious of the unintended bias in the recruiting procedure. This bias was introduced both by the universities at which the company recruited and by the recruiters themselves. (In this case, the senior researchers, who conducted most of the interviews, were primarily interested in idea generating.) As a result of the analyses, upper management was careful to have a mix of the critical functions represented by the people who interviewed job candidates.

The analyses led to other results that were less tangible than the above but equally important. Jobs were no longer defined solely in technical terms, i.e., in terms of required educational background or work experience. For example, if a job involved idea generation, the necessary skills and the typical activities for that critical function were included in the description of the job. Furthermore, the need for a new kind of teamwork developed since it was rare that any single person could perform effectively all five of these essential functions. Finally, the critical functions concept provided the framework for the selection of people and division of labor on the innovation team that became the nucleus for all new R&D programs.

Conclusion

We have examined the technology-based innovation process in terms of a set of informal but critical behavior functions. Five critical roles have been identified within the life cycle of activities in an R&D project. These roles are idea generating, entrepreneuring or championing, project leading, gatekeeping, and sponsoring or coaching. In our surveys of numerous North American R&D and engineering organizations, we have made two key observations: Some unique individuals are able to perform concurrently more than one of the critical roles; and patterns of roles for an individual often change over the course of his or her productive work career.

These critical functions concepts have managerial implications in such areas as manpower planning, job design, objective setting, and performance measurement and rewards. They provide a conceptual basis for design of a more effective multiladder system to replace many R&D organizations' ineffectual dual-ladder systems.

Several years of development, testing, and discussion of this critical functions perspective have also led to applications outside of R&D organizations. We have seen the perspective extended to such areas as computer software development and architectural firms. Recent discussions with colleagues suggest an obvious appropriateness for marketing organizations. A more difficult translation is expected in the areas of finance and manufacturing. To the extent that innovative outcome rather than routine production is the output sought, we have confidence that the critical functions approach will afford useful insights for organizational analysis and management.

2

Entrepreneurs, Champions, and Technological Innovation

Modesto A. Maidique

Successful radical innovation requires a special combination of entrepreneurial, managerial, and technological roles within a firm. As the firm grows and changes, these roles also change, and they tend to be performed by different people in different ways. The author draws conclusions from several cases of radical technological innovation to support these hypotheses. *SMR.*

There is plenty of reason to suppose that individual talents count for a good deal more than the firm as an organization.   –Kenneth J. Arrow[1]

At all stages of development of the firm, highly enthusiastic and committed individuals who are willing to take risks play an important role in technological innovation. In the initial stages of the technological firm's development, these entrepreneurial individuals are the force that moves the firm forward. In later stages, they absorb the risks of radical innovation, that is, of those innovations that restructure the current business or create new businesses. As Ed Roberts has pointed out, "In the large firm as well as in the founding enterprise, the entrepreneur is the central figure in successful technological innovation."[2]

Successful innovation, however, requires a special combination of entrepreneurial, managerial, and technological roles. Furthermore, the characteristics of this network[3] of roles are a function of the stage of development of the firm. In this article, the theory of entrepreneurial roles—what we know about entrepreneurship and technological innovation—is combined with Scott's theory of corporate development to generate several hypotheses regarding the evolution of entrepreneurial roles as the firm evolves from a small firm to a large, diversified firm.[4]

From *Sloan Management Review,* Winter 1980, Vol. 21, No. 2. Reprinted with permission.

47

Three principal arguments are made: First, that the entrepreneurial role is essential for radical technological innovation, but that it manifests itself differently depending on the firm's stage of development. Second, that radical technological innovation, to be successful, requires top management participation in the entrepreneurial network. Third, that in addition to the independent entrepreneur and the product champion, an important intermediate entrepreneurial role is especially prominent in diversified firms—that is, the executive champion.[5]

Radical technological innovation, at any stage of development, can be viewed as requiring a recreation of the original entrepreneurial network—a merging of the roles the original entrepreneurial team performed: business definition, sponsorship, technical definition, and technical communication. As a business grows or becomes more diverse, the original entrepreneurial network becomes fragmented; these critical roles are decoupled, and a conservative bias is often introduced into subsequent innovations. Business definition becomes separated from technical definition by administrative systems, organizational hierarchy, and market and technological diversity. The business readjusts more slowly, or not at all, to technological discontinuities. Nonetheless, this decoupling is natural and necessary. It is impossible for the original entrepreneur to be closely tied to an increasingly large number of diverse innovations. He or she must, however, seek out and complete the network of entrepreneurship for that handful of radical innovations that will have significant impact on the future of the firm.

This article is organized into five sections. First, the literature on entrepreneurial roles and corporate development is briefly summarized. In the following three sections, the evolution of the network of entrepreneurial roles is examined by analyzing radical innovations in three different contexts: the small, the integrated, and the diversified technological firm.[6] In the last section some hypotheses are drawn from this analysis regarding the task of top management in the technology-based firm.

Entrepreneurship and Corporate Development: A Brief Review of the Literature

A rich literature exists on heroic, independent, technological entrepreneurs such as Thomas Watson, Jr., Henry Ford, and Edwin Land. During the last two decades, a new literature on entrepreneurship has also developed that emphasizes the role of individuals within the firm who exhibit entrepreneurial characteristics.

Entrepreneurs and Champions

The significance of the role of the entrepreneur has been recognized for at least two centuries. Schumpeter credits J. B. Say, an early nineteenth-century French economist, for being the first to recognize that the entrepreneur in a capitalist society is "the pivot on which everything turns."[7] According to Schumpeter, the entrepreneur

reforms or revolutionizes the pattern of production by exploiting an invention or, more generally, an untried technological possibility for producing a new commodity or producing an old one in a new way, by opening up a new source of supply of materials or a new outlet for products by reorganizing an industry. . . .[8]

On the other hand, the critical role that "champions" of technological change play within industrial organizations has been recognized only during the last two decades. In a seminal study of radical military innovations, Schon observed that certain committed individuals, *champions,* played the key role in successful innovations. Schon lists some fifteen major inventions of the twentieth century, such as the jet engine and the gyrocompass, in which individuals played a major role. In his studies, Schon found that "the new idea either finds a champion or *dies."* To Schon, the "product champions" are critical, for

no ordinary involvement with a new idea provides the energy required to cope with the indifference and resistance that major technical change provokes. . . . Champions of new inventions . . . display persistence and courage of heroic quality.[9]

Schon's analysis led him to four basic conclusions:

1. At the outset, the new idea encounters sharp resistance.[10]
2. Overcoming this resistance requires vigorous promotion.
3. Proponents of the idea work primarily through the *informal* rather than the formal organization.
4. Typically, *one person* emerges as champion of the idea.

The product champion served as a catalyst for the development of a literature on internal entrepreneurial roles. In the decades following Schon's work, several new entrepreneurial (and related) roles and new names for old roles appeared in the innovation literature, such as "business innovators,"[11] "internal entrepreneurs,"[12] "sponsors,"[13] "change agents,"[14] "Maxwell demons or mutation selectors,"[15] "technical and manager champion,"[16] and "administrative entrepreneur."[17]

Collins and Moore[18] found very strong similarities between traditional or "independent" entrepreneurs and certain managers within the firm who operated like Schon's product champions: They called them "administrative entrepreneurs." Collins and Moore developed a psychological profile of the 150 independent and administrative entrepreneurs in their study and concluded that the "entrepreneurial personality, in short, is characterized by an unwillingness to submit to authority, an inability to work with it, and a consequent need to escape from it."[19] Some potential entrepreneurs find ways, at least temporarily, to satisfy their psychological needs by pursuing—sometimes in unorthodox ways—high-risk projects *within* the organization; others finally break away and create a new structure.

In two recent studies, Duchesneau[20] and Olsen[21] obtained statistical data on the presence of champions in the footwear and textile industries, respectively. Duchesneau interviewed senior managers in sixty-nine footwear firms and found that about two-thirds of them recognized the presence of "product champions" in their firms. In his study of twelve textile firms, Olsen found a "strong correlation" between early adoption of innovations and the existence of an identifiable champion. Olsen found identifiable champions in eight of the twelve firms in his study.[22]

SAPPHO

One of the first studies that attempted both to quantify the product-champion function and to break it down into subroles was the SAPPHO study.[23] In phase I of the SAPPHO project, twenty-nine pairs of successful and unsuccessful innovations were studied. Of the forty-three pairs of innovations in SAPPHO II, twenty-two were in the chemical industry and twenty-one in scientific instruments.[24] The forty-three pairs were compared along 122 dimensions, fifteen of which were found (on an aggregate basis) to have statistical significance higher than .1 percent (as determined by the binomial test). Another nine variables had statistical significance higher than 1 percent. The SAPPHO investigators used multivariate analysis to extract from these twenty-four variables five underlying areas of difference between successful and unsuccessful innovations:[25]

1. Strength of management and characteristics of managers.
2. Marketing performance.
3. Understanding of user needs.
4. Research and development (R&D) efficiency.
5. Communications.

To study the first of these factors—the role of key managers and technologists—the SAPPHO investigators defined four categories of key individuals:

1. *Technical innovator.* The individual who made the "major contribution on the technical side" to the development and/or design of the innovation.

2. *Business innovator.* The individual within the managerial structure who was responsible for the overall progress of the project.
3. *Product champion.* Any individual who made a decisive contribution to the innovation by "actively and enthusiastically promoting its progress through critical stages."
4. *Chief executive.* The "head of the executive structure" of the innovating organization, but not necessarily the managing director or chief executive officer.

The forty-three pairs of innovations were then tested to determine how, if at all, the presence of such key individuals explained the success of the innovation. The results for the five most significant parameters are summarized in Table 2.1. Sup3risingly, the individual who emerged as the principal factor was *not* the product champion, but the "business innovator." In particular, the business innovator's power, respectability, status, and experience were important. However, the role of the product champion was also shown to discriminate significantly for success.

Thus, the SAPPHO study provides systematic evidence in favor of the champion hypothesis. The study also indicates that besides commitment and

Table 2.1   Five Main Characteristics of Executives in Charge of Successful Innovations

Variable*	S	N**	F	%S†	Binomial Test††
1. The executive in charge of the successful innovation has more power.	20	19	4	75%	7.7×10^{-4}
2. The executive in charge of success has more responsibility.	18	20	4	72%	1.3×10^{-3}
3. The executive in charge of success has more diverse experience.	20	18	5	73%	2×10^{-3}
4. The executive in charge of success has more enthusiasm.	14	27	2	71%	2×10^{-3}
5. The executive in charge of success has higher status.	18	21	4	72%	2×10^{-3}

Notes:

* S = variable discriminated for success; F = variable discriminated for failure; N = variable did not discriminate in either direction, *or* insufficient data were available to form the comparison.

** The N grouping presents a data interpretation problem since it's not clear how this group broke down between the "insufficient data" category or situations where the variable had a "neutral" effect or none at all.

† The %S was calculated by assuming that the N group was *equally* split between the insufficient data group and the neutral grouping. The "insufficient data" half was discarded and the remainder was split equally between the S and F groups. The "%S" was then calculated as a percentage of the new total S + F population.

†† Calculated by SAPPHO group.

Table 2.2   Key Roles and Functions According to Different Investigators*

Function	Bower (1972)	Schwartz (1973)	SAPPHO (1974)	Kusiatin (1976)	Roberts** (1968, 1972, 1977, 1978)	This Article†
Business, Structure & Definition	Context	Context	Chief Executive	—	—	Business Definition, Technological Entrepreneur
Sponsorship	Impetus	Impetus	Business Innovator, Product Champion	Manager Champion, Technical Champion	Sponsor, Product Champion, Project Manager, Internal Entrepreneur	Executive Champion, Product Champion, Sponsorship, Technological Entrepreneur
Technical Definition	Definition	Technical Definition, Factoring	Technical Innovator	Technical Champion	Creative Scientist	Technical Definition, Technologist
Technical Information	—	—	—	Technical Champion	Gatekeeper	—
Market Information	—	—	—	—	Market Gatekeeper	—

Notes:
*   Roles and definitions vary from researcher to researcher and are only roughly comparable.
** See also Rhoades, Roberts, and Fusfeld, 1978 (reference 28).
†   See list of definitions in Table 2.3.

enthusiasm, the power and status of the sponsoring executive also play an important role in determining the success of an innovation. Often this latter role is played by someone other than the "product champion"—that is (using the SAPPHO terminology), the "business innovator."

The significance of the SAPPHO data is made clearer by using Bower's model for the resource-allocation process.[26] He proposed a three-stage model for resource allocation in a large firm: Top management provides a business and structural *context* for decision making; within this context, middle management selects the projects that they support; higher level sponsorship, *impetus,* is required for successful completion of funding. At the root of the resource-allocation process are the specialists and lower level managers who give *definition* to the projects.

Using Bower's terms, the technical innovator provides technical *definition,* the business innovator provides *sponsorship* or *impetus,* and the chief executive provides business definition or *context.*[27] Viewed from this vantage point, the role of the product champion is to serve as a catalyst for increased sponsorship or impetus.

Similarly, the innovation process can also be viewed from the perspective of

Table 2.3 Definitions of Key Roles

Technological Entrepreneur	The organizer of a technological venture who exercises control of the venture (typically by owning a substantial percentage of the equity) and assumes the risks of the business. Usually he is the chief executive officer.
Product Champion	A member of an organization who creates, defines, or adopts an idea for a new technological innovation and who is willing to risk his or her position and prestige to make possible the innovation's successful implementation.
Executive Champion	An executive in a technological firm who has direct or indirect influence over the resource allocation process and who uses this power to channel resources to a new technological innovation, thereby absorbing most, but usually not all, the risk of the project.
Technical Definition	The basic performance requirements and associated specifications that characterize a proposal for a new technological innovation.
Sponsorship	The actions by which executives channel resources to innovative projects that they have chosen to support.
Business Definition	A description of the business within which a firm chooses to compete and of the overall administrative practices that the firm will follow in that business.

the key roles defined by Roberts. He expands the set of critical functions to include a technical-information role and a project-management role (see Tables 2.2 and 2.3 and Figure 2.1). The project manager anticipates the need for sponsorship by planning for the requirement of the innovation. The gatekeeper, a function characterized originally by Allen, acts as a clearing house for technical information for the technologists in the firm. In a subsequent paper, Roberts suggests that marketing and manufacturing gatekeepers, who can usually be identified, play important roles in the innovation process.[28]

Stages of Development of the Firm

While the literature on entrepreneurs and champions is primarily concerned with static behavior, a substantial literature exists on corporate development. However, this literature is concerned with overall description of the stages of corporate development, not with the specific issue of the entrepreneurial team. Nonetheless, the corporate-development literature does provide a framework for analyzing the development of entrepreneurial networks.

Galbraith proposed that the three stages of company evolution are small,

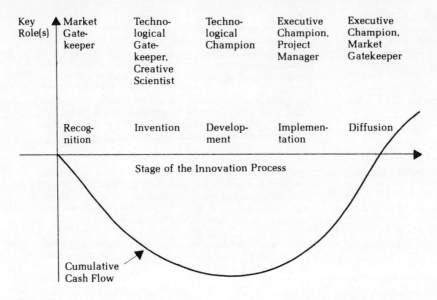

Figure 2.1

medium, and large.[29] Chandler, on the other hand, suggested that the three basic stages are small, integrated, diversified. Scott, Salter, and others concur.[30]

Based on his study of the histories of about seventy large U.S. firms, Chandler proposed that, in most cases, firms follow a typical sequence of development.[31] After the initial entrepreneurial stage, the firm becomes vertically integrated and managed by a centralized functional organization. Normally, this stage is followed by diversification, which is managed by a decentralized divisional organization.

This basic idea was further developed and extended by Scott, while he was working with Christensen and McArthur. A set of propositions delineating the various stages of corporate development resulted from a cooperative effort by Scott and Salter (see Table 2.4).[32]

Wrigley further elaborated on the three original stages and proposed three subclasses of diversified businesses: dominant business diversified, related business diversified, and unrelated business diversified.[33] Scott's classes, as modified by Wrigley, include the following:

Small (or entrepreneurial): single product or single product line company, with little formal structure, controlled by owner-manager.

Integrated: single-product line firm with vertically integrated manufacturing

Table 2.4   The Three Stages of Organizational Development

Company Characteristics	Stage I: Small	Stage II: Integrated	Stage III: Diversified
Product Line	Single product or single line	Single product line	Multiple product lines
Distribution	One channel or set of channels	One set of channels	Multiple channels
Organization Structure	Little or no formal structure; "one-man show"	Specialization based on function	Specialization based on product-market relationships
R&D Organization	Not institutionalized; guided by owner-manager	Increasingly institutionalized search for product or process improvements	Institutionalized search for new products as well as for improvements
Performance Measurement	By personal contact and subjective criteria	Increasingly impersonal, using technical and/or cost criteria	Increasingly impersonal, using market criteria (return on investment and market share)
Rewards	Unsystematic and often paternalistic	Increasingly systematic, with emphasis on stability and service	Increasingly systematic, with variability related to performance
Control System	Personal control of both strategic and operating decisions	Personal control of strategic decisions, with increasing delegation of operating decisions through policy	Delegation of product-market decisions within existing businesses, with indirect control based on analysis of "results"
Strategic Choices	Needs of owner versus needs of company	Degree of integration; market-share objective; breadth of product line	Entry and exit from industries; allocation of resources by industry; rate of growth

and specialized functional organizations. Owner-manager retains control of strategic decisions. Most operating decisions are delegated through policy.

Diversified: multiproduct firm with formalized managerial systems that are evaluated by objective criteria, such as rate of growth and returns on investment. Product-market decisions within existing business are delegated. Within the diversified group, there are three subcategories:

1. *Dominant business firms* that derive 70–95 percent of their sales from a single business[34] or a vertically integrated chain of businesses (e.g., General Motors, IBM, Xerox, U.S. Steel).

2. *Related business firms* that diversify into related areas where no single business accounts for more than 70 percent of sales (e.g., Du Pont, Eastman Kodak, General Electric).

3. *Unrelated business firms* that have diversified without necessarily relating new business to old, and where no single business accounts for as much as

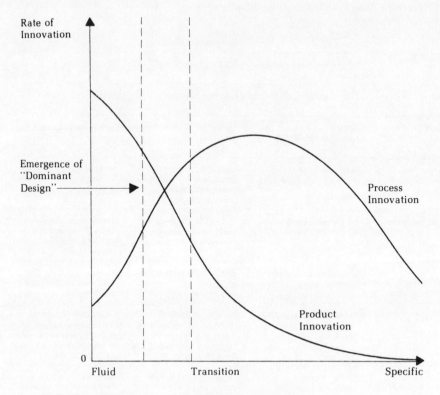

Figure 2.2   Stage of Development of the Manufacturing Process

70 percent of sales (e.g., Litton, North American, Rockwell, and Textron).

Abernathy and Utterback have studied the process of corporate evolution using the "productive unit."[35] An economist might call the productive unit a simple firm: Abernathy and Utterback use the term to describe a related line of products, the manufacturing process, and the overhead structure required to develop, make, and market the products. Their work has significantly extended the literature on corporate evolution, but their focus has been on the evolution of the process segment rather than on managerial characteristics.

Abernathy and Utterback visualized newly created manufacturing processes as initially having some slack: Procedures are not fixed, and job design and material flow are informal and flexible. In short, the process is *fluid*. At the other extreme, once the process has been "perfected" by accumulation of experience, jobs become standardized, manual procedures are automated, and rigid specifications are instituted. The process becomes, in Abernathy and Utterback's term, *specific*. A transition phase joins these two external conditions.

In this model (Figure 2.2), product and process innovation proceed at different rates. Product innovation is highest in the fluid phase and declines monotonically through the transition and specific phases, as the slack is managed out. Process innovation appears slowly and rises as the accumulated flow of products through the processing stages increases the opportunity—and managerial pressures—to formalize the process and reduce costs.

A product or family of products emerges from the initial crops of new products and attains wide market acceptance and high volume. These products, called "dominant designs," make it possible to increase the rate at which the manufacturing process becomes systematized. As standardization increases, process innovation declines (see Figure 2.2).

Although we might expect some major transformations in managerial relationships as a process follows the path described above, Abernathy and Utterback do not discuss these transformations. Yet, in an earlier article, Abernathy and Townsend acknowledged (following Bright) that "management has a critical role in causing the process to evolve and in readying it for technological innovation."[36] These transformations in managerial relationships were not studied in the subsequent article, which used the extensive Myers and Marquis[37] data base (567 innovations, 120 firms, 5 industries), partly because the data base did not contain data on managerial issues.[38] Thus, regarding the evolution of managerial relationships in innovations, Abernathy and Utterback do not go beyond referring to the broad "organic" and "mechanistic" descriptions of organizational relationships suggested by Burns and Stalker.[39]

In the next three sections, we use the three major corporate evolution contexts defined by Scott to examine entrepreneurial roles in radical innovations. We start with the small, or entrepreneurial, technological firm.

Stage I: The Small Technological Firm

The technological entrepreneur, in addition to defining the firm's business, plays (and enjoys playing) the dual role of sponsor and definition agent. Technological entrepreneurs often intervene (sometimes excessively) in the definition phase of innovations.

At Redactron Office Automation, a start-up firm specializing in automatic-editing components, founder and President Evelyn Berezin[40] explained her part in the defining of her company's first product:

When we reached the stage of spelling out detailed specifications, it became apparent that the engineers simply hated to commit things to writing. So I wrote out all the detailed specifications myself, usually dictating them while I was commuting back and forth to the plant. That's how the system got designed.[41]

And it wasn't by whim that Berezin decided on the specifications. Prior to the definition phase, she had spent weeks in the field observing people who used IBM automatic-editing equipment. Berezin considered closeness to the market imperative:

If you don't go there yourself but rely instead on what other people tell you, the information is likely to be distorted or the impressions incomplete. When you're designing a new product, you simply cannot afford to have layers of people between you and the eventual product users.[42]

Clearly, Berezin believed that the power and vision of the CEO should be brought into intimate contact with both technical experts and customers.

A similar pattern becomes evident from studying Henry Kloss, the founder of Advent Corporation. For Kloss, a classic technological entrepreneur, Advent was his third technology venture. He was a founder of Acoustic Research (AR). From there, he moved on to start KLH (both AR and KLH make high-quality consumer audio products). One of Kloss's principal reasons for starting Advent was his desire to retain control: He sold his shares of AR "under duress, and his share of KLH Corporation with mixed feelings."

Like Berezin, Kloss was familiar with the market and the most advanced technologies. He directed Video Beam, Advent's large-screen television project, from start to finish. According to Kloss, "I am responsible for the concept of the product and the initial demonstration that the idea is feasible. . . ." He delineated personal contributions, such as

choosing the optimal size of tubes; deciding the critical tolerances in the final product, making tradeoff choices between costs and qualities; working with consultants in the tube-making business and making the best judgment out of their recommendations as to production processes, specifications and material tolerances. . . .[43]

Kloss laid out the manufacturing and assembly plant when the time came to make the product. He was at the time the chief executive officer of Advent, which then had annual sales of $16 million.

The Kloss-Berezin phenomenon can occur in other countries. Efraim "Efi" Arazi, an Israeli electrical engineer educated at MIT, founded Sci-Tex in 1968. The company makes electro-optical systems, and it now has annual sales of over $10 million. Sci-Tex had an appointed administrator of R&D, but "Efi felt that would not preclude him from being involved, from continuing to participate very actively in the problem-solution process which had become his own lifeblood."[44]

In all three cases (Advent, Redactron, and Sci-Tex), the entrepreneur helped define new products while retaining control as CEO. For the entrepreneur sees the company as a giant erector set and retains the right to play with *any* of the pieces. For Kloss, the ideal situation would be that of Edwin Land, chairman and technical director of billion-dollar Polaroid. Land reputedly has access to any level of R&D while functioning as CEO.

Stage II: The Integrated Firm

Thus what the enterpreneur created passed inexorably beyond the scope of his authority. . . . What the entrepreneur created, only a group of men sharing specialized information could ultimately operate.[45]

If the entrepreneur succeeds, he or she creates a dilemma. Growth means more products, more people, more managers—a transition from a small to an integrated firm. Continued growth requires changes in the entrepreneur's role. Technological progress and organizational complexity act as dual forces on the entrepreneur to cause him or her to give up technical definition and sponsorship of most new projects.

Robert Noyce, the coinventor of the integrated circuit and cofounder and chairman of Intel, puts it this way:

Maybe you can do good technical work for ten years, if you work hard at it, but after that the younger guys are better prepared. It's a question of technical obsolescence, if you will.[46]

Like Noyce, Ken Olsen, chairman of Digital Equipment Corporation (DEC), has moved away from technical definition, though he, like Henry Kloss, is reputedly a "shirt-sleeved engineering type."[47] After a recession, Olsen explained in an interview: "I let the engineers do the designing; my concern was to keep the team together."[48] Olsen is vitally concerned with maintaining open communications to ensure that the best proposals come to his attention. He meets regularly with an engineering committee comprised of about twenty engineers from all levels of DEC. Olsen sets the agenda and periodically disbands and reconstitutes the committee to maintain a fresh flow of ideas. He sees his role as that of a catalyst, or a "devil's advocate": He expects that the best solutions to technical problems will be developed by his technicians.

Often Olsen's role is that of a sponsor. One DEC manager had been championing a project whose approval had become mired in red tape. Olsen sat in on a meeting in which this man's difficulties emerged. Olsen asked about the project and wondered out loud why such a promising idea was finding such little support. The manager describes what followed: "Suddenly the barriers to my project came down. What normally might have taken a year or more to complete became a six-month project."[49] Sponsorship had replaced technical definition.

Such sponsorship of product champions is critically important for continued innovation. Schwartz studied innovation in two major technology-based firms (one was DEC) and concluded that middle managers served as integrators between technical specialists and top management.[50] The middle managers decided which proposals would be submitted for approval, negotiated terms of support for a proposal, and selected the criteria for program evaluation. According to Schwartz, these functions "tended to add a conservative bias to proposals. As a result, the innovations studied were incremental rather than radical."[51] The technological or product champion seeks to break through these barriers, but his or her attempts meet with little success without adequate sponsorship.

The development of the float-glass process at Pilkington Brothers, an integrated British glass manufacturer, is a classic case of technological championing. A few years after joining the firm, Alistair Pilkington, a distant relative of the founding family, conceived a radically new way of making plate glass one evening while he was washing the family dishes. That evening was the beginning of a risky crusade to develop the float-glass process, during which, according to Pilkington, "chaps were literally taken off on stretchers from heat exhaustion, yet [they] came back for more."[52]

Developing this process was a big financial gamble for Pilkington Brothers. After the fundamentals of the process had been proved in the lab, over 100,000 tons of unsalable glass costing $3.6 million were produced in the pilot plant. Month after month, Alistair Pilkington faced the firm's directors with a new request for $280,000 of operating funds and with promises of progress on the project. For a company with net profits of about $400,000 per month, this was a major risk; yet Pilkington continued to get approval until salable glass was finally produced in 1958. Alistair Pilkington succeeded by persisting in his role as technological champion, despite continued setbacks and high risks.[53] His credit, however, must clearly be shared with Harry Pilkington, the entrepreneurial chairman of the board, who absorbed the risks of young Alistair's innovation and who made it possible for the company later to reap $250 million in licensing fees from its competitors. The Pilkington story is often given as a classic example of the product champion. In fact, it is a classic example of the entrepreneur and the champion working in unison—the simplest entrepreneurial network. The champion proposes, the entrepreneur disposes.

Both at DEC and at Pilkington Brothers, the entrepreneur's role evolved from technical definition to sponsorship. But the entrepreneur was still the primary impetus for new projects, especially large ones. Other people, like the young engineering manager at DEC and Alistair Pilkington, had assumed the role of technical definition and had become technological champions for their projects. Olsen and the senior Pilkington found it easy to continue to act as sponsors for key projects in their firms. This was possible partly because the technologies of their integrated, single product line firms could be grasped by top management more easily than could the technologies of a diversified firm.

Stage III: The Diversified Firm

Diversified firms that have a dominant business (one that accounts for over 70 percent of sales) operate that business as if they were integrated, single product line firms. Such dominant businesses are usually controlled by top management through a functional structure, while the remainder of the businesses are managed through product divisions.[54] In these firms, the relationship between entrepreneurs and champions in the dominant business resembles that which we found in integrated, single product line firms like DEC and Pilkington. The entrepreneur gives up definition of products in the dominant business, but he keeps tight reins on sponsorship, particularly for major products. IBM in the late 1960s is a case in point.

Outsiders see IBM as a reflection of its products—a model of orderliness and rationality. To many, IBM is the epitome of the modern corporation: technologically powerful and highly innovative, but predictable and smoothly managed. Yet in 1964, after months of chaotic infighting, Tom Watson, Jr. (then IBM's CEO), made the extraordinarily risky decision to commit IBM to a revolutionary new line of computers, the System 360. The program's projected cost, $5 billion, exceeded the total assets (or, for that matter, the annual sales) of IBM that year. The System 360 was revolutionary in three major ways:

1. It depended heavily on microcircuitry (technology now commonplace, but then in its infancy).
2. The series was comprised of six basic computers designed so that users could scale up from one machine to another without having to rewrite existing programs.
3. The six models (30, 40, 50, 60, 62, 70) were to be made available simultaneously.

Bob Evans, the line manager who acted as technological champion for the new computers, explained: "We called this project 'you bet your company.' "[55]

According to one IBM executive, Watson had grown up with the IBM computer business and therefore "was able to use the informal organization to obtain the knowledge necessary to make the right decisions."[56] Watson once invited Fred Brooks, who at that time was the 360 project-design manager, and other technical experts to his ski lodge in Vermont for a detailed discussion of the critical programming-compatability issues. Watson also relied on T. Vincent Learson, a group executive whom he had tapped in 1954, to head IBM's entry into computers. Learson, a "tough and forceful personality," was "impatient with staff reports and committees," and he tended to "operate outside the conventional chain of command."[57] Learson was known to go directly to lower level management when he needed information.

The decision to go ahead with the 360 system shook IBM to its core. Sweeping organizational changes were instituted (three reorganizations over a six-year period), technically oriented executives diluted some of the traditional power of the marketing staff, IBM World Trade stopped trying to develop its own computers. IBM shifted from being simply an assembler of computer components to making its own components. In the process it became for a time the world's largest manufacturer of integrated circuits.

The success of IBM's System 360 is now legendary. It became the dominant design in business computers, and Learson was promoted to president of IBM shortly after its introduction. But in 1966 it was far from clear that Watson's gamble would be successful, and IBM's management agreed that "no meaningful figure could be put on the gamble." But a decade later it was clear that Watson had bet his company—and won.

Like Harry Pilkington and Ken Olsen, Watson and Learson communicated directly with the technical experts, and they relied on informal information networks to supplement the data they were able to obtain directly. Middle managers, like Brooks, Evans, and Alistair Pilkington, championed the new products. But top management made the major resource-allocation decisions, and they had the insight to make winning decisions, because they were dealing with single product line businesses, with which they had grown up.

When diversified firms enter fields with which the dominant entrepreneur is not intimately familiar, the process changes. Now a new kind of champion emerges, bridging the gap between the entrepreneur and the technological champion. Within the scope of their authority and responsibility, these "executive champions" are modeled after the independent entrepreneurs discussed above. Sometimes, they are simply the original independent entrepreneur in a new corporate context, in which their power is circumscribed. In other cases, they grow out of the roots of the existing corporate culture.

In 1975, for example, Redactron, facing financial difficulties, agreed to merge with the Burroughs Corporation. Though Evelyn Berezin kept her title of president of Redactron, she became a Burroughs employee in 1976. In an interview shortly after joining Burroughs, she explained her philosophy of management:

In a small company the real cost is not in the operating expenses, or in buying some new pieces of gear, or hiring a new person—it's time. Reducing your development or commercialization time is worth virtually whatever you have to pay.

Redactron and three other companies in the Burroughs structure operated as relatively autonomous businesses within Burroughs, which was then a $2 billion corporation with 50,000 employees and fifty plants. At Burroughs, Berezin's role had changed considerably, partly as a result of her continued quest to gain precious time. Now she was far more concerned with resource allocation than with product definition. She explained her new role:

Burroughs's product management is involved in the resource-allocation process, thus I am constantly involved in funding decisions. I have told my managers "you go do it, I'll get the funds." But there are limitations: For instance, I don't have authority to increase the engineering budget, but I can determine how programs are carried out. Secondly, all raises go through Detroit. I can't unilaterally increase people's salaries, but my people know that I will champion them.

Berezin cited a specific example:

We had developed a new peripheral device which was very sophisticated yet inexpensive. It was a new technology. It was, in a word, "gorgeous." Yet corporate engineering said no, they were working on something else and this project could not be supported. The tooling that was required was on the order of $50,000 and had to be approved by corporate. My capital budget, however, had been approved at the beginning of the year, and I could only approve new items below $5,000.

What did I do? I took the device to top management. What happened? The project was approved. I had to fight for four months, but I won the fight. In a good large company, if you fight—long enough—you win.

Evelyn Berezin, similarly to Tom Watson, Jr., was sponsoring a member of her organization who had proposed a promising new project. The key difference was that the circumscription of her authority required that she seek higher level sponsorship to implement the project. Berezin was an "executive champion" several times removed from the detailed technical definition, but without the entrepreneurial clout to be the ultimate sponsor. Thus, in this example, we find a new kind of champion—more senior in the managerial structure than the technological champion, who, in fact, is often a sponsor for the latter within the limits of his or her responsibility.

In 1974 just after Ronald Peterson had returned to Grumman Aerospace from a year as a Sloan Fellow at MIT, he was tapped by the president of Grumman to head an exploratory group on advanced energy systems. His immediate concern was with resource allocation, and in particular, with the authority that would go with his new position. Peterson, who had done his MIT thesis on innovation, felt that unless he reported directly to chief executive Joseph G. Gavin, Jr., the probability of success for his project would be reduced. "I've learned enough about new ventures," explained Peterson, "to know they don't work unless they get top level attention." Soon after, Peterson became manager of the Energy Program Department, and he reported directly to Gavin.[58]

After studying the alternatives open to Grumman, Peterson decided not to follow in the footsteps of aerospace firms bidding on proposals for esoteric new technologies, such as giant wind machines, oceanic platforms, and orbiting power stations.[59] Peterson decided instead to shun government proposals and to concentrate first on low-technology solar hot-water and space-heating installations. He knew that, in order to achieve his goals, he needed the freedom to operate the business differently and independently from the traditional management style of the parent firm.

In 1977 when Joseph G. Gavin, Jr., was appointed president of the Grumman Corporation, the parent company of Grumman Aerospace, he appointed Peterson general manager of the Grumman Advanced Energy Systems Division. "I've been fortunate that Gavin has had a long-term interest in energy and since the beginning has played the sponsor role on this project." Peterson explained why the new division was established:

One of the main reasons for establishing this division was not to be hampered with aerospace procedures, salaries, and infrastructure. . . .

In this position I have a lot of authority. . . . I can sign for anything up to a million dollars on the annual plan without any counter signature. I have the power to raise salaries and hire and fire people. In effect, I am the president of a virtually independent corporation.[60]

Peterson had become, within the limits approved by Gavin, an executive champion who was willing and able to risk Grumman's resources on projects proposed by technological champions in his organization.

Conclusion: Evolution of the Entrepreneurial Network

The relatively small number of cases and industries studied, the incompleteness of some of the secondary data, and the complexity of the processes examined limit us to hypothesis generation. But the data suggest a framework to explain how the relationship between the network of entrepreneurial roles and radical innovation changes with stage of process development and increasing organizational complexity. The proposed framework is illustrated in Figure 2.3.

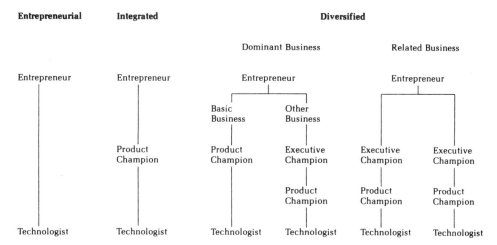

Figure 2.3   The Evolution of the Entrepreneurial Network

The small firm is easiest to analyze. Here, there is usually one business unit and one source of managerial sponsorship for technological projects: the entrepreneur. However, as in Efi Arazi's case, problem solving is part of the technological entrepreneur's lifeblood. Thus, most technological entrepreneurs continue to hold on to most, or all, of the reins of product definition, often until it is too late: Henry Kloss neglected financial and other duties of corporate management until he eventually lost control of his firm. Involvement in product definition without upsetting the firm's organizational hierarchy is not difficult for entrepreneurs in small firms. Most of the technical people are generally old colleagues of the entrepreneur or were hired directly by him or her. But even the most capable entrepreneur has limits. One of the most brilliant entrepreneurs I've met thought himself impervious to these limitations when he moved into his plant, cot and all. Within a few months, after a divorce and a nervous breakdown, he too realized that he had a limit.

Unless the entrepreneur recognizes that at some point—two or three projects for some, perhaps a dozen for others—he or she must retreat from the product-definition role, the firm is likely to fail. Berezin, as is evident from our second encounter with her, had begun such a transition.

The integrated technology firm, such as DEC and Pilkington Brothers, illustrates the entrepreneur's transition from the definition role. In these firms, the CEO was technically knowledgeable and still played a pivotal role in the innovation process—for radical innovations. Harry Pilkington and Ken Olsen did not define the new products, but they used their technical expertise and their organization's informal channels to gather information from their technical people. Although Pilkington and Olsen were managing firms several times smaller than Watson's IBM, all three chief executive officers viewed providing impetus to at least the radical technical innovations as a key part of their role. Nonetheless, there is a limit to how many projects a chief executive can sponsor. Olsen, for instance, could afford to be very visible in his firm's resource-allocation process. Watson, as CEO of a $4 billion firm, could be involved only in those projects that might reshape the entire future of his firm—like the System 360. Similarly to the small company entrepreneurs, Watson and Olsen had excellent informal information networks that made available to them vitally important data for their decision making without destroying the firm's organizational structure. And that is precisely what they did: they made the major technological decisions and absorbed risks. Sponsorship replaced definition.

Increasing organizational complexity requires that others also sponsor innovations. The CEO, or the overall top management team, should be the sponsor for radical changes in large organizations; yet many other important projects also need sponsors.[61] Ronald Peterson argued that Joseph G. Gavin, Jr., had been the "sponsor" for his energy group. It was clear, however, that by the time Grumman Advanced Energy Systems had become a division, Peterson, not Gavin, had become the sponsor for most new projects. Gavin primarily helped to set overall business direction. In short, Peterson and Berezin functioned as executive champions who, *within their business units,* behaved similarly to Olsen, Watson, and Pilkington, Sr.

The inherent disorder produced by direct interaction of the central sources of sponsorship with the defining or proposing agents is a unifying thread in all the cases studied. By promoting informality in communications, interacting with first-line technical people, reviewing proposals outside of the "conservative bias" of middle management, and finally *deciding,* the entrepreneurial heads of the executive structures studied helped to perpetuate the fluidness, slack, and disorder that Abernathy and Utterback found in the highly innovative initial stages of process development.

In a study of the evolution of the structure of the firm,[62] Abernathy and Utterback suggest that the "normal" direction of transition in a business unit, and more generally, in a firm, is toward a more rigid process that implies more product homogeneity, increased automation, and more bureaucratic management. In this phase, both product and process innovation begin to approach zero (see Figure 2.2).

However, Abernathy and Utterback do not propose that the "normal" direction of process and organizational evolution is inexorable. They leave the door open for reversals. Utterback has argued that major innovation, usually originating outside the existing industry, is the key catalyst for a reversal. New ventures—larger firms entering a new business—are credited with the lion's share of the innovations that create important threats for the present competitors.[63] In a later article, Abernathy and Utterback concluded that government sponsorship, through either purchases or direct regulation, can also have a major impact on innovation in an industry.[64] The recent downsizing of automobiles is a case in point.

Some firms, however, do revolutionize themselves from within. We argue here that when this happens it is the consequence of entrepreneurial sponsorship. This lever for change is not often used. Established firms generally respond to technological invasions by perfecting their present technology. The history of the fountain-pen, steam-locomotive, and razor-blade industries and their response to ballpoint pens, diesel locomotives, and electric razors are illustrative examples.[65]

When the sources of sponsorship are buffered, major changes either do not come about, or, alternatively, occur through a spinoff. Soon after the System 360 had been introduced at IBM, Gene Amdahl, a brilliant designer who had been part of its creation, proposed a new generation of computers based on advanced integrated circuits. After failing to get sponsorship for his proposals, Amdahl quit IBM in frustration and set out to develop his own computer in 1971. The result was the Amdahl 470, introduced in 1975, that was 1.4 to 1.8 times faster than the IBM 370/168 while costing 8 to 12 percent less. Amdahl's sales, four years after the introduction of the 470, were running at an annualized rate of over $400 million.[66] Although IBM later introduced a system with comparable performance, the attitude toward technological champions seems to have changed significantly since the Watson days. Frank Cary, IBM's present chairman, says, "From now on, change will be evolutionary rather than revolutionary."[67]

In summary, managing radical technological change is a fundamental element of top management's task in the technology-based firm. To succeed in coping with new waves of technology, the chief executive must, in Ted Levitt's words, "attack the problem of change."[68] He or she should develop an environment where risk taking by executive champions and product champions will lead to new ventures and products. Most important, if the top manager is to thwart the drift toward rigidity and organizational inertia that usually accompanies success, he or she must be personally involved in the entrepreneurial networks that lead to radical technological change, for only the chief executive can make decisions, provide the resources, and absorb the risks necessary for such change.

3

Leadership, Conflict, and Project-Management Effectiveness

Hans J. Thamhain

David L. Wilemon

This article deals with key problems faced by project managers in managing complex tasks. The emphasis is on the focal position of the project manager—how he or she develops support from functional specialists and handles the ever-present conflict situations in managing projects, and how these activities influence managerial performance. The report is based on a continuing research study of project managers in various high-technology organizations. A situational approach to project-management effectiveness is developed, and specific guidelines are provided to help project managers become more effective. *SMR*.

Project management is an organizational system used for the effective execution of multidisciplinary, one-time undertakings of finite duration. Examples of this system include high-technology R&D programs, political campaigns, crime control efforts, and foreign-assistance programs.[1] A project organization is usually an overlay to the functional structure of the host or parent organization. This overlay organization is characterized principally by horizontal lines of communication and work flow and by the necessity for planning, integrating, and controlling various multidisciplinary tasks across functional lines.

The central figure in any project organization is the project manager who is accountable to both top management and the client for delivering acceptable performance within schedule and budget constraints.

In their search for solutions to complex problems, project managers often must cross functional lines within their parent organization to gain support for

From *Sloan Management Review*, Fall 1977, Vol. 19, No. 1. Reprinted with permission.

their projects from different disciplines. More often than not, project managers have little or no formal authority[2] over those individuals who can provide the needed advice and assistance. Equally important is the project manager's ability to manager intense conflict situations.[3] This ability often can mean the difference between successful and unsuccessful project performance.[4]

This article reports on a field investigation, the objectives of which were to examine:

- The relationship between managerial style and conflict in various project settings, and
- The relationship between managerial style and project management effectiveness.

The variables and specific typology used to collect data are described in the next section, followed by a discussion of the results, and concluding with recommendations for improving project-manager effectiveness.

Data Collection and Research Methodology

Data were collected from project managers during a series of project-management seminars. Project managers attending these seminars came from a variety of technology-oriented companies, such as aircraft manufacturers, computer companies, and electronic equipment manufacturers. A judgment sample of 100 project managers was obtained.

The data were collected via a questionnaire and supplemented by discussions before and after completion. The process was designed to measure values of the four sets of variables:

1. Managerial influence style,
2. Managerial conflict-resolution style,
3. Conflict cause and intensity, and
4. Effectiveness rating of project managers.

Managerial Influence Style

A manager's ability to gain support from others depends on his or her managerial style. By definition, influence style is composed of certain bases of influence such as authority and reward or punishment. In project management, the study of managerial style is especially important, because many of the traditional influence bases, such as direct reward and punishment, are in the hands of functional colleagues. The project manager usually selects the per-

Table 3.1 Nine Key Influence Bases Available to Project Managers

Influence Base (Rank Ordered)	Characteristics
EXPERTISE	The ability to gain support because project personnel perceive the project manager as possessing special knowledge or expertise; that is, he is perceived as possessing expertise that they consider to be important.
AUTHORITY	The ability to gain support because personnel supporting the project perceive the project manager as having the power to issue orders.
WORK CHALLENGE	Based on personal enjoyment while executing a particular type of work; oriented toward the intrinsic motivation of personnel.
FRIENDSHIP (REFERENT POWER)	The ability to gain support because project personnel feel personally attracted to the project manager, to the project, or both. Expert and referent power, unlike authority, reward, and penalty power cannot be delegated by senior management to project managers but is earned through their relationship with project personnel.
FUTURE WORK ASSIGNMENT	The ability to gain support because personnel perceive the project manager as being capable of influencing their future work assignments.
FUND ALLOCATION	The ability to gain support because personnel perceive the project manager as possessing the power to dispense financial resources (budgets).
PROMOTION	The ability to gain support because project personnel perceive the project manager as being capable of indirectly dispensing valued organizational rewards.
SALARY	The ability to gain support because project personnel perceive the project manager as being capable of directly dispensing monetary rewards.
PENALTY	The ability to gain support because project personnel perceive the project manager as being capable of directly or indirectly dispensing penalties they wish to avoid. Penalty power usually derives from the same sources as reward power, with one being a necessary condition for the other.

sonnel he or she wants from the functional pool and negotiates their availability with the functional manager and with the individual. Project personnel stay connected to functional managers, who decide on salary adjustments, performance appraisals, and promotions. However, project managers can usually influence such decisions through formal and informal performance reports and recommendations to functional managers.

Moreover, the manager's power may vary over the life of the project due to changes in project scope, his charter with senior management, and his relationship with the client. Effective project leadership, therefore, is a critical attribute that relates interpersonal influence and situational variables in a complex fashion. Even so, results of a particular leadership style are not always predictable.[5]

For the current investigation, nine influence bases were identified. Table 3.1 lists these influence bases in order of importance as measured by the aggregated response of 100 project managers.

To minimize potential bias that might have resulted from the use of social-science jargon, specific statements were used to describe each of the nine influence bases. Project managers were asked to indicate on a six-point scale (very important; important; somewhat helpful; I am indifferent about it; might do more harm than good; might be detrimental) how important each influence method was in gaining support from project personnel. For example, to measure the perceived importance of authority, three statements were used for scoring:

- The project manager should have formal authority.
- The project manager should inform his personnel that he has this formal authority.
- The organization should inform the project personnel who is in command.

Hence, an independent set of scores was obtained on the perceived importance of each influence base. This method allowed the researchers to rank the project managers according to their perceived style for each of the nine sources of influence.[6]

Conflict-Resolution Style

Because conflict is basic to human behavior, it is inevitable in the management of complex social systems. In project organizations, conflict is often attributed to the limits placed by the structure on divergent individual interests. However, conflict can be beneficial; individuals may be pushed to higher performance levels and encouraged to make additional progress.[7]

Five approaches, or modes, for dealing with conflict can be defined.[8] Table 3.2 lists these conflict-resolution approaches according to the particular frequency used by project managers. Thus, *confronting* was used most frequently, while *withdrawing* was used least often in handling project-related conflict.

In order to obtain a measure for the modes used by project managers to resolve conflicts, questions have been asked based on aphorisms or statements of folk wisdom. Three aphorisms were used to represent each conflict-handling mode. Project managers were asked to indicate (on a standard four-point scale) their agreement with each aphorism based on how accurately it described the means by which they handled conflicts in their work environments.

Examples of these aphorisms are: "Might overcomes right," representative of forcing; and "Better half a loaf than no bread," representative of compromising. The sources obtained on the total of fifteen aphorisms represent a

Table 3.2   Five General Modes for Handling Conflict

Conflict-Handling Modes (Rank Ordered)	Characteristics
CONFRONTING OR PROBLEM SOLVING	Involves a rational problem-solving approach. Disputing parties solve differences by focusing on the issues, looking at alternative approaches, and selecting the best alternative. Confronting may contain elements of other modes such as compromising and smoothing.
COMPROMISING	Bargaining and searching for solutions which bring some degree of satisfaction to the parties involved in conflict. Since compromise yields less than optimum results, the project manager must weigh such actions against program goals.
SMOOTHING	Emphasizes common areas of agreement and de-emphasizes areas of difference. Like withdrawing, smoothing may not address the real issues in a disagreement. Smoothing is a more effective mode, however, because identifying areas of agreement may more clearly focus on areas of disagreement; and further, project work can often continue in areas where there is agreement by the parties.
FORCING	Exerting one's viewpoint at the expense of another - characterized by competitiveness and win/lose behavior. Forcing is often used as a last resort by project managers since it may cause resentment and deterioration of the work climate.
WITHDRAWING	Retreating from a conflict issue. Here, the project manager does not deal with the disagreement. He may ignore it entirely, he may withdraw out of fear, he may feel inadequate to bring about an effective resolution, or he may want to avoid rocking the boat. If the issue or disagreement is important to the other party, withdrawal may intensify the conflict situation. In some cases, a project manager may elect to use the withdrawing mode as either a temporary strategy to allow the other party to cool off or as a strategy to buy time so that he can study the issue further.

measure of how strongly project managers believe in certain methods of handling conflict, in effect profiling each manager's conflict-resolution style.

Conflict Causes and Intensity

The average conflict intensity perceived by the project managers was measured for seven potential conflict sources. Project managers were asked to indicate the intensity of conflict they experienced for each source on a four-point scale. The seven potential conflict sources are characterized in Table 3.3.

Table 3.3 Seven Potential Causes of Conflict in Project Management

Potential Cause of Conflict	Characteristics
SCHEDULES	Disagreements which develop around the timing, sequencing, and scheduling of project-related tasks.
PROJECT PRIORITIES	The views of project participants differ over the sequence of activities and tasks which should be undertaken to achieve successful project completion.
MANPOWER RESOURCES	Conflicts which arise around the staffing of the project team with personnel from other functional and staff support areas or from the desire to use another department's personnel for project support.
TECHNICAL OPINIONS AND PERFORMANCE TRADE-OFFS	Disagreements may arise, particularly in technology-oriented projects, over technical issues, performance specifications, technical trade-offs, and the means to achieve performance.
ADMINISTRATIVE PROCEDURES	Managerial and administrative-oriented conflicts which develop over how the project will be managed; i. e., the definition of the project manager's reporting relationships, definition of responsibilities, interface relationships, project scope, operational requirements, plans of execution, negotiated work agreements with other groups, and procedures for administrative support.
COST	Conflict that develops over cost estimates from support areas regarding various project work breakdown packages. For example, the funds allocated by a project manager to a functional support group might be perceived as insufficient for the support requested.
PERSONALITY CONFLICT	Disagreements which tend to center on interpersonal differences rather than on "technical" issues. Conflicts often are "ego-centered."

Effectiveness Rating of Project Managers

A measure of managerial effectiveness was obtained by contacting the superiors of the 100 project managers investigated. Each superior was asked to rate the project manager relative to his peers on two measures: ability to resolve conflict, and overall project performance. A 0–100 percent scale was used, and a usable sample of thirty superiors was obtained.

Results

The results are presented here in four parts: (1) the effects of the project managers' influence style on conflict intensity; (2) the effects of conflict-resolution modes on conflict intensity; (3) the relationship between influence style and conflict-resolution modes; and (4) the relationship between influence style and project managerial effectiveness. All associations were obtained by using Kendall Rank Order correlation techniques.[9]

Influence Style and Conflict Intensity

Table 3.4 presents a summary of the correlation between managerial influence style and conflict intensity. The influence bases of managerial style are listed in the order of importance perceived by project managers. As shown, expertise, authority, and work challenge were particularly important, while fund allocation, salary, and penalty were less important to project managers.

The correlation figures in Table 3.4 show that the various influence methods have different effects on conflict intensity. For example, in the first column, the two highest correlation figures of $\tau = -0.25$ suggest that the more project managers rely on expertise or penalty, the less conflict they experience in dealing with schedule problems. However, the effectiveness of a particular influence method for minimizing conflict must be judged over the whole spectrum of work situations. For instance, while penalty methods seem to be effective in minimizing conflict over schedules, they increase conflict in most other areas, particularly when dealing with manpower and personality issues.

To avoid cluttering Table 3.4 with insignificant data, only those correlation figures that have confidence levels of greater than 70 percent are listed. Particularly significant associations of $p \geq 95$ percent are indicated by framing the correlation figure with a broken line $\lceil -\tau \rceil$ for favorable associations and with a solid line $\boxed{\tau}$ for unfavorable associations between influence method and conflict intensity. The reader is reminded, however, that the correlation figures in Table 3.4 represent only the relationship between various influence methods and conflict intensity and do not permit any conclusions as to the effectiveness of these influence methods regarding overall project performance. Research data on overall project effectiveness are discussed in Table 3.8.

Table 3.4 Kendall τ Correlation Between Influence Style and Conflict Intensity (Correlation Figures are Shown only if Confidence Level p > 70 Percent)

MANAGERIAL INFLUENCE * INFLUENCE BASES AS RANKED BY PROJECT MANAGERS	CONFLICT CAUSES **						
	INTENSITY OF CONFLICT PERCEIVED OVER						
	SCHEDULES	PROJECT PRIORITIES	MANPOWER RESOURCES	TECH OPINIONS	ADMINISTR PROCEDURES	COST OBJECTIVES	PERSON'TY CONFLICT
EXPERTISE	-.25	-.15	-.30	.35		.20	.15
AUTHORITY	-.15	-.10		.25	-.20		.25
WORK CHALLENGE			.15				-.35
FRIENDSHIP	.15	.25	-.10			.20	
FUTURE WORK ASSIGNMENTS		.10	-.20			.15	
FUND ALLOCATION	-.10	.10	-.20				
PROMOTION	-.10		-.20				
SALARY	.15		-.20	-.15			.10
PENALTY	-.25	.20	.25	-.15	.20	-.15	.35

* Influence Bases as perceived by Project Managers dealing with Project Personnel.

** Variables of influence and conflict have been measured independently, hence the rows or columns in the table do not necessarily total zero.

[τ] Favorable Association at Confidence Level p ≥ 95%.

[τ] Unfavorable Association at p ≥ 95%.

[Blank] Correlation Figures are too low and insignificant (p ≤ 70%) to draw any conclusions.

Conflict-Resolution Style and Conflict Intensity

In Table 3.5, the association between conflict-handling approaches and perceived conflict intensity for the conflict causes is presented. Again, only correlation figures with a confidence level greater than 70 percent are listed; cells with insignificant correlation remain blank. The conflict-resolution modes are ranked by frequency of use. Confrontation or problem solving was favored by approximately 70 percent of the number of project managers. This implies that 70 percent of the project managers indicated that the proverbs that represent the confrontation mode "accurately" or "very accurately" describe the way they resolve conflict in actual project situations.

Similar to the associations of influence methods, the various conflict-resolution modes have different effects on conflict intensity. Focusing on the more significant correlations (confidence level greater than 95 percent), Table 3.5 data indicate that conflict over schedules seems to increase the more project managers rely on compromise or withdrawal, while forcing seems to reduce this type of conflict. On the other hand, the positive correlation figures of 0.25 and 0.30 associated with forcing indicate that forcing increases conflict intensity when dealing with manpower issues or technical opinions.

Another interesting finding is that conflict over project priorities seems to decrease if project managers rely on confrontation, smoothing, or even forcing; but increases with withdrawal. An explanation may be found in the fact that priority problems usually must be solved promptly and in a manner that focuses squarely on the issues. By contrast, retreating from the conflict issue may intensify a conflict situation, because it does not address the real issue of disagreement; it provides only a temporary solution.

In summary, as in the case of managerial influence style, the effectiveness of each conflict-resolution mode is situational. Although certain modes appear to minimize conflict, the data presented thus far do not yet show any particular management style as being clearly more effective than the others regarding overall project performance.

Influence Style and Conflict-Resolution Style

The interrelationship between managerial influence style and conflict resolution style, summarized in Table 3.6, indicates that certain influence bases tend to be used with particular conflict-resolution modes. All correlation figures in Table 3.6 have a minimum confidence level of 70 percent. Black cells indicate associations of lower significance. The most important statistical relationships are listed separately in Table 3.7.

These results indicate that project managers who emphasize expertise and

Table 3.5 Kendall τ Correlation Between Conflict Resolution and Conflict Intensity (Correlation Figures Are Shown only if Confidence Level p > 70 Percent)

| CONFLICT RESOLUTION * | CONFLICT CAUSES ** | | | | | | |
| CONFLICT-RESOLUTION MODES AS RANKED BY PROJECT MANAGERS | INTENSITY OF CONFLICT PERCEIVED OVER ...... | | | | | | |
	SCHEDULES	PROJECT PRIORITIES	MANPOWER RESOURCES	TECH OPINIONS	ADMINISTR PROCEDURES	COST OBJECTIVES	PERSON'TY CONFLICT
CONFRONTATION	-.20	-.20	-.10	.25 (box)		.10	
COMPROMISE	.25 (box)	.10			-.25 (dashed)		-.20
SMOOTHING	-.15	-.25 (dashed)			-.20	.20	
FORCING	-.25 (dashed)	-.15	.25 (box)	.30 (box)	.20		
WITHDRAWAL	.25 (box)	.25 (box)			-.15		

* Conflict-Resolution Modes as perceived by Project Managers dealing with Project Personnel.

** Variables of influence and conflict have been measured independently, hence the rows or columns in the table do not necessarily total zero.

[τ] Favorable Association at Confidence Level p ≥ 95%

τ Unfavorable Association at p ≥ 95%

Blank Correlation Figures are too low and insignificant (p < 70%) to draw any conclusions

Table 3.6   Kendall τ Correlation Between Managerial Influence Style and Conflict-Resolution Style (Correlation Figures Are Shown only if Confidence Level p > 70 Percent)

MANAGERIAL INFLUENCE * — INFLUENCE BASES AS RANKED BY PROJECT MANAGERS	PROJECT MANAGER'S ** CONFLICT RESOLUTION STYLE				
	CONFRONT	COMPROM	SMOOTHING	FORCING	WITHDRAWAL
EXPERTISE	.30	.10	- .20	.20	- .25
AUTHORITY			- .10	- .15	
WORK CHALLENGE	.25		- .20		- .20
FRIENDSHIP		.30	.25		.25
FUTURE WORK ASSIGNMENTS	- .10	- .10		- .15	
FUND ALLOCATION	- .25	.10	.10		.20
PROMOTION		- .30			- .10
SALARY	- .40	- .10	- .10	.30	.20
PENALTY	- .40	- .20	- .10	.30	- .15

* Influence Bases and Conflict-Resolution Modes as perceived by Project Managers dealing with Project Personnel.

** Variables of influence and conflict have been measured independently, hence the rows or columns in the table do not necessarily total zero.

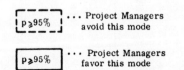

$p \geqslant 95\%$ ... Project Managers avoid this mode

$p \geqslant 95\%$ ... Project Managers favor this mode

Blank Correlation Figures are too low and insignificant (p ≤ 70%) to draw any conclusions

work challenge as influence bases tend to resolve conflict by confrontation and to avoid withdrawal. It would seem odd if this were not the case, since the more expert project managers are, the greater is their ability to evaluate and question work progress and quality. In other words, they are better prepared to face problems and deal directly with conflict situations.

The data in Tables 3.6 and 3.7 also show that those project managers who rely on friendship as a means of gaining support are more likely to favor con-

Table 3.7 Summary of the Most Significant Relationships Between Managerial Influence Style and Conflict-Resolution Style

MANAGERIAL INFLUENCE	CONFLICT RESOLUTION	
Project Managers who rely on these Influence Bases	. . . . Favor these Conflict-Resolution Modes	. . . . Avoid these Conflict-Resolution Modes
EXPERTISE	CONFRONTATION	WITHDRAWAL
WORK CHALLENGE	CONFRONTATION	SMOOTHING WITHDRAWAL
FRIENDSHIP	COMPROMISE SMOOTHING WITHDRAWAL	
FUND ALLOCATION		CONFRONTATION WITHDRAWAL
PROMOTION		COMPROMISE
SALARY	FORCING	CONFRONTATION
PENALTY	FORCING	CONFRONTATION

All Relationships are significant at the 94% Level or better.

flict-resolution modes of compromise, smoothing, and withdrawal. Discussions with project personnel revealed that managers with low expertise or low position power often resort to referent-type leadership styles and, further, prefer indirect methods of handling conflict. While indirect methods might be the best ones for a manager under given circumstances, he or she might have to accept suboptimal solutions. For example, the findings discussed earlier in Table 3.4 reveal that project managers who rely predominantly on friendship experience greater conflict with project priorities, cost objectives, and schedules. One explanation for this is that project managers may be reluctant to jeopardize their relationships with those who support them by using a more direct mode.

It is interesting to note the statistically significant relationship of the two least important influence bases—salary and penalty. The more project managers rely on those two bases as a method of influence, the stronger they favor forcing and avoid confrontation as a mode for conflict resolution. The results are not surprising, however, since both salary and penalty are organizationally derived influence sources, and their use suggests a more leader-centered management approach.[10] It is also this type of manager who might favor forcing over a problem-oriented approach such as confrontation.

Thus far, the focus has been on the effect of leadership style on conflict intensity. The data presented provide a foundation for an analysis of project-management effectiveness.

Project-Manager Effectiveness

Table 3.8 summarizes the correlation data between influence style of project managers and their effectiveness rating as given by their superiors. This table lists correlation figures with a minimum confidence level of 70 percent. Blank cells indicate associations of lower significance. The positive correlation for expertise and work challenge associated with a confidence level of $p = 0.9$ indicates their important role in the improvement of project effectiveness. The more project managers use expertise and work challenge to gain support, the greater appears their ability to resolve project-related conflict (τ_1) and the better their overall performance (τ_2). The negative correlation associated with punishment power, authority, and salary indicates (at a confidence level of $p = 0.95$) that the use of each leads to lower effectiveness.[11]

It should be noted, however, that the perceived importance of a particular influence base is not necessarily an indication of its effectiveness. As shown in Table 3.8, authority, for example, is perceived by project managers as being very important, but its use leads to a lower rating regarding both the ability of the project manager to resolve conflict and his or her overall project performance. One explanation for this may be that project managers employ influence methods depending upon the particular situation. While authority (if they have it) might be an important basis of influence, project managers must use it judiciously depending upon the particular situation. Overuse of authority might influence the project manager's ability to gain sustained support from project personnel and might also have a negative effect on overall project performance.

Table 3.8 Kendall τ Correlation Between Influence Style of Project Managers and Their
Effectiveness Rating for Resolving Conflict and Managing Projects

MANAGERIAL INFLUENCE INFLUENCE BASES AS RANKED BY PROJECT MANAGERS	EFFECTIVENESS RATING OF PROJECT MANAGERS REGARDING	
	CONFLICT RESOLUTION τ_1	PROJECT PERFORMANCE τ_2
EXPERTISE	$\boxed{.25}$	$\boxed{.40}$
AUTHORITY	$\overline{\underline{-.25}}$	$\overline{\underline{-.25}}$
WORK CHALLENGE	.20	$\boxed{.30}$
FRIENDSHIP		.05
FUTURE WORK ASSIGNMENTS	.10	
PROMOTION	.10	
FUND ALLOCATION		.15
SALARY		$\overline{\underline{-.25}}$
PENALTY	$\overline{\underline{-.35}}$	$\overline{\underline{-.30}}$

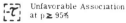

$\boxed{\tau}$ Favorable Association at
Confidence Level $p \geq 95\%$

$\overline{\underline{-\tau}}$ Unfavorable Association
at $p \geq 95\%$

Blank Fields indicate Correlations
with Confidence Levels of $p < 70\%$

Discussion

Our research explored the relationships between the project manager's influence style, the conflict-resolution approaches he or she uses, and each manager's overall performance level. The following discussion is an attempt to bring

these research findings into perspective and relate them to actual project management practices.

● *It appears that project managers do not select a management style that minimizes the overall conflict experienced in managing their projects.*

The findings indicate that, while influence bases are perceived in a particular order of importance, their effect on the degree of conflict experienced varies. That is, the influence bases perceived as being most important by project managers—expertise, authority, and work challenge—are not associated with lower degrees of conflict across the spectrum of conflict determinants. This might be explained by both the project manager's concern for overall project performance and his or her assessment of the role of conflict in the attainment of performance. In complex projects, conflict is inevitable, and task performance often depends on how effectively the manager can handle a myriad of delicate conflict-oriented issues without jeopardizing schedule, budget, or performance parameters. His concern might be the outcome of a conflict situation and its impact on overall project effectiveness, rather than the level of conflict associated with his management style and actions.

● *The effectiveness of conflict-resolution modes in minimizing conflict is largely determined by the situation.*

Conflict over different issues (such as schedules, priorities, or manpower resources) often originates because of the project manager's interactions with different organizational and behavioral elements. In confronting these issues, the project manager must negotiate with a diverse range of functional experts. Thus, managing various conflict situations requires a high degree of adaptability on the part of the project manager in finding the most appropriate conflict-resolution mode.

● *Project managers generally have more flexibility in altering their conflict-resolution modes than in modifying their influence styles.*

In dealing with a wide range of functional experts, project managers have more flexibility in modifying their conflict-resolution modes than in changing their managerial influence style. For example, the forcing mode may be best suited for dealing with an administrative problem, whereas smoothing or compromising may be most effective for a conflict over priority. As the data in Table 3.5 suggest, some modes may work better than others in reducing conflict over a given issue. Equally important, some modes may be more effective in encounters with certain individual contributors to the project than other conflict-handling approaches.

Altering managerial influence style, however, appears to be more difficult for project managers. Although a project manager may attempt to deal with his various interfaces differently, he is likely to use a relatively consistent influence style in his relationships with a specific interface. The continual change of influence style by a project manager is likely to lead to confusion and distrust by his interfaces. Moreover, managerial influence style is often inherent in the values of the manager and is continually reinforced by interaction with others.

- *The less project managers emphasize organizationally derived influence bases—such as authority, salary, and penalty—and the more they rely on work challenge and expertise, the higher they are rated in their ability to effectively resolve conflict and manage projects.*

One of our most interesting findings is the importance of work challenge as an influence method. Work challenge appears to deal with integrating the personal goals and needs of project personnel with project goals more than do other influence methods (such as authority), which appear to be more concerned with adapting project personnel to project goals without regard to their preference and needs. That is, work challenge is primarily oriented toward the intrinsic motivation of project personnel, while other methods are oriented more toward extrinsic rewards. The study suggests that attempts to enrich the assignments of project personnel in such a way as to be professionally challenging may indeed have a beneficial effect on project performance. Additionally, the assignment of challenging work is a variable over which project managers may have a great deal of control. While in most cases the total task structure is fixed, the method by which work is assigned and distributed is discretionary.

The use of authority requires special consideration. If the project manager is perceived as having earned authority, he or she is better able to use authority in handling conflict over schedules, priorities, and procedures. If authority is thought to be undeserved, the use of it may increase conflict.

Recommendations for Improving Project-Manager Effectiveness

The findings presented in this article should help both the professionals who operate in a project-organized environment and the scholars who study and research contemporary organizational concepts to understand the complex interrelationships among managerial influence, conflict resolution approaches, and project-management effectiveness.

A number of suggestions are derived from the broader context of this study that can potentially increase the project manager's effectiveness in resolving conflict and ultimately improve overall program performance.

1. Project managers need to understand the interaction of organizational and behavioral elements in order to build an environment conducive to their team's motivational needs. This will enhance active participation and minimize disfunctional conflict. The effective flow of communication is one of the major factors determining the quality of the organizational environment. Since the project manager must build teams at various organizational layers, it is important that key decisions are communicated properly to all project-related personnel. By openly communicating both the project objectives and those of its subtasks, unproductive conflict can be minimized. Regularly scheduled status-review meetings can be an important vehicle for communicating project-related issues.

2. Because their environment is temporary and often untested, project managers should seek a leadership style that allows them to adapt to the often conflicting demands of their project organization, "parent" organization, specific contributors, and client requirements. They must learn to "test" the expectations of others by observation and experimentation. Although difficult, they must be ready to alter their leadership style as demanded by both the status of the project and its participants.

3. Since the ability to manage conflict is related to their overall performance, project managers should (1) recognize the primary determinants of conflict in their environment and when these are most likely to occur in the life of particular projects; (2) consider the effectiveness of the conflict-handling approaches they have used in the past to manage these conflicts; and (3) consider experimenting with alternative conflict-handling modes if they feel that better performance is warranted.

4. Project managers should try to accommodate the professional interests and desires of supporting personnel when they negotiate their tasks. Project effectiveness depends upon how well they provide work challenges to motivate those individuals who support them and how well their goals match with objectives of the project and of the overall organization. Although the scope of a project may be fixed, the project manager usually has a degree of flexibility in allocating task assignments among various contributors.

5. Project managers should develop or maintain technical expertise in their field. Without understanding the technology they are managing, they will not win confidence among team members or build credibility with the customer community.

6. Effective planning early in the life cycle of a project is another action that

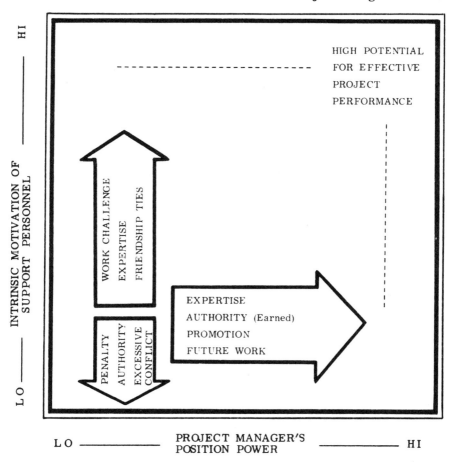

Figure 3.1   Variables of Project-Management Effectiveness

may have a favorable impact on the organizational climate. This is particularly so because project managers have to integrate various disciplines across functional lines. Insufficient planning may eventually lead to interdepartmental conflict and discontinuities in the work flow.

7. Finally, project managers can influence the climate of the work environment by their own actions. Their concern for project team members, their ability to integrate the personal goals and needs of project personnel with project goals, and their ability to create personal enthusiasm for the work itself can foster a climate high in motivation, work involvement, open communication, and resulting project performance.

A situational approach to project-manager effectiveness is presented in Figure 3.1. It summarizes the effects of managerial influence style on two variables of the project environment: motivation of support personnel and position power of the project manager.

Figure 3.1 indicates that the intrinsic motivation of project personnel increases with the project manager's emphasis on work challenge, his or her own expertise, and his or her ability to establish friendship ties. On the other hand, emphasis on penalty measures, authority, and inability to manage conflict effectively lowers personnel motivation.

The figure further illustrates that the project manager's position power is determined by such variables as formal position within the organization, the scope and nature of the project, earned authority, and ability to influence promotion and future work assignments. It appears to be important for sustaining continuity, resources, and organizational commitment to the project over its life cycle.[12]

Some of the most important findings of this research are reflected in Figure 3.1. Project managers who foster a climate of highly motivated personnel not only obtain higher project support from their project personnel, but also achieve high overall project performance ratings from their superiors. In addition, the higher the perceived position power of project managers, the better their potential for effective project performance.

Taken as a whole, Figure 3.1 projects some of the important elements of managerial leadership regarding project effectiveness that seem to be related to the manager's ability to foster an environment conducive to high motivation and favorable to his or her personal position power.

The project manager's role is a difficult one. Only by understanding those variables that contribute to more effective role performance can one develop meaningful insight into project-management effectiveness. This article, it is hoped, has contributed the building blocks for a theory of project management effectiveness and added understanding for project managers themselves.

PART II

Structure

4

Performance of Information Channels in the Transfer of Technology

Thomas J. Allen

There is rather general agreement that the existing channels for communication both within and between the scientific and technological communities are not performing as well as they should.[1] There is also a great lack of understanding of the way in which these channels actually function.

To increase our knowledge of the communication process in science and technology, a number of research studies have attempted to develop descriptive models of the existing communication systems. An understanding of the manner in which scientists and engineers obtain their information, while a major contribution, is not quite sufficient for our purposes. We would like to know more about the impact of various information-gathering practices upon the quality of the research being performed.[2] This would allow us to predict the effects of changes in the information services on the scientist's or engineer's work.

To do this, we obviously require criteria by which to measure research performance. Satisfactory techniques for determining absolute performance measures on an R&D project have yet to be devised, but the relative quality of solutions can be assessed rather easily by a competent judge. This is the technique employed by experimental psychologists in studies of certain kinds of human problem-solving behavior (creative thinking, for example). Several persons are presented with a problem, and a panel of judges is asked to evaluate the relative quality of their answers. The parallel nature of the experimental design allows the psychologist to compare the behaviors observed and relate certain general behavior characteristics to the quality of the solutions produced.

From *Sloan Management Review,* Fall 1966, Vol. 8, No. 1. Reprinted with permission.

Since we cannot yet afford to hire a sufficient number of scientists and engineers and assign them the same research problem, we must search for cases in which parallelism either occurred adventitiously or was consciously planned. The results presented here come from our first study of parallel research and constitute the third interim report on a continuing research program. The first series of parallel projects studied is made up entirely of government supported efforts performed in industrial laboratories. All but one set of these projects are quite clearly developmental in nature and can be considered to fall within the realm of technology. The single deviant pair involved a rather fundamental investigation in physics and displays some rather interesting consequent differences in the information-gathering behavior of the investigators. Some of the differences will be pointed out as we go along, but first a word about the methods by which the data were obtained.

Research Methods

Once a parallel project has been located, its work statement is obtained from the government laboratory awarding the contracts and is analyzed and factored into a number of subproblem areas (generally subsystems). The breakdown is then checked with the technical person who prepared the work statement, and data collection forms are designed. After all data have been collected from the contractors, the technical monitor is asked to provide a confidential evaluation of each lab's performance on each subproblem. The data presented today were gathered by means of a form dubbed the Solution Development Record and from pre- and postproject interviews with individual scientists and engineers.

The Solution Development Record is a research tool that provides a record of the progress of an individual engineer or group of engineers (or scientists) toward the solution of a research and development problem. The lead engineer responsible for each subproblem is asked to provide an estimate each week for each alternative approach of the probability that it will be finally chosen as the solution to that subproblem.

Figure 4.1 illustrates the list of alternative approaches identified from the contract work statement, when so specified, or from the responsible engineer when he or she is interviewed prior to beginning the task. Blank spaces are always provided, so that new approaches may be reported as they arise. If at some point in the design the respondent was equally committed to two technical approaches to rendezvous at Uranus, he would circle 0.5 for each, as shown. Eventually, as the solution progresses, one alternative will attain a 1.0

Manned Uranus Landing in an Early Time Period Study   General United Aerospace Corporation

Date .... Name ....

Subproblem #1: Method of rendezvous at Uranus	Estimate of Probability that Alternative will be Employed										
Alternative approaches:											
orbital rendezvous mission with excursion vehicle	0	0.1	0.2	0.3	0.4	0.5	0.6	0.7	0.8	0.9	1.0
orbital rendezvous mission without excursion vehicle	0	0.1	0.2	0.3	0.4	0.5	0.6	0.7	0.8	0.9	1.0
direct mission	0	0.1	0.2	0.3	0.4	0.5	0.6	0.7	0.8	0.9	1.0
_____	0	0.1	0.2	0.3	0.4	0.5	0.6	0.7	0.8	0.9	1.0
Subproblem #2: Design of the electrical power supply subsystem for the space vehicle											
Alternative approaches:											
hydrogen-oxygen fuel cell	0	0.1	0.2	0.3	0.4	0.5	0.6	0.7	0.8	0.9	1.0
KOH fuel cell	0	0.1	0.2	0.3	0.4	0.5	0.6	0.7	0.8	0.9	1.0
Rankine cycle fast reactor	0	0.1	0.2	0.3	0.4	0.5	0.6	0.7	0.8	0.9	1.0
Rankine cycle thermal reactor	0	0.1	0.2	0.3	0.4	0.5	0.6	0.7	0.8	0.9	1.0
Brayton cycle reactor	0	0.1	0.2	0.3	0.4	0.5	0.6	0.7	0.8	0.9	1.0
_____	0	0.1	0.2	0.3	0.4	0.5	0.6	0.7	0.8	0.9	1.0
_____	0	0.1	0.2	0.3	0.4	0.5	0.6	0.7	0.8	0.9	1.0
_____	0	0.1	0.2	0.3	0.4	0.5	0.6	0.7	0.8	0.9	1.0

Figure 4.1   Solution Development Record

probability and the others will become zero. By plotting the probabilities over time, we obtain a graphic record of the solution history.

The Solution Development Record, by economizing on the respondent's time, provides quite an efficient record of a project history. When the project is completed, each respondent receives a time plot of his probability estimates and is interviewed at some length to determine causes and effects of design changes reflected in this record.

In considering the sources of ideas, the unit of analysis employed is "messages received" [8]. In other words, each message the engineer or scientist receives that suggests an alternative solution is coded for its source.

A list of the most frequently cited information channels is shown in Table 4.1. This does not imply that each idea can be traced to a single channel. More often than not a single alternative will result from messages received from several channels. For example, someone on the lab's technical staff might refer

Table 4.1   Typical Information Channels Considered in the Study

Literature	Books; professional, technical and trade journals; and other publicly accessible written material.
Vendors	Representatives of or documentation from suppliers or potential suppliers of design components.
Customer	Representatives of or documentation from the government agency for which the project is performed.
External sources	Sources outside the laboratory which do not fall into any of the above three categories. These include paid and unpaid consultants and representatives of government agencies other than the customer agency.
Technical staff	Engineers and scientists in the laboratory who are not assigned directly to the project being considered.
Company research	Any other project performed previously or simultaneously in the lab regardless of its source of funding.
Personal experience	Ideas which were used previously by the engineer for similar problems and are recalled directly from memory.
Analysis and experimentation	Ideas which are the result of an engineering analysis, test, or experiment with no immediate input of information from any other source.

the engineer to an article in a trade journal, which in turn leads him to a vendor who provides more complete information. In such a situation, where several channels contribute to a single alternative, equal credit is given to each.

The nineteen projects under consideration involved the following nine general problems:

1. The design of the reflector portion of a rather large and highly complex antenna system for tracking and communication with space vehicles at very great distances.
2. The design of a vehicle and associated instrumentation to roam the lunar surface and gather descriptive scientific data.
3. An investigation of passive methods for transfer of modulation between two coherent light beams.
4. A preliminary design of an earth-orbiting space station.
5. The design of a deep space probe, and appropriate instrumentation.
6. The preliminary design of an interplanetary space vehicle.
7. The preliminary design of a special-purpose manned spacecraft for lunar missions.
8. The development of a low-thrust rocket engine for maneuvering manned spacecraft.
9. An investigation of possible mission profiles for manned expeditions to another planet.

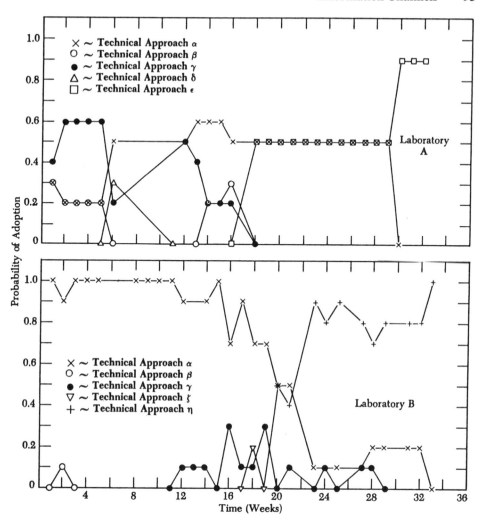

Figure 4.2   Design of Subsystem to Determine Antenna Position

Results

An example of the time plot of solution-development records for a typical
subproblem is shown in Figure 4.2. The problem, in this case, is the design
of a position-feedback subsystem for a very large and complex antenna system. The work statement for both labs suggests approaches α, β, and γ.
Both rejected these, however, and generated two new approaches each (δ,
ε, ζ, and η). In both labs one of the new approaches resulted from difficul-

Table 4.2 Messages Received and Messages Accepted by R&D Scientists and Engineers as a Function of Information Channel—Nine Parallel Sets Comprising Nineteen R&D Projects

Channel	Messages received	Messages accepted	Acceptance ratio
Literature			
Scientists	18	6	0.33
Engineers	53	21	0.40
External sources			
Scientists	5	5	1.00
Engineers	67	32	0.48
Vendors			
Scientists	0	0	—
Engineers	101	33	0.33
Customer			
Scientists	0	0	—
Engineers	132	41	0.31
Technical staff			
Scientists	1	0	0
Engineers	44	24	0.55
Company research			
Scientists	1	0	0
Engineers	37	20	0.54
Analysis and experimentation			
Scientists	3	1	0.33
Engineers	216	72	0.33
Personal Experience			
Scientists	7	4	0.52
Engineers	56	17	0.30
Unknown	75	6	—

Differences in acceptance ratios between the following channels are statistically significant at the 0.01 level: technical staff and vendors, external sources and vendors, technical staff and customer, company research and customer, external sources and customer. The difference between ratios for external sources and vendors is statistically significant at the 0.05 level.

ties incurred by the currently preferred approach; the other resulted from receipt of new information and was independent of the state of approaches currently under consideration.

Alternatives such as these can now be evaluated at two levels. First the engineer decides that one of several possibilities is preferable to the others under consideration. At a second level, the customer's relative evaluation of the solutions reached by the two or three research groups is available. So, each group selects one alternative as its solution to the problem, and then the solutions submitted by the two or three groups are evaluated relative to each other by the government technical representative. Working from the solution evalua-

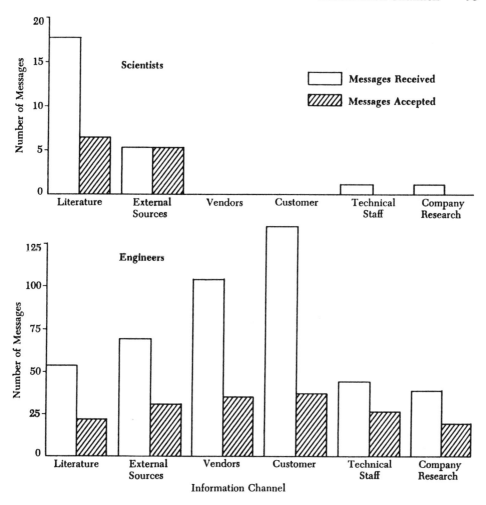

Figure 4.3 Messages Received and Messages Accepted by R&D Scientists and Engineers as a Function of Information Channel

tion back to the sources of the alternative provides two measures of performance for the information channels that we will now examine.

Acceptance by the Engineer

Table 4.2 and Figure 4.3 show total frequency counts for messages received and accepted from each of the eight channels. Seventy-two alternatives could not be attributed to a channel, either because the engineer was unavailable or it was impossible to obtain this information during the interview.

These data show quite a variance in both the relative use and performance of the eight channels. Considering those channels located outside of the project, we find that customer and vendors are used most by engineers, and that literature is the least used channel.[3] For scientists, on the other hand, literature is most often used, and no ideas whatsoever originate with vendors or the customer.

The most important finding, however, is that the channels used with the greatest frequency are not the ones that provide the greatest number of acceptable ideas. A chi-squared test performed on the data for both scientists and engineers shows a significant ($X^2 = 19.55$, $p < 0.01$) difference in the allocation of acceptances and rejections among channels.

Relative performance on this basis shows the three channels involving "expert" sources to have the highest performance. These three channels—technical staff, company research, and external sources—all produce very high acceptance rates among engineers. None of the expert channels was used to any extent by the scientists, but the one external source that produced more than a single message had the highest acceptance rate found. This finding, however, might be spurious, since the external source in this case was the scientist's former mentor, which could suggest a distortedly high acceptance rate for his ideas. So, while no hard conclusions can be drawn concerning scientists, it is quite clear that engineers are quite prone to accept ideas from someone they consider "expert." This does not generalize to all interpersonal sources, as the very low standing of vendors and customer representatives shows. While low acceptance of the former's ideas should surprise no one, the low acceptance rate for the customer's ideas indicates a rather refreshing amount of intellectual honesty on the part of our engineers.

Evaluation by the Customer

For twenty-seven of the eighty-two subproblem pairs, relative evaluations of the solutions were obtained from responsible technical monitors in the customer agencies. In the remaining fifty-five pairs, scores were either tied or no evaluation was available.[4] This relative evaluation permits a comparison of the information channels used to arrive at solutions judged superior to those presented by other teams.

Table 4.3 shows the proportion of both higher and lower rated solutions derived from information obtained through the eight channels. In other words, taking literature as an example, 11 percent (or three) of the twenty-seven higher-rated solutions were based, at least in part, on information obtained

Table 4.3 Sources of Messages Resulting in Higher and Lower Rated Solutions—Twenty-seven Subproblem Pairs

Information channel	Percentage of solutions suggested by messages received through each channel		
	27 High-rated solutions	27 Lower rated solutions	Level of statistical significance
Literature	11%	22%	0.14
External sources	7.4	26	0.03
Vendors	30	30	0.50
Customer	56	44	0.21
Technical staff	22	15	0.24
Company research	22	7.4	0.06
Analysis and experimentation	44	52	0.29
Personal experience	11	11	0.50

The percentages in Tables 4.3 and 4.5 are distilled from 2 × 2 contingency tables in the following manner: Taking the first row, *Literature* as an example, the original contingency table looked like this:

Solution rating

	high	low	
Number of solutions based at least in part on messages from the literature	3	6	3/27 = 11%
			6/27 = 22%
Number of solutions not based on messages from the literature	24	21	
	27	27	

from the literature. Twenty-two percent (or six) of the twenty-seven lower-rated solutions derived, in whole or in part, from information gained through this channel.

Again, the "expert" channels stand out. Two of the three, external sources and company research, demonstrate significant differences in performance, and the differences are in opposite directions. The performance difference for the third "expert" channel is not statistically significant.

The hypothesis to be tested here is based upon the findings of Allen and Marquis [1] for R&D proposal competitions. The use of information sources outside of the laboratory was found in that case to be inversely related to the technical quality of proposals, while use of sources within the lab was weakly but positively related to quality. The hypothesis predicts that poorer performing groups will rely more heavily upon sources outside of the lab, and better performing groups more upon sources within the lab.

In order to test the hypothesis, the actual number of solutions derived from

Table 4.4 Sources of Messages Resulting in Higher and Lower Rated Solutions—Twenty-seven Subproblem Pairs

Information channel	Number of higher rated solutions suggested	Number of lower rated solutions suggested
Channels outside the laboratory External sources or vendors but not technical staff or company research (ES∪V) ∩ (TS∪CR)	6	10
Channels inside the laboratory Technical staff or company research but not external sources or vendors (TS∪CR) ∩ (ES∪V)	7	1
Other channels Both or neither (TS∪CR) ∩ (ES∪V) or (TS∪CR) ∩ (ES∪V)	14	16

$x^2 = 5.63, p<0.03$

each set of channels is aggregated in Table 4.4. Since a solution can result from several messages, each received over a different channel, those solutions to which only internal channels contributed are compared with solutions resulting only from external channels. To complete the set, a third category has been included. This category comprises solutions deriving from neither internal nor external sources and solutions derived from both in combination. A chi-squared test rejects the null hypothesis of no difference in the performance of internal and external channels at the 0.03 level of statistical significance.

A somewhat more general test of the information-gathering behavior of the engineers is a comparison of the sources used in generating all of the solution alternatives. In other words, general information-seeking behavior varies as a function of the individual and his or her particular circumstances. Table 4.5 shows that a comparison at this level strengthens the conclusions reached on the basis of comparing the sources of solutions alone.

Higher and lower performers again show little difference in their use of the literature, vendors, and analysis and experimentation, and in their reliance upon personal experience in generating solution alternatives. Poorer performers once again rely more heavily upon external sources, and better performers upon sources within their own laboratory, i.e., upon their technical staff and other company research programs.

Table 4.5   Sources of Messages Resulting in All Technical Alternatives Considered by Engineers Submitting Solutions Receiving Higher and Lower Ratings—Twenty-seven Subproblem Pairs

Information channel	Percentage of alternatives suggested by messages received through each channel		Level of statistical significance
	85 Alternatives associated with higher rated solutions	85 Alternatives associated with lower rated solutions	
Literature	8.2	14.0	0.11
External sources	5.9	15.0	0.02
Vendors	21.0	28.0	0.23
Customer	44.0	46.0	0.38
Technical staff	12.0	4.7	0.05
Company research	15.0	3.5	0.004
Analysis and experimentation	48.0	38.0	0.08
Personal experience	11.0	8.2	0.30

Discussion

Three rather striking differences are observed in the performance of the information channels studied. First, there is a wide variance in the frequency with which the several channels are used. Considering only the channels external to the project group, the customer agency and vendors are found to supply almost three times as many suggestions of solution alternatives as do the lab's technical staff or its other research programs. Second, the actual acceptance of these messages is inversely related to the frequency of use. Two of the least used channels, technical staff and company research, yield the highest acceptance ratios. It appears that "expert" channels show the highest probabilities of having an idea accepted.

Finally, comparing the sources of both solutions and rejected alternatives for higher and lower rated problems shows a marked difference in the performance of channels, depending upon whether they originate within or outside of the laboratory organization. Those originating within the lab perform far better than those originating outside.

The importance of this finding to those concerned with promoting the transfer of technology cannot be overstressed. But before delving into its implications in more detail let us marshall a bit more support for its existence.

As we have noted, this is not the first time this phenomenon has appeared. It was first revealed in the study of R&D proposal competitions [1]. The proposal competitions studied varied widely in the nature of their problem and ranged throughout the research spectrum from quite fundamental basic research studies to hardware-oriented development and test projects. Across this wide range of problem types, teams that relied more heavily upon outside information sources were found to produce poorer quality solutions. In fourteen of fifteen cases correlations between the extent to which outside sources were used and rated technical quality of the proposals were found to be negative. The mean rank order correlation for fifteen competitions was -0.30 ($p < 0.001$). The data indicate that lack of technical capability within the lab was largely responsible for at least the decision to use outside sources. Inverse relations were found between the use of such sources and both the size of the lab's technical staff and its ratio to the total employment of the lab. Laboratories lacking the necessary technical manpower resources attempted unsuccessfully to substitute through reliance upon outside technical personnel.

Similarly the study of Shilling and Bernard [10] shows consistent inverse correlations between the extent to which "paid consultants" are employed by industrial bioscientists and eight measures of laboratory "productivity and efficiency." All of these correlations are statistically significant at the 0.05 level or beyond. Furthermore, the authors found the use of paid consultants to be the only factor "which clearly and unequivocally differentiates [university from government and industrial] laboratories."

The present data (Tables 4.3, 4.4, and 4.5) reveal a similar performance differential. So the evidence that has accumulated is indeed quite convincing, but it does not as yet explain the situation. One clue lies in the finding of an inverse relation between the size (both absolute and relative to total company employment) of a lab's technical staff and the extent to which outside sources are used during proposal competitions. This suggests that two factors must be operating. First, those teams, or more precisely those laboratories, whose research teams rely on outside help possess other characteristics that more likely are the actual cause of the poor performance. The most plausible of these is simply the lack of the required technical competence within the lab. Certainly the use of an information source can seldom be held to *reduce* quality directly. It is, rather, the initial lack of knowledge on the part of the R&D team members that is directly responsible. Some information sources are more capable of counteracting this initial condition than others, which introduces the second factor: Sources outside are either less well informed, which is unlikely, or the flow of information is restricted at the organizational boundary. Why should the organization impose an effective barrier to communication? Before considering the question directly, let us first examine an instance that at first appearance runs counter to the evidence thus far.

Hagstrom, who studied 179 prominent researchers in the formal (mathematics, statistics, and logic), physical, and biological sciences, found a strong positive correlation (Q = 0.85) between extradepartmental communication and productivity in terms of papers published.[5] The correlation between productivity and intradepartmental communication is considerably lower (Q = 0.42). Now, how does this relate to the earlier findings and how can the apparent contradiction be resolved? First of all, Hagstrom's measure of extradepartmental communication was restricted to communication within the individual's academic discipline. Furthermore, the organization in Hagstrom's case is somewhat different. It was a university department; all of the other results stem from studies of industrial organizations.

It follows that the differences in the effectiveness of extraorganizational communication in the two situations can be attributed in large part to two factors:

1. The relative commitment of the individual to the organizations or social systems at hand, and
2. The degree to which the boundaries of these organizations are formally structured.

In this context, Hagstrom's scientists confronted a low impedance in communicating across the bounds of their academic departments (but within their disciplines), because the academic department elicits a lower degree of commitment from most academic scientists than does their professional discipline, or "invisible college." Here we should expect to find a higher impedance than at the bound of the academic department, but not so high as at the periphery of a more formalized organization such as an industrial or government laboratory.

At this point our second consideration becomes relevant. As many social scientists in recent years have noted, the difficulty lies in the impermeability of bureaucracy to the influx of information and technology. Bennis, for example [3], in cataloging the many criticisms leveled at bureaucracy includes the charge that it, "cannot assimilate the influx of new technology or scientists. . . ." Katz and Kahn [7] provide us with some explanation for this, revolving about two major points:

1. In order to control its intake of information and thereby avert the possibility of being so overwhelmed that the resulting condition is one of pure noise, the organization establishes a "system boundary" which defines the appropriate region for organizational activities, and "constitutes a barrier for many types of interaction between people on the inside and people on the outside."
2. Every organization like every individual develops a coding system with which to order its world. This coding scheme, in turn, enhances the effi-

ciency of communication among those who hold it in common. It can, however, detract from the efficiency of communicating with the holders of a different coding scheme.

The two points are clearly complementary. The first is accomplished, in part, through the second. System boundaries are to some degree defined and maintained by a distinction in coding schemes. The boundary, of course, is not intended to be completely impenetrable; the organization must have some exchange with its environment. In order to allow this and yet control the degree, it establishes a limited number of officially recognized channels through which communication must be directed—for example, libraries, purchasing departments, and field offices. Engineers (often to the dismay of librarians and field office managers) are generally quite uninhibited in circumventing such channels. The development of coding schemes best explains the evidence we have seen.

Let us now briefly review these results. First, several studies of industrial and government scientists and engineers have shown an inverse relation between extraorganizational communication, contrasting with a direct relation between intraorganizational communication and performance. Second, in Hagstrom's study where the organization (an academic department) appears to occupy a subsidiary position to a more inclusive social system ("invisible college" or academic discipline), and where the communication process measured was external to the first entity but *internal to the second,* a strong positive relation was found between the extent of communication and performance. Third, in the instances in which external communication bears an unfruitful relation to performance, there is evidence that it is not this communication per se that degrades performance but other factors, such as lack of the required knowledge by the engineer or scientist seeking information. The internal channels are better able to compensate for this deficiency than are external ones.

The rationale of the shared coding scheme produces a rather simple and straightforward explanation. In industrial and governmental situations the laboratory organization dominates the scene. These organizations demand a degree of loyalty and affiliation far outweighing that required by academic departments. In addition, the members of industrial and governmental organizations acquire through common experience, and organizational imposition, shared coding schemes that can be quite different from the schemes held by other members of their discipline. This is not true of the academic scientists. They generally feel more aligned with scientists in similar research areas than with a particular university or department, and therefore tend to use a system of coding in common with other researchers. In other words, the "invisible college" now becomes the mediator of the coding scheme. Following this line of reasoning a step further, one would predict that were interdisciplinary communication among scientists measured, the results would show some loss in communicative efficiency. An inverse relation with performance in this case might or might not exist, depending upon other factors, but we would predict some loss in efficiency when compared with intradisciplinary communication. The problem is compounded when, as is often the case, incompatibilities between the two coding schemes go unrecognized, or when identical coding systems are assumed that do not in fact exist.

There are possible measures that can be applied to reduce the organizational boundary impedance. One which may take place under uncontrolled circumstances is a two-step process in which certain key individuals act as bridges linking the organization members to the outside world. Information, then, enters the organization most efficiently when it is channeled through these individuals, who are capable of operating within and translating between two coding schemes.

The possible existence of such individuals, who in effect straddle two coding systems and are able to function efficiently in both, and perform a transformation between the two, promises their potential utilization in technology transfer. In other words, it appears that information must be obtained by an indirect route. Attempting to bridge the organizational bound directly is not the most efficient path. Rather, the "technological gatekeepers" in the lab must first be reached, and it is only through these people that the boundary impedance can be effectively surmounted.

Conclusions

This study has measured the relative performance of six channels in transferring technical information. The research technique employs the vehicle of parallel R&D projects to provide a control over the substance of the problem and a relative evaluation of solutions. Data are gathered by means of Solution Development Records and lengthy interviews with engineers. The ideas considered for solving each problem are thus associated with the channels whence they came, and measures of performance are generated for the channels.

The principal conclusions of the study are:

1. There is a serious discrepancy between the quality of the ideas generated through the channels studied, and the frequency with which these channels are used by engineers.
2. Literature is not greatly used and is mediocre at best in its performance.
3. Better performing groups rely more than the poorer performers upon

sources within the laboratory (the technical staff, and other company research programs) as contrasted with sources outside the lab.

4. A mismatch in information coding schemes appears to be responsible for the ineffectiveness of communication across the organizational boundary. The possible existence of key individuals (technological gatekeepers) shows promise of providing a means of surmounting this organizational boundary impedance.

5

Has a Customer Already Developed Your Next Product?

Eric A. von Hippel

It has been conventional wisdom to assume that first-to-market products are usually designed by the manufacturers of such products. As a result of extensive research, the author has found that, in some industries, the conventional wisdom does not hold, and that successful designs for what later become successful products are typically available from customers or others *before* the first-to-market manufacturer begins his design work. In this article, the author provides managers with a method for identifying and utilizing such free sources of product design data. Manufacturers who build on this information can eliminate duplication of effort by their own staff and streamline their operations—strategies that contribute significantly to the goal of maximizing profits. *SMR*.

"Find a need and fill it" is the accepted strategy for developing a successful new product—a strategy that research into the innovation process has proved correct. But what is a "need," and where do you most successfully look for it? During the past three years, a study carried forward at the Sloan School has systematically examined the need information that triggered the manufacture of several hundred innovative and successful new industrial products, and has developed some answers which should be of use to managers interested in such products.[1] The key findings discussed in this article include:

- Information about the need for a new product is often found bundled together with valuable product design data. This data may be missed even by experienced market researchers looking for "needs only," with the result that a manufacturing firm has to invest in redeveloping what it could have gotten for free. Sensitivity to the amount of product design data usually present in a "new" product can pay off handsomely.

From *Sloan Management Review*, Winter 1977, Vol. 18, No. 2. Reprinted with permission.

• Information about new product needs in some industries proves to come consistently from the same type of source in case after case. Once this source is identified, management can do a great deal to use it more efficiently.

Managers who use our findings and apply the methods proposed in this article should be able to say as a result, "In *our* industry, need information leading to successful new products typically also provides us with X amount of free product design data, and comes from Y source—and we can organize to pick up and process this type of information more efficiently."

Product Design Data Contained in Need Information

The conventional wisdom is that customers provide the needs, while manufacturing firms develop the solution to the needs. But, if one thinks about it, one sees that any information about a need provides information about the nature of a product responsive to the need as well. Consider the following statements of a need. Each succeeding phrase adds more data about what a responsive product should look like:

I need higher profits
—which I can get by raising output
—which I can best do by getting rid of the bottleneck in process step D.
—This can best be done by designing and installing new equipment
—with the following operating characteristics
—and the following design.

Clearly, much work is involved if a manufacturer is to convert the first need statement—"I need higher profits"—into a responsive new product. He must employ skilled analysts to study the business of the potential customer and to conceptualize a new product opportunity that will affect the customer's felt need for higher profits. On the other hand, if he receives information containing the maximum amount of product design data shown, he need only have his manufacturing people poised by the telephone ready to follow customer instructions. An example from our research data may be helpful. Consider the following case of a product innovation for which a product *user* did most of the innovation work.

In the late 1950s, IBM designed and built the first printed circuit card component insertion machine of the X-Y Table-type to be used in commercial production. (IBM needed the machine to insert components into printed circuit cards, which were in turn incorporated into computers.) After building and

Table 5.1   Source of Innovative Product Designs in Two Industries

Industry Studied	Innovative Products First Developed by:		Data Not Available	Total Sample Size
	Users	Manufacturers or "Others"		
Semiconductor and Electronic Subassembly Process Equipment[a]	67%	33%	6	49
Scientific Instruments[b]	77%	23%	17	111

[a] Source: von Hippel [2], Table 2
[b] Source: von Hippel [1], Table 4

testing the design in-house, IBM, in 1959, sent engineering drawings of its design to a local machine builder along with an order for eight units. The machine builder completed this and subsequent orders satisfactorily and later (1962) applied to IBM for permission to build essentially the same machine for sale on the open market. IBM agreed, and the machine builder became the first commercial manufacturer of X-Y Table component insertion machines. The episode marked that firm's first entry into the component insertion equipment business. Today the firm is a major one in the business.

For process equipment manufacturers or instrument manufacturers, the pattern in the example should seem familiar. We have found that most of the innovative products (see Table 5.1) commercialized in those industries were invented, prototyped, and used in the field by innovative users *before* equipment or instrument manufacturing firms offered them commercially.[2] In such instances, the manufacturer who takes advantage of user efforts needs only to contribute product engineering work to obtain a first-to-market product innovation. (Preliminary data indicates that this type of *user-dominated* innovation pattern plays a major role in many other product areas as well, including computer software and medical products.)

Need Information May Contain a Large Amount of Product Design Data

A user will do some of your innovation work, and provide you with new product need information containing a great deal of product design data, if he

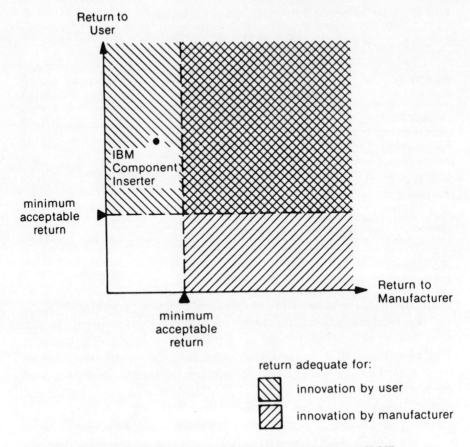

Figure 5.1   Return to Users and Manufacturers from Innovation Investment (ROII)

needs the new product as much as or more than you do. Consider the two-axis diagram in Figure 5.1. One axis represents the level of return on innovation investment (ROII) a *user* of an innovative product might expect if he made the investment to develop a given product. The second axis represents the level of return on innovation investment (ROII) a *manufacturer* of that same product might expect if he invested in its development. The marker on each axis represents the minimum ROII that would induce a product user or product manufacturer to do the innovation work on a given product. Dotted lines from each of these minimum-return markers divide the total innovation-return space into four segments, namely:

1. (Upper left) in which only the innovation *user* will have sufficient incentive to innovate;

2. (Upper right) in which *both* user and manufacturer will have sufficient incentive to innovate—where one therefore expects to see cases of *both* user and manufacturer-dominated innovation;
3. (Lower left) in which *neither* party will have the incentive to innovate; and
4. (Lower right) in which only the innovation *manufacturer* will have sufficient incentive to innovate.

Having completed the diagram, we can theoretically place any new product innovation opportunity on it at a point that reflects the ROII that opportunity offers to user and manufacturer. (In practice it is often difficult to make exact ROII calculations; nevertheless, ROII diagrams are a useful conceptual tool.) As an example, consider the component insertion machine innovation described earlier. As shown on the diagram, the opportunity to develop the basic invention into a new product was attractive to IBM, the innovative user, but not to the product manufacturer. IBM had to invest more than a million dollars to develop the concept, but justified the expenditure in terms of potential savings through the use of the equipment. The machine builder, on the other hand, could never have justified such an innovation investment in anticipation of sales of only a few hundred thousand dollars. The result of this combination of circumstances—high (estimated) ROII to user and low (estimated) ROII to manufacturer—is that the user did most of the innovation work and then triggered the manufacture of the innovative product by transferring a great deal of product design data to the manufacturer along with information about his new product need.

New Product Need Information and Design Data from Nonusers

Up to this point, the discussion and examples have focused on new product need information coupled to design data which comes from innovative product users. In reality, such new product information can come from any person or group with the incentive to generate it. The development of bread wrapped in polyethylene film is an example of a case in which a *materials supplier* did much of the innovation work and gave the product manufacturer need information with a large amount of product design data.

Polyethylene-film-wrapped bread was developed by Crown Zellerbach, a materials supplier, to replace the cellophane wrap then used by many baking companies. Crown introduced the film commercially in 1957–58 along with an inexpensive machine adapter, also of its design, to allow baking companies to use the new film on their existing wrapping machines.

Material suppliers as a group stood to gain far more from this innovation than did machine builders or baking companies. In 1958, the total potential market for polyethylene bread-wrapping film was about $25 million annually, divided among only a few suppliers. Total *one-time* sales of machine adapters, on the other hand, amounted to about $20 million, while annual materials savings divided among hundreds of bread manufacturing companies was only $3–6 million.

Sources of Need Information Containing Product Design Data

It is important to recognize whether your firm gets, or can get, need information containing a significant amount of new product design data, for this is free information that costs a good deal to generate from scratch. To ascertain whether your firm gets need information, draw ROII maps of the product types that interest you to see whether or not it is in someone's interest to provide you with product design data. Then, if the ROII analysis shows you should be getting such data, look into the firm's past history for the need information that triggered your past new products, to see how much product design information was provided, from whom, and how.

Mapping ROII

Mapping ROII cannot be precise. Indeed, many aspects of ROII important to innovators, such as improvements in product quality, are not easily measurable. But you can use your understanding of your markets to ask, "Who gained what from past product innovations my firm brought to market or would have liked to have brought to market?"[3] If plastic bread wrap is a product innovation that interests you, for example, draw a three-axis ROII chart, because three parties—bread-wrap user (bakery), wrapping-machinery builder, and plastic-wrap supplier—would seem to have something to gain from the innovation. Consideration of the figures given in the bread-wrap case would lead you to place the innovation at the point in the ROII chart shown in Figure 5.2.

As we see, the only significant incentive lay with the plastic-wrap supplier. We would therefore predict that the *supplier* would provide need information to the manufacturer that contains a large amount of product design data. As the case history has demonstrated, this is in fact what happened. As a result, while the ROII for the manufacturer was below the minimum acceptable had he undertaken the entire innovation job, the return on manufacturing a plas-

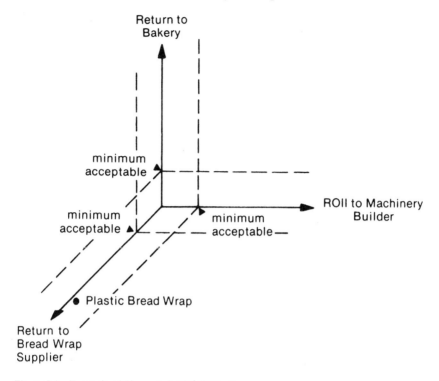

Figure 5.2   Example of Three-Axis "ROII Map"

tic bread-wrap machine product became quite acceptable when the material supplier had undertaken the risk and expense of developing the product.

Of course, receiving free product design data in instances where one's ROII would be attractive even if one *did* have to shoulder the entire innovation investment would be even more desirable. You may be able to find such instances as well by looking in areas where your ROII and that of some other parties are *both* high. Areas of the ROII map that would be most attractive to a bread machinery manufacturer (to continue with the example), are shown as shaded in Figure 5.3.

Get the Past History of Your Successful Products

Suppose that your ROII map exercise shows that there may be new product need information containing free product design information potentially available in product categories of interest to you. The next step is to study a sample

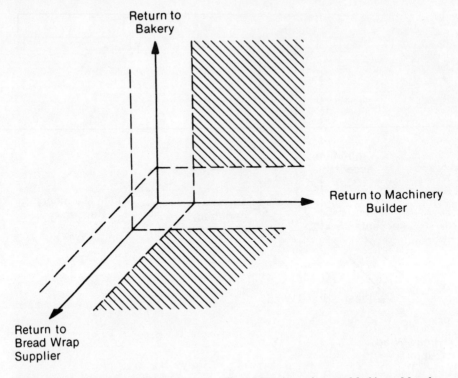

Figure 5.3   Shaded Areas of ROII Map Are Those Most Attractive to a Machinery Manufacturer Seeking Free Product Design Data

of past product successes to see what need information containing product design data was available at the time. By discovering a historical pattern, you will learn what to look for in the future.

The process of getting a proper sample is a technical matter beyond the purview of this article. (The references on p. 274 can be helpful in such an analysis.) However, it is important to look at a sample of ten to twenty cases in order to make a valid judgment about the product design data you might expect in conjunction with new product need information. A judgment made on the basis of just one or two product histories, no matter how successful those products were, will almost inevitably be misleading.

After ascertaining the kind of need and solution information you have—or could have—obtained in the past that led you to your present line of successful products, compare these data to a chart of stages of the innovation process, such as the IBM case shown in Figure 5.4. Note that in this instance, the user has done everything except product manufacturing and sales.

Typically, the work necessary to bring an innovation from the idea stage to the marketplace is divided between yourself and others. If the pattern is con-

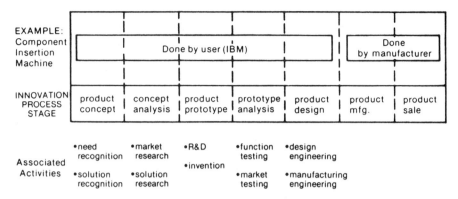

Figure 5.4 Charting Product Design Data Provided Free to a Manufacturer Against Stages of the Innovation Process

sistent from case to case, and our research shows that often it is, then you will want to *undertake only that portion of the innovation process that history shows you actually do.* If, for example, the pattern you find in your firm looks like the one shown in Figure 5.4, you have learned that you do only product engineering in house, and so you should hire only product engineers. If you hire engineers skilled in the earlier stages of the innovation process, they will want to exercise their skills and will very likely repeat the R&D, at your expense, that the customer has already provided you for free.

The same approach applies to marketing research. For example, consider a recent conversation we had with a major consumer goods company. The company had established that its highest payout products had been innovative rather than product repositionings and repackagings. The conversation focused on how to plumb the consumer's psyche, until we asked if there was another source of data representing a later stage of the innovation process that might also be tapped. The answer was "Yes." All of the more innovative products under discussion had been preceded by a similar product put out by a small company! Analysis of the "experiments" performed by these small companies could provide the major company with much richer need and product design data than consumers could provide via interviews. The company *could* start the innovation process over from scratch, but what a waste![4] (See Figure 5.5.)

Getting Your People to Recognize the Facts

It is easy enough to use the ROII mapping and case-sampling approach to prove that a particular firm has sources of need information that also provide

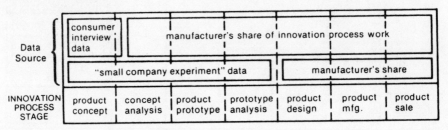

Figure 5.5   Amount of Free Product Design Data Available Varies by Source

free product design data, but it is often difficult to convince a firm's product development group that this is so. Consider the reasons why the casual observer might think that the product manufacturer is the innovator, even when it can be proved that the product user was, in fact, the innovator:

- New product design data from a user that is noted and utilized by your new product group may happen only once per new product. On the other hand, instances in which your people train customers to use the product are as frequent as sales, and continue for the lifetime of the product.
- Everyone is surrounded by advertising that says, "Process Electronics Co. introduces a terrific innovation to the market for the first time." Process Electronics means that it was first to produce and market the product *commercially*. But in the absence of countervailing advertising by inventing users and suppliers, the impression develops that the manufacturer is the inventor.
- Prototypes developed by users or suppliers are seldom manufactured as received by a manufacturing firm. Firm personnel will typically contribute some product engineering work to the prototype in order to make it more reliable, manufacturable, etc., while preserving the operating principles of the prototype.

Since there is no sense in redoing what you can get for free, it is important that your people understand the situation, at least enough to make effective use of such design data.

Organizing to Match Up with the Source of Your Need and Product Design Information

In addition to learning how much product design data is contained in the need information available to your firm, it is important to learn where the useful need information comes from, how it comes, and at whose initiative. Data on these matters can also be derived from a sample of past innovations. Once the pattern is visible, the organizational changes needed to match up properly will be clear.

To give the flavor of what we mean, let's walk through an example. Consider a study we did of the nature and source of need information leading to product innovations in two categories of process machinery—machines used to make semiconductors, and machines used to make electronic subassemblies. Our first step was to select a sample of new products developed in the past that were very successful.

Our second step was to search carefully for the product design data content and source of the need inputs that lay behind each of these successful new products. In the case of our process machinery sample, we found the need information came overwhelmingly from product users and, in about two-thirds of all cases, contained product design data on field-proven prototypes of the new products. So far so good, but *how* did the manufacturer get this need information and product design data? We studied our sample of cases further and found two main patterns:

- In 35 percent of the cases, manufacturers got the data from innovative user customers who did not mind sharing process know-how. While selling their existing products to these users, the manufacturers took the initiative to ask user engineers: "What have you done that's new and useful lately?" Usually the engineers were happy to explain.
- In 26 percent of the cases, manufacturers were sought out by innovative users and given the need and design data, because the innovative user needed an outside source of supply for an equipment innovation. Usually in these cases, the user chose to deal with a manufacturer from whom he had bought in the past.

Interestingly, in another 26 percent of the cases, we found that new product needs plus extensive product design *were* available from users had the manufacturer looked for them. But he did not. Instead, he incurred the expense of reinventing what he could have had for free.

Given these patterns, the strategy of a manufacturer seeking new industrial products is clear:

1. He should get into the market with a standard product of interest to innovative users—anything that will allow him to establish a sales and service relationship with the right group of user engineers.
2. He should hire people to deal with users who can recognize potential new products as well as sell the standard line. (Not all of a manufacturer's sales

and service people must meet this standard, only those who deal with innovative users. The sample should identify these key users. In our sample, they were the few user companies with the greatest annual sales.)

3. He should organize his new product development group so that it is easy and normal for new product ideas with a large amount of free product design information to come from sales and service, pass to marketing research for assessment of market potential, and then pass to product engineering, manufacturing, and sales.

This example derives from data generated from our research. Your own best strategy may look very different, but it can be developed with the help of an ROII analysis such as the one described in this article.

6

Technological Innovation, Entrepreneurship, and Strategy

James Brian Quinn

Historically, Western societies have largely relied on the individual inventor/entrepreneur for many of their most startling innovations. In order to meet the enormous challenges of our times, large institutions must understand and exploit the individual entrepreneurial system. The author details the factors that have made this system so effective and outlines the current shortcomings of large institutions with respect to those factors. He then draws on his experiences in major enterprises that have successfully undertaken large-scale innovation, and develops strategies to respond to the enormous challenges ahead. *SMR.*

Innovation—creating and introducing original solutions for new or already identified needs—must be one of the central themes for society and for technological management during the next few decades. The challenges are new and on a scale never before attempted by mankind. If one believes the most prevalent projections, the U.S. and world must within the next fifteen to twenty years:

- Feed a new population as large as the world's entire population in 1940, but with less massive use of chemical fertilizers and biocides.[1]
- Develop and deliver as much new energy as has been produced in all history to date—with each increment harder to find and develop—and yet eliminate acid rains like those which have reached pH_3 levels in Sweden and New England.[2]
- Meet additional demands for foods, raw materials, and products 100 percent greater than today's with land resources ever more marginal and safe waste disposal ever more difficult.[3]

From *Sloan Management Review,* Spring 1979, Vol. 20, No. 3. Reprinted with permission.

- Generate net real capital at an annual rate at least twice as high as today's despite governments' preemption of capital for social redistributions.
- Genuinely improve the living, working, educational, urban, and environmental habitats of people in both industrialized and developing countries.
- Simultaneously increase each nation's health standards, shift from disease-cure to morbidity-prevention systems, and restrain population growth within reasonable bounds.
- Employ 30 to 50 percent more people, many in service industries, while increasing productivity enough to halt inflation.
- Accomplish all this without fatally disturbing natural equilibria or creating resource crises that lead to war.

Although some elitists might choose to ignore them, these demands represent the genuine needs of the world's population. Despite some claims to the contrary, we cannot accomplish these aims using today's technologies, much less yesterday's.[4] To live even as well tomorrow as today, in real material and social terms, is impossible without significant inventions, innovations, and institutional changes. Because of the massive investments needed for many solutions, much of this innovation will have to occur in large institutions.[5]

The Individual Entrepreneur

Unfortunately in the past, although some large institutions have been quite innovative, most have not. Historically, western societies have depended on the individual inventor/entrepreneur for many of their most startling innovations.[6] In fact, this "individual entrepreneurial system" has proved history's most successful method for meeting new human needs. Policy makers should try to understand why this system has worked so well and what problems and potentialities exist in adapting its approaches to larger organizations and the huge-scale problems of the future. In my experience, I have had the opportunity to observe and study scores of technical/entrepreneurial ventures. While one could select from many specific examples, two well-documented classics typify successful individual technical/entrepreneurial patterns.

◊ Starting in 1947–48, Howard Head, then an aerospace designer, metals expert, and ski enthusiast, began to design, build, and test metal skis. Working in his home shop he would create a ski, produce a few, and then beg ski professionals to test them. Despite their disparaging comments and three years of broken and twisted skis, Head persisted. He was described as "possessed by his idea," a "fanatic" on the subject. After each test—and failure—he would redesign the ski, make some more, and take them out for tests. Head worked night and day out of his own home. He ran out of his own money and his company, incorporated with only $8,000 of Head's capital, almost went under. An infusion of $60,000 (for 40 percent of the company) at the right moment saved the concern. Only after six to seven years and scores of design failures did Head finally begin to make some money from his enterprise. Hundreds of others had tried to design metal skis, but had failed. Head's skis worked so well they were called "cheaters" by the trade. They sold for $100 in a market used to paying only $25, and helped create the ski boom of the 1950s.[7]

◊ Around 1935, Chester Carlson, former carbon chemist, printer, and patent lawyer, was working in the patent office of Mallory Company. He was disturbed by the cost and errors involved in typing and copying patents for transmission to outsiders. Carlson began to work nights and weekends, at home and in the public library, to create a copying process. He experimented with various photoelectric plate surfaces and adhering black powders. Working with very simple equipment and a part-time employee in a rented room, Carlson got his first image in October, 1938. With a crude demonstration device, he agonizingly went from company to company seeking development support. But they all turned him down. No one could visualize the potential of the process; there was no significant copying business then. By 1942, Carlson had obtained patents on basic concepts in the process. But by then Carlson was, in his words, "in desperate straits" financially, although he had only some $3,000 invested in the process. Finally, in 1944, a "vest pocket" division Battelle had set up to sponsor new ideas agreed to use some of its own money for development in return for a share in potential royalties.

In 1947, as a result of reading about one of Carlson's patents, a small company named Haloid agreed to license and develop the process. The company's existing products were stagnating, and its president, Joseph Wilson, was willing to take risks to develop an entirely new market. Although xerography became one of the great success stories of all time, it was not profitable until the early 1950s, thirteen to seventeen years after its conception.[8]

These and many other similar examples reveal clear patterns as to why this form of entrepreneurship has been so effective.

Fanaticism/Commitment.   The system allows talented fanatics a way to pursue their ideas without the personality pressures and second guessing typical in large organizations. For success, the individual must be fanatically committed in order to endure the pain, frustration, and effort of overcoming the technical and market obstacles that always confront a new idea. The system permits the match-up of personalities, opportunities, and incentives under which such people thrive. It frees the innovator to interact flexibly with other experts and users without intervening bureaucracies.

Chaos Acceptance. The inventor/entrepreneur is not bound to formal plans or PERT charts of progress. Progress on a new innovation typically comes in spurts among unforeseen delays and setbacks. He accepts and even enjoys the essential chaos of development. And he does not have to waste time explaining his progress—or lack thereof—to a board or legislature with less commitment and with false expectations concerning the speed and orderliness of progress.[9]

Low Early Costs. Because the inventor/entrepreneur works out of his own home, his overhead cost is minimal. He invents to avoid costs. He uses sweat capital instead of dollars for materials or equipment. As a result, failure cost is low and not publicly visible. Although many failures occur, there are no formal inquiries when the entrepreneur is wrong. Future progress is not inhibited by past failure or fear that such failure could be represented as a fraud against the public or stockholders.

No Detailed Controls. In the early stages, detailed market estimates are costly, inaccurate, and perhaps misleading. Early estimates of such things as computers, xerography, and metal skis were all misleading. No market existed for such products. Consequently, market estimates both seriously understated potentials and entirely missed the products' opening market niches. For example, Head skis were first successful for beginning, not expert, skiers; xerography started as a method for making cheap lithographic originals. Early market estimates repeatedly indicated that only 5,000 Xerox machines would ever be sold; that the total computer market was limited to 30–300 units operating at millisecond speeds; and that "metal skis were no good and would never sell," especially at a $100 price.

Incentives/Risks. The individual inventor/entrepreneur can satisfy his personal desires for money, achievement, or recognition, and is motivated to do so. Because he is a committed expert in the field, he perceives the risk as less than any review group would. He does not panic when others might. This becomes especially important when risking money on very large-scale systems.[10]

Long Time Horizons. The inventor/entrepreneur is undeterred by the seven to fifteen years that typically elapse between invention and financial success.[11] He does not make detailed financial calculations of such matters. He defines success as of the time of exploitation, and he provides a continuity of interest and support for the entire development cycle.

Flexible Financial Support.   The inventor/entrepreneur is not dependent on any single financial source. If one source will not satisfy, others may. At crucial times there are specialized venture capitalists used to taking "one out of twenty" development risks. They are not bound by the bureaucracies or the inflexibilities of large organizations or government agencies. They do not rely on detailed analyses of financial projections to make their judgments. They evaluate the *concept* of the business, the *capabilities* of the entrepreneur, and the *broad dimensions* of the opportunity rather than the details of its finances. They recognize that, in any new venture, forecasts are so inaccurate that they must trust their judgment of *people* much more than numbers.[12]

Multiple Competing Approaches.   For every success there are hundreds of failures. Thus, although the probability of any one individual succeeding is low, the large number of contenders actually makes the probability of satisfying any real need very high.

Need Orientation.   Because the only solution that survives is the one that will sell, the individual inventor/entrepreneur keeps his eyes glued to the market need. He gets as close as he can to the marketplace and opportunistically snatches anything that will help solve his problem. The entrepreneur's lack of resources and risk of his own property force invention and rapid adoption of any new solutions. There is a minimum of the NIH (Not Invented Here) complex. The entrepreneur's loyalties are to the idea and its success—not to promotion in a vertical organization.

Unfortunately the individual entrepreneur is unlikely to resolve completely many of the large-scale technological problems now facing our society and the world. But he is likely to help in their solutions. Thus, as policy makers approach today's major problems, they should both maintain the health of the individual entrepreneurial system and try to design its most important success characteristics into any new institutions formulated. Similarly, large existing institutions should try to learn from such experiences and adapt the best characteristics of this remarkable system.

Large Institution Problems

Instead, many large organizations operate in a mode that actively discourages entrepreneurial innovation. Their most common shortcomings are outlined below.

Fanatics versus Organization.   The "fanatical" entrepreneur is not political, nor is he power oriented. He is obnoxious, impatient, egoistic, and perhaps even a bit irrational in organization terms. As a consequence, he is not hired. If hired, he is not promoted or rewarded. He is regarded as "not serious," "embarrassing," or "disruptive." He quickly builds up resistance to him in the organization. He rarely stays long enough to complete his innovation, often preferring to go it alone.[13]

Expect Orderly Advance.   Various groups within large organizations expect technological advance to be orderly. They insist on PERT or CPM methodologies to plan or track the innovation. When, as predictably happens, the innovation does not follow plan, it is deemed a failure. Consequently, the technical group begins to work to prove the plan rather than to achieve innovation on the shortest and least costly cycle. By definition, the things that go wrong are the things the planners could not anticipate. This is why Murphy's Law works. It is also the reason why projects constantly run behind schedule, cost more than anticipated, and bring technical groups under fire for "low productivity." One well-known organization even went so far as to charge its technical management for failures to achieve anticipated profits on products not yet invented.

Spend Too Much.   In many organizations, as soon as a new technical project is identified, it is charged with its full personnel, materials, overhead, and back-up costs. The innovator cannot lower his costs by using his sweat capital. No one is encouraged to work all night because all speed-ups lead to increased charges for overtime or doubletime. As a result, progress is slow, and early stage costs soar. The project quickly becomes unattractive in present value terms. As costs mount, the political exposure of the project becomes ever higher, as does its criticism. Consequently, much of the really innovative technical work in such organizations is hidden from management and carried on "underground," for fear it will be killed.

Detailed Control Too Soon.   As soon as a project is defined, professional managers seek market-research information to justify its potential returns. They ignore the facts that an adequate market-research study might actually cost more than the risk of carrying the project ahead, or that the market information might be positively misleading. Parallel approaches to the same goal are unacceptable, for they appear "chaotic," "wasteful," or "duplicative" to professional managers used to order. Formal procedures are instituted to obtain drawings or special shop work or to obtain equipment and technical assistance. As a result, the time between experiments lengthens, the cost of each experiment soars, and innovative productivity plummets.

Don't Reward Risk.   Most organizations, business or political, operate under the management-control concept of "no surprises." But development is by its very definition a surprise. Subordinates are penalized if they work on something and are wrong, but no penalties are attached to missing an opportunity entirely. Rewards do not accrue to those who perform superbly on a failing project. And if successful on high-payoff projects, technical people are rarely made millionaires or given rewards perceptible to outside peers.

Time-Scale Conflict.   As noted, the typical major innovation takes some seven to fifteen years from first discovery to profitability.[14] At any reasonable rate of return, present value calculations decrease future returns to extremely low levels. Because of long time horizons, uncertain market information, and high early costs, major innovations appear essentially irrational if analyzed by standard financial techniques. Consequently, many companies purposely undertake a "strong second" posture, letting others undertake the initial innovation. They then try to move powerfully with their established marketing, large-scale manufacturing, or finance capabilities to take over the already proven market. Unfortunately, if a whole industry follows this policy, that industry is likely to become strongly second rate, and the nation's trade suffers.

Control Systems.   Most companies' control systems are dominantly financial. Because other factors like product quality, image, and innovativeness are difficult to measure, they do not become bases for rewards. Producing units are held accountable primarily for ROI-profit performance. And they have little incentive to undertake longer-term development or investment programs that will not meet these criteria in the short run. Corporate financial results are published monthly and quarterly, forcing top management and all lower levels of management toward very short time horizons.[15] This problem is compounded when managers are not penalized for underinvesting in crucial nonmeasurable areas like skills development, plant maintenance, and technological innovation. Since a manager is likely to move from his existing job within three to four years, he is unlikely to be there when the results of his underinvestment take place.

Top-Man Problems.   If only one out of twenty advanced development projects really pays out, how can an organization reward a manager who, in his investments, is right even twice as often as one would expect? After all, he will still be wrong 90 percent of the time. Large enterprises tend to make decisions based on forecast data, rather than the venture capitalists' criteria of the "concept, the people, and (only then) the finances." And people willing to take venture-capital risks rarely survive the financial controls of these organizations. Hence those who make capital allocations in large enterprises are seldom intuitively comfortable with true "venture financing."

Because of such difficulties, many organizations have tried to centralize risk, taking on new ventures in "development," "entrepreneurial," "new enterprise," or similar groups. Although some such approaches have been successful, most have failed. The main reasons are: (1) corporate time horizons were not long enough to play the probability game and wait for results; (2) venture teams were staffed with professional managers balanced as to their marketing, financial, and technical skills, rather than infused with the deep-seated expertise and personal commitment a real entrepreneur needs; and (3) full costing of ventures (including all overheads) made those ventures difficult to justify in financial terms and excellent targets for cutbacks during short-term economic or organizational crunches.[16]

Large-Scale Innovation

Nevertheless, some major enterprises have an extremely fine record in large-scale innovation. We investigated many successful organizations and their practices to see if any clear patterns did appear. We will focus our illustrations here on a few well-documented organizations and innovations known to most technical audiences: the IBM 360 introduction,[17] the practices of Bell Telephone Laboratories,[18] the Xerox 914 introduction, the development of synthetic rubber and catalytic cracking by the oil/chemical industry, and the innovation of float glass at Pilkington Brothers, Ltd.[19]

Many formal management techniques can assist in planning and controlling the continuous small-scale innovations that are characteristic of almost any successful enterprise.[20] Some of these are also useful at various stages in managing major large-scale innovations. However, for the latter, other processes seemed to dominate. The following patterns—not surprisingly, quite similar to those found in smaller scale enterprises—applied to most of the major innovations studied:

1. *A Strong Incentive* existed for successful development. Each private company had at risk millions to billions of dollars. However, if successful, IBM or Xerox would achieve powerful positions in their expanding fields; Pilkington would make millions in royalties and control access to important world markets; the oil/chemical industry would meet urgent wartime demands; and Bell-AT&T could defend its monopoly position, expand its revenue base, and defend from obsolescence the largest privately held asset base in the world.

2. *A Clearly Defined Need* was specified in economic/technical performance terms for the whole system, each important subsystem, and the interaction of various subsystems. Great care was taken at the outset not to define these needs in terms of particular technologies or solution sets. IBM and Bell at first defined their needs in terms of "user needs," "functions to be performed," "systems architecture," or "black boxes" of input/output characteristics. Pilkington decided early that, to be introduced, its float process must "perform to *obsolete* existing plate technologies."

3. *Multiple Competing Approaches* were encouraged at both the basic research and development levels. This technique serves a different purpose in large company development programs. It (a) creates a positive competitive spirit among the people on each program team, (b) stimulates scientists' and engineers' commitment to their programs, (c) instills a sense of urgency to the work, (d) allows the discipline of knowledgeable people critiquing each other's approaches, (e) encourages people to invent and to use basic research knowledge to improve their approach to the problem, and (f) prevents premature commitment to any single approach. Final system choices can be made as late as possible consistent with the information available. Multiple competing approaches, by being more effective, ultimately end up by being more efficient. For such reasons, almost all large-scale innovating companies consciously encouraged parallel development.

4. *User Guidance* and participation in programs ensured that specifications remained current and that people who would manufacture, install, service, or use the system had a hand in its development. This interface occurred at all levels of the organization, not just at the technical or top level alone. To facilitate this interface, development groups were placed in physical proximity to research, producing, and, when appropriate, marketing groups. People were often moved to locations where face-to-face contacts could more easily occur.

5. *High Expertise* and research discipline were maintained by assembling first-rate people and supplying them with a leader possessing extensive knowledge about programs and their underlying art.[21] Nonperformers were removed from programs. Bell Laboratories, for example, constantly conducted peer reviews of its highly selected basic researchers' performance, and over a decade some nine out of ten of these researchers moved on to other tasks. IBM reassigned its most talented technical people to head its 360 programs and systematically weeded out nonperformers.

*6. **Time Horizons*** in successful innovative enterprises were longer than those common in their fields. Bell, Xerox, and IBM all had planning and advanced systems groups looking decades ahead, and their top managements began major innovative programs even when product lines appeared solidly positioned for seven to ten years into the future. Pilkington was privately held, was not concerned about short-term stock movements, and was headed by a vigorous chairman in his mid-forties. Each company was willing to absorb the fiscal drains associated with significant developments. Pilkington, for example, experienced negative cash flows for eleven years on its float-glass introduction.

*7. **Committed Champions*** were encouraged to carry forward major developments. Chairman Vincent Learson created this style at IBM during that company's most innovative period. He encouraged different groups to bring forward proposed designs for "performance shoot-outs" against competing proposals. At one time it was, in fact, difficult to find a successful major IBM innovation that derived directly from formal product planning rather than this championship process. Similarly, Alastair Pilkington, who championed float glass, is now chairman of Pilkington Bros.—the first person outside the direct lineage of the founder to hold that position. And Bell Labs fostered its own breed of Nobel Prize winners and champions (like Shannon, Shockley, and Pierce) for various products and causes. Each system found appropriate ways to reward such champions, sometimes even for extraordinary contributions on projects that failed in the marketplace.

*8. **Top Level Risk-Taking Support.*** For large-scale innovations to reach fruition, some top executive must be willing to take risks. At IBM, Messrs. Watson and Learson, successive chairmen of the company, were behind the 360 development and maintained close contact with both the program and its potential customers during crucial periods. Pilkington established a special Directors' Flat Glass Strategy Committee at the Board level to coordinate float's introduction.

*9. **Morale-Discovery Mode.*** Two common elements in highly productive innovative programs were that objectives were clear to all and identified as genuinely worthwhile by those on the program. High morale occurs when team members intensely share a common goal.[22] "Making more profits" rarely achieved such identity in larger organizations. But creating a significant technical advance did prove energizing. For example, at Pilkington, "people would literally work until they dropped of fatigue and then come back for more," because they saw their innovation as exciting, challenging, and capable of making St. Helens the "creative center of their industry." In successful programs there was a fervor to solve a problem, to genuinely invent, or to create something new for a purpose. Challenging goals stimulated people to look beyond the feasible to the possible.

A Control to Today

It is fascinating to contrast these characteristics and those in the preceding section with the nation's approaches to today's major problems in energy, environmental improvement, health care, public transportation, productivity, or even urban housing. Sanctions are substituted for incentives. Two-to-four year political horizons dominate. There is a search for the one all-encompassing policy (or preplanned solution) rather than tolerance for the chaos of multiple competing approaches, each vying for its piece of the action. Productive fanaticism and commitment are alien to many of the institutions working on such problems. Instead, researchers and technologists are offered civil-servant-like security. And bureaucracies rather than markets or potential users guide major programs.

Political policies discourage top-level risk taking by establishing price controls or "windfall profits" taxes in areas where needs are high. Regulations change too often and on too short a time horizon to develop significant new technologies or to get a payback on them. The media pillory those who do take risks (as in auto-exhaust or mpg innovations) by calling them "foot draggers" if they are not successful and "liars" if they said the task was difficult and then succeeded. Incorrect predictors of doom are lionized, while successful problem solvers' patents are taken away. Whole programs, like that for controlled fusion, are laid out to the year 2000 on the assumption that little new will be discovered in the future, that nothing will be invented, and that the innovator must solve every problem his technology might possibly create before it can be introduced or even tested. There is no assumption that future inventions might resolve problems if they do appear.

Far from encouraging much needed solutions, today's institutions and practices frequently discriminate against the very innovations essential to a constantly improving future.

Major Organizational Strategies

Nevertheless, major organizations can develop real strategies to respond to the large-scale challenges ahead.[23] The process must start at the very top of the organization. People of courage and vision do head many of the nation's largest organizations. These people have such credibility that, if they were willing to take the risks, they could convince both the financial and press communities to report their cases in favorable terms. The response to GM's "downsizing" decisions provides an excellent example. Despite the negative effects of financial controls and reporting, such efforts can be made worthwhile to the companies themselves. After all, favorable P/E ratios are really premiums for anticipated *future* earnings. Further, with a challenging vision of the future, organizations can more easily attract valuable people committed to solving major problems and willing to put forth the entrepreneurial efforts that characterize great enterprises—like IBM, Xerox, Pilkington, Intel, Control Data, or Texas Instruments—in their most productive years. However, this vision must be backed by a number of specific practices that stimulate invention and entrepreneurship throughout the entire organization.

Unlimited Access Concept.   Most corporate managers approach the planning-budgetary process as if they were rationing a limited available stock of capital or resources. Venture capitalists and financial houses take another approach: that there is no real limit to available capital. They simply seek ideas or business opportunities of sufficient quality to attract capital at the current price. Even when capital was scarcest, capable people like Gene Amdahl and Seymour Cray were able to obtain backing for worthy ventures. Similarly, corporations can develop an "unlimited access" attitude and be willing to seek outside capital if necessary to support ideas of adequate quality. The real task, then, is to challenge the organization to produce high-quality ideas directed toward its goals and market needs.

Opportunity Planning.   To accomplish this, the whole planning process must be converted from a resource-rationing process into an opportunity-seeking process. Essentially, the enterprise can define its major areas of expertise and interest broadly. It can then encourage and evaluate proposals to achieve these in the same way the venture capitalist does: first in conceptual terms only, using very broad figures; then through a careful appraisal of the *individual* or *team* making the proposal; and finally by considering the company's capacity to support the concept if it is successful. Only if the concept passes muster as a high potential idea would more detailed numerical analysis be used. Then the process must purposely allocate resources to major new innovations as a portion of a "total portfolio." For example, the organization can protect itself by investing the *bulk* of its resources in traditional, less risky, cash-generating ventures. But overall strategy could purposely define a *portion* of its total portfolio as investable in longer-term, higher risk ventures and thus yield new concepts.

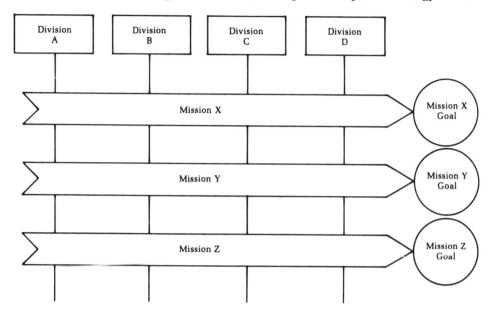

Figure 6.1   Schematic Diagram—Missions Crossing Divisions

Portfolio Planning.   Many companies have found such portfolio planning to be an
effective way to break out of the short time horizons and risk averse tendencies of normal control systems. In essence the corporation's total product/busi-
ness strategy is broken out into its most important thrusts. Each of these
thrusts is defined as a coordinated "mission" cutting across all of the several
groups or divisions which must support it.[24] For example, the development of
a second generation of products might require support from marketing, production, engineering, research and development, and/or specific geographical
groups. Figure 6.1 illustrates how planning in each of several existing divisions
could be laterally coordinated toward "mission goals."

Planning within each of the functional groups must ensure that sufficient resources are committed to each mission and that these commitments are coordinated laterally among divisions. Some missions, such as technical work to
build the quality leader for a product line or to take care of anticipated environmental requirements, might have negative or very low present values for
specific divisions or functional groups. Nevertheless, these investments might
be crucial to the success of the total strategy. In short, the requirements of the
major missions within a strategy must override the raw ROI or PV rankings of
projects within a particular function or division. Otherwise, "current product
lines" and "cash cows" obtain all of the organization's attention. Long-term,

developmental, and growth-related activities will be systematically driven out of the technical mixture, and the future of the enterprise can be jeopardized. The strategy's major thrusts define the components for the portfolio of missions. These can be segmented by criteria, such as time horizon to payout, risk category, product life cycle, product or geographical area supported, or other criteria appropriate to the specific strategy.

Control System.   Clearly, the control system must then be adjusted to measure performance along mission lines. Within each mission, it might be appropriate to rank projects by ROI, PV, or other similar criteria. However, the control system should be dominated by the strategy. It must ensure that *all* of the important goals of the enterprise are served in the patterns intended, not just current profitability. With sophistication and care, this end can be accomplished.

Motivation Systems.   Motivation systems must then reward performance toward these goals.[25] In most corporations and government laboratories, the motivation for research and development personnel quickly becomes the completion of publishable papers, the expansion of budgets, and the "carrying out of investigations." Rarely do such organizations make their technical entrepreneurs into millionaires or give them other perquisites representing success. A few conglomerating concerns, however, have learned that they need to reward richly the people who headed their intended growth divisions, or those people will grow similar enterprises elsewhere. Similarly, outstanding technical entrepreneurs have been recognized, even if belatedly, by some large enterprises. Although admittedly tricky to implement, such awards do have stimulating effects.

Skunk Works.   Many companies have found that a most effective way to stimulate truly innovative development is to place a highly talented team of engineers, technicians, and model builders "in a shed" where they can work closely and informally together—without the formal procedural structures of larger units. This was the approach used by Cray at Control Data, the Pilkington floatglass development team, Kelly Johnson at Lockheed, Issogonis at British Motor Corporation, Bruekner at KMS, and numerous other successful innovative groups in large companies. The approach tends to orient the group toward its task, rather than toward organizational promotion. It speeds turnaround time, increases the number of experiments, and encourages all technical, design, and shop personnel to join in the venture as productive coequals.

Goal Identity.   The organization must then recruit people with the necessary entrepreneurial, inventive outlooks. Often, in recruiting, research-technical groups squander enormous time checking the applicant's course work, publications, and detailed technical knowledge, and neglect the question of whether he or she might really invent something or have the will to see it introduced. The organization must make clear that its major objectives include innovation and the directions toward which those innovations should lead. Goals must appeal to and stimulate technical people, and the organization must seek to promote identification with these goals by ensuring that employees: (1) participate in goal establishment, (2) make their own proposals for specific technical approaches, and (3) are measured and rewarded against challenging performance goals. The more people can understand, identify with, and internalize stimulating goals, the more likely they are to work productively on their own, create in relevant directions, and follow through to ultimate use of their results.

Win a Few.   Finally, management must allow a sufficient number of projects and a long enough lead time for the "one in twenty" success ratio to have effect. Initially, entrepreneurial managers may need to undertake projects with somewhat lower risk ratios in order to build management confidence. Once top managements develop a "comfort factor" with a few entrepreneurial investments, they tend to be more willing to accept venturesome risks farther from traditional approaches, and innovation flourishes.

Conclusions

There are, of course, no panaceas leading to instant innovativeness. However, such broad guidelines do seem to increase the probability of entrepreneurial action in larger organizations. They are consistent with current knowledge about the entrepreneurial process and, given the enormous challenges of our times, such practices would seem to offer the opportunity for large institutional, national, and profit yields at minimal risks to sponsors. It is essential that technological managers and policy makers learn from past successes and failures those patterns that lead to important innovations. Only then may there be hope that we can reverse some of the tragic trends in our current national posture. There is little doubt that innovative large institutions could solve many of the huge-scale problems of the late twentieth century. But they must be consciously managed to do so.

PART III

Strategy

7

Managing Technological Innovation: Three Ideal Modes

Mel Horwitch

C. K. Prahalad

Technological innovation has long been considered a complex management issue. In this article, the authors suggest that a great deal of the confusion in this area has resulted from the tendency to see technological innovation as occurring in a universally applicable pattern. To address this problem, the authors have constructed a new framework to characterize technological innovation and to contribute to the understanding of the process in its various settings. This framework categorizes present-day technological innovation into three ideal modes and illuminates the different sets of managerial skills required by each. *SMR*.

The assumption that there exists an independent and universally applicable process called "technological innovation" has led to a great deal of confusion in understanding the variety of ways new technology is developed and implemented. In particular, this assumption of universality has resulted in the virtually impossible task of trying to assimilate essentially incompatible pieces of information. It is the purpose of this article to suggest a new framework for understanding and characterizing much of the technological innovation taking place in modern society. We will delineate certain broad types of technological innovation. We will also address the managerial implications of operating within the proposed structure.

The framework is structured around three ideal modes representing much of the technological innovative activity occurring today. For the purposes of discussion, a mode is the manner in which technological innovation takes place. It encompasses both the actual process by which, and the setting where,

From *Sloan Management Review*, Winter 1976, Vol. 17, No. 2. Reprinted with permission.

innovation occurs. Although three ideal modes will be described, in reality a technological innovation process often exhibits characteristics of more than one mode. No attempt is made here to discuss explicitly the issue of transition between modes, nor is it assumed that these three modes cover all present-day forms of technological innovation. They represent, however, a new approach to categorizing a wide variety of technologically innovative activities, and they are illustrated with several case histories where technological innovation played a critical role.

The three ideal modes of technological innovation presented in this article are:

- Mode I—the technological innovation process found in small, high-technology firms;
- Mode II—the process that occurs in large, divisionalized corporations;
- Mode III—the process found in multiorganization and, usually, multisector settings.

The key characteristics of each mode can be classified along the following dimensions:

1. Available technology/skills
2. Environment
3. Market
4. Internal Processes
5. Innovation: product line, process, or system.

The critical inputs to the technological innovation process include the available technology/skills, the general environment that affects the innovation process, and the specific markets that are ready for possible exploitation. Each has significant impact on the activities actually involved with managing innovation. These activities can be termed the internal processes. The internal processes include the goal-setting mechanisms, the communications systems, and the organizational structure. Finally, innovation is the result of the internal processes.

Innovation can be a single product (e.g., an Advent Videobeam), a manufacturing process (e.g., automation), or a system (e.g., a personalized rapid-transit system). By delineating the three modes along the key characteristics suggested, the critical managerial differences between these three modes of technological innovation can be seen more clearly.

Mode I. Technological Innovation in the Technology-Based Small Firm

Technological innovation is often associated with the technology-based small firm. The Route 128 area in Boston and the Palo Alto, California, region, for example, are rich in such companies. Typically, these firms have sales revenues in the $2–20 million range. Technological skills and innovation are usually their key strengths and raison d'être.

A key characteristic of the Mode I firm is that it usually has an extremely limited product line. Often its success depends on the skills, background, or interests of the founder and/or a small top-management group. Metpath, Inc., is representative of a Mode I firm and exhibits the strong influence of its founder, Paul Brown, M.D. Using a machine called the AGA Autochemist, Metpath performs a wide range of clinical laboratory tests on blood and urine samples at great accuracy, speed, and low cost. Between 1968 and 1974, sales grew from $35,090 to $8,468,726. Dr. Brown recognized that a market for low-cost, accurate service existed and located the technology. Furthermore, he provided Metpath with an entrepreneurial momentum. In effect, Metpath's success is due directly to the actions of its founder.[1]

The identification and exploitation of markets is perhaps the greatest difficulty Mode I firms face. The technology may be unfamiliar and, therefore, a substantial marketing effort may be required before potential customers will accept the new product. In addition, initial demand for a new product may be small, or potential buyers may be difficult to reach. A common weakness of the Mode I firm's marketing posture is a lack of attention to marketing issues within the organization and an overconcentration on purely technological matters. An illuminating example of the danger of investing too much effort on improving the technology is the experience of Photon, Inc., between 1949 and 1964. Photon, a pioneer in phototypesetting technology, continually put more and more funds into R & D, thereby improving its machines. Photon's "100 series" was introduced in the early 1950s; the "200 series" in the mid-1950s; the "500 series" in the early 1960s; and the "Zip" machine in the mid-1960s. In many ways, each successive product not only represented a technological improvement, but also appealed to different markets (such as multipurpose printing, daily newspapers, and computer printouts). Photon maintained a purely technological focus. After spending substantial funds on R&D, it could not mobilize the resources or the will to launch a concentrated marketing effort and losses continued to mount through 1965. Like many Mode I high-technology firms, Photon was enamored with further improving its technology, leaving the market to be exploited by less technologically sophisticated competitors.[2]

The internal processes in a Mode I firm are usually relatively simple and informal. Goal-setting, for example, is done basically by the founder or the few individuals who make up top management. The structure of a Mode I firm also remains relatively simple and informal. Communication and coordination between various managerial functions (such as manufacturing, marketing, and engineering), if these areas are separated at all, can be frequent and extensive. In fact, it is not uncommon for one manager to have responsibility for several functions. Moreover, all the important parameters of the internal processes in a Mode I firm—goal-setting, communication flow, and organization structure—are often centered around a single key individual, usually the founder or head of the firm. An illustration of the internal processes of a Mode I firm and of the significance of a single critical individual is Advent Corporation. Advent was the creation of Henry Kloss, president of the firm. Kloss had a long and distinguished history as an innovator in the quality consumer-electronics field, having founded AR and KLH. Until 1975, Kloss dominated the organization at Advent. He set goals and decided which products and markets would be exploited. Kloss's strategy at Advent was to produce high-quality, low-cost products (such as loudspeakers and Dolbyized cassette recorders) to help generate funds needed to develop a major new innovation, a large-screen T.V. called the Advent Videobeam. Kloss remarked, "I started this company with one major goal in mind: The development of a projection T.V. system."[3] It was Kloss who matched what he called the "floating knowledge" of technology with his perception of the needs in the marketplace. To exploit the market, he relied on his own intuition and experience, rather than any formal market-research studies.[4] However, in 1975 Kloss ran into severe financial pressure and was forced to sell a large block of Advent stock to an outside investor.

A significant point of vulnerability for the Mode I firm can be its limited access to financial resources. This lack of funds can often limit a Mode I firm's scope of activities and its rate of growth. Furthermore, the constant pressure to manage cash needs can reinforce a short-term operational perception of business issues. The history of Strang Corporation, a highly innovative manufacturer of carriers and test sockets for the electronics industry, illustrates this problem area. By 1971, Strang had 60 percent of the market and, for five years, had been growing at a rate of 70 percent. Its sales volume in 1971 was $7 million. However, it suddenly experienced a severe drop in sales of almost 50 percent below forecast for three consecutive months, which led to a situation where Strang was unable to meet its operational cash needs, let alone finance continued growth. Within six months, Strang was taken over by another firm.[5]

Finally, even if the Mode I firm is successful in developing a market for its innovation and carefully manages its finances, it still has to deal with the problem of growth. Some Mode I managers, such as Henry Kloss, do not want to grow past a certain point. In fact, one reason Kloss left AR and KLH was because they had grown too large for his taste. However, other firms, such as Polaroid and Xerox, have successfully passed through the transition from Mode I to Mode II. In these firms, the managers of technological innovation were then challenged by a whole new set of issues.

Mode II. Technological Innovation in the Large Multimarket, Multiproduct Corporation

The setting for Mode II includes corporations with extensive product lines servicing multiple markets and corporations that manufacture relatively few but ex⁺remely complex product lines. Thus, Mode II includes such disparate giant corporations as IBM and Xerox, which have a few dominant product lines, and Rockwell International, Textron, and Litton, which are involved in multiple product lines organized into several businesses.

This segment is extremely interesting within the context of this discussion, since R&D expenditures in the U.S. are heavily concentrated in large corporations. Companies with 10,000 or more employees were responsible for over four-fifths of U.S. industrial R&D funds in 1971; furthermore, approximately 100 large corporations accounted for more than three-fourths of all industrial R&D in that year. These 100 largest R&D performing corporations also accounted for 39 percent of sales and 38 percent of all employment in R&D performing companies.[6] The large amount of industrial R&D funds found in this Mode suggests that the management of the innovation process in this Mode is critical to our overall understanding of the process of technological innovation.

Technological innovation in Mode II is characterized by a wide range of outcomes. Mode II is associated with product innovations (e.g. hand-held electronic calculators), process innovations (e.g. the float-glass process), and innovations that combine a product with application engineering (e.g. programmable terminals in airline reservations).

Mode II corporations operate in diverse environments; this diversity results from the variety and complexity of products they manufacture and sell as well as from the peculiarities of geographical regions in which they operate. One large multinational chemical producer not only offers 400–500 distinct products, but often alters the base specifications of such products to suit the needs of various geographical regions. For example, the specification for polyethylene film resin in Brazil may be different from that in the U.S. Managing the diversity that arises from the differences in markets and products is one of the central managerial problems in Mode II corporations, especially in multinationals.[7]

The decision to innovate is more complex in Mode II than in Mode I. This complexity is due in part to the multiple opportunities that result from the diversity of markets in which the large corporation operates. Priorities for exploitation must be established and innovations selected according to set criteria, since all opportunities cannot be exploited simultaneously. Selection of relevant market segments requires substantial managerial attention. Several Mode II corporations, like GE, attempt to rank potential corporate resource commitments to its various businesses using such categories as: (1) deserving full resource support, (2) deserving medium resource support, or (3) deserving no support. Such a selection system can be based on criteria such as present and future market share, technological strengths, estimated growth, employee loyalty, and profit potential.[8] Other approaches such as market segmentation, R&D policy, product policy, product specification, application engineering and ad hoc evaluation committees are also frequently used to define the market and select the innovation. Once businesses and market segments are clearly identified, Mode II enterprises can apply massive resources—financial and manpower—to achieve a desired result. IBM reportedly spent $5 billion to develop System 360.[9]

Mode II differs substantially from Mode I in terms of the internal processes that impact on innovation. In Mode II, the organization must constantly balance strategic considerations with short-term operational requirements. Resources such as manpower, capital, and management attention must be divided between R&D for generating new products, processes, and businesses, as well as R&D for improving the performance of existing products and for minimizing the costs of existing manufacturing operations. This allocation process becomes more complex with increasing product diversity. The management system at Texas Instruments, called OST (Objectives, Strategy, Tactics) is an example of an attempt to balance formally such conflicting goals.[10]

As well as having to set priorities among markets, resource allocation, etc., top management must decide on what sort of management system will direct its technological innovation process. For example, the top management at IBM created a system that enabled them to be directly involved in making key technological decisions. In the development of the IBM System 360, several significant technological alternatives were discussed, evaluated and decided upon by top management.[11] At Infotech Systems (a disguised name for a large, diversified corporation), by contrast, top-management involvement in divisional technological decisions was minimal. Top-management control was exercised by indirect means, such as through the budgetary process.[12]

Mode II innovative activity is further complicated by the fact that needed skills are frequently scattered throughout the organization and are organized formally into various departments or units such as Corporate R&D, Product R&D, Engineering, Marketing, Finance, and Manufacturing. Communication among these groups becomes conditioned by a variety of organizational filters, and may result in the departmental parochialism and narrow perspectives so familiar to students of behavior in large corporations. Consequently, managers have developed several formal structural mechanisms such as task forces, project teams, and matrix organizations in the hope that innovations that would otherwise go unrecognized or unexploited due to difficulties in communication between functions can be realized. Therefore, while the Mode II corporation commands great technical, marketing, financial, and managerial skills, it must deal with its inherent complexity and contradictions in pursuing technological innovation.

Mode III. Technological Innovation in the Multiorganization and Multisector Enterprise

Mode III refers to the process of technological innovation that takes place in a multiorganization and, usually, multisector setting. Modern society has many examples of this kind of innovation, including the SST, Apollo, the Breeder Reactor, solid-waste disposal systems and such interindustry innovations as the development of a standard symbol in the U.S. grocery industry.

Perhaps the most important reason for the evolution of the Mode III enterprise is that such endeavors demand a technology and set of skills that cannot be found in entirety in any one of the largest corporations. The technology may not exist and therefore must be developed; this development process calls for a diverse group of experts. In addition to the technical skills needed, the Mode III enterprise requires a host of managerial talents—from operational skills to systems-application abilities, from skills in managing R&D facilities to skills in dealing with Congress and public opinion. Therefore, a common attribute of practically all Mode III endeavors is their demand for manpower of great technical and managerial diversity.

The environment for a Mode III enterprise is different from that of Mode I or Mode II. First, it is much more complex both in the number and diversity of actors. In fact, it is often difficult to distinguish between Mode III's environment, market, and internal processes. At times, Congress is a consumer and target of information. At other times, it is a decision maker. The same is true for most other points in the system: the managing agency, the President, the contracting manufacturers, and the public at large.

The market for a Mode III enterprise is also very complex. One reason for this is that there are many different kinds of markets encountered in a Mode III setting. There is a user market, the organizations that will operate the Mode III innovation (e.g., the municipal governments for solid-waste disposal systems). There is also the technical specification market, usually the actual manufacturers of the Mode III innovations (e.g., TRW for personalized mass-transit systems). Finally, there exist a variety of policy-influencing markets, which demand information and impact heavily on the overall decision-making and resource-allocation processes (such as the press, Congress, the mayor, and the President). Each of these markets has different needs, yet each is critical if the Mode III enterprise is to be successfully implemented. Furthermore, unlike the Mode I market (which is relatively easy to define) or a Mode II market (which is also definable through vigorous though often difficult monitoring and forecasting systems), critical points in the Mode III market are frequently never completely identified. Because of the extreme diversity of Mode III markets and their susceptibility to rapid change, they are often not totally amenable to definition, even using the most effective and sophisticated corporate marketing systems associated with Mode II. The Mode III decision-making process is extremely vulnerable to change, because the environment can be transformed from a narrow setting into a broadly based, highly politicized arena. For example, originally the breeder reactor was primarily the concern of the nuclear-power industry, the utilities, the old AEC, and the Joint Atomic Energy Committee in Congress. However, with the entrance of the Natural Resources Defense Council, other environmental organizations and ad hoc citizen groups, the breeder reactor became a highly visible issue.[13]

The internal processes can be distinguished in a number of ways. The Mode III goal-setting system is extremely complex and fragmented. First, different organizations can set goals. Typically, the funding level is set by one organization, and the technical parameters of the innovation are designed by a number of organizations. The process is further complicated by the tendency among Mode III enterprises to continue altering such goals. Other organizations outside the formal goal-setting system may seek to intervene and impact on a Mode III enterprise. The system is also exposed to the public and therefore vulnerable to outside interest-group pressure (as in the ABM or breeder reactor programs).[14]

The communications system in such a structure is usually highly fragmented and incomplete. Mode III is populated with organizations and individuals of different cultures and interests, and the perceived stakes can be quite different for the various players. For the bureaucrat, the concern may be his or her job or career. For the public advocate, moral or policy issues may be important. It is difficult to use a purely informal communications process or to institute formal systems in such a fluid situation. Consequently, participants rarely attempt to communicate purposely throughout the whole structure on a single issue. Communication is usually done on an incremental basis using a variety of mechanisms depending on the information and target audience. At times, important communication takes place outside the relevant decision-making organizations. An example of this situation is when information is purposely "leaked" to the press.[15]

The structure of Mode III is usually highly fragmented. Different key activities are frequently the responsibilities of completely separate organizations. For example, in the SST Program, funding approval was the responsibility of Congress, but the basic research was done by the Air Force, NASA, and the manufacturers. Overall policy making was carried out (until 1968) by a high-level interagency Presidential Advisory Committee. Direction and coordination of the SST Program was the responsibility of the FAA and later of the Department of Transportation. The day-to-day operations were carried out by the major airframe and engine manufacturers and their subcontractors.[16]

The life cycles of Mode III enterprises vary. For example, the TVA, a massive technological innovation on a regional level, became a permanent institution. On the other hand, many units established to manage a Mode III endeavor, such as the Apollo Program, are quasi-permanent in that they exist for the life of the program, usually a number of years.

Mode III enterprises, however, can also exhibit highly temporary organizational structures. An example of this involves the subcommittee established to study the feasibility of a standard symbol to be used in the U.S. grocery industry. Until 1971 this industry was considered extremely conservative and uninnovative, and the technology it used was relatively simple. The attempt to initiate studies on the feasibility of a standard symbol represented a radical industry-wide shift into the age of computers and automation. This attempt exhibited several characteristics of a Mode III enterprise. It involved representatives of grocery manufacturers, retailers, and technical and management experts from the Batelle Memorial Institute, MIT, and McKinsey & Co. Several other groups, such as the electronic-equipment manufacturers and the printing industry, were also consulted, and the Federal Trade Commission and the President's Council on Productivity exhibited interest. Funds for the effort were contributed by both the manufacturing and retailing members of the grocery industry. The result of the effort, the development of a standard symbol, is expected to revolutionize the U.S. grocery industry and spawn a new line of business in point-of-sale systems. This new business area is expected to grow into a $2–3 billion industry by 1980.

It would have been impossible to reach agreement on a standard symbol for the grocery industry without the participation of all the groups mentioned above. The process was managed by the Standard Symbol Subcommittee, which was comprised of high-level representatives from the retailers and food-processor groups. Although it had an important decision-making responsibility, it had no formal power of enforcement nor did it have a role in implementing the innovation, once it had decided upon the final design. The major tasks of the subcommittee were to gain credibility for the standard symbol from the entire industry and to decide on a feasible format for it. Once this was accomplished, the subcommittee's activities were to cease.[17]

It is interesting to note that when a Mode III enterprise is involved with *only* the idea-generation and design phase of an innovation, it frequently tends to exhibit many of the characteristics of a temporary organization. However, when the Mode III endeavor is involved with the implementation of the Mode III innovation, it tends to take on attributes of permanence and is very difficult to terminate. (Four years after the SST Program was cancelled by Congress, there was still an SST contract office in the Department of Transportation.)

The resulting Mode III innovation is characterized by the enormous amount of diverse support needed for its successful development. Support is defined not only in terms of funds but also as the mobilization of diverse kinds of expertise and favorable public opinion. There appear to be at least three basic types of Mode III innovations:

1. A single complex product* developed for a single customer (usually the government), such as Apollo or Polaris;
2. A single product* developed for multiple customers, such as the breeder reactor or the SST;
3. A complex system of organizations and hardware to accomplish some end or deliver some service, such as personalized rapid transit or solid waste disposal.

A main source of strength for the Mode III enterprise lies in the diverse resources that can be mobilized in its behalf. Mode III has the additional feature of being able to allow the public, or at least groups purporting to represent the public interest, to enter the fragmented Mode III decision-making process. Such intervention may at times enlarge the scope of the debate. Finally, if successful, a Mode III enterprise may have enormous impact on society as a whole.

On the other hand, the Mode III enterprise has significant weaknesses. It is highly vulnerable to public opinion, and therefore its outcome can never be totally assured even using effective modern managerial techniques. Even support from within—the internal coalition of organizations—can never be totally relied upon, and complete control over the system becomes almost impossible. Finally, the support-building activity among the many actors is time consuming and never ending, especially if the interests of the constituent parts of the internal processes and the involvement of actors in the environment and market change radically.

---

*However, this end product is usually made up of a number of complex components supplied by a number of manufacturers.

Implications for Management

Having described three ideal modes, it is now possible to compare the distinguishing characteristics of these forms of modern technological innovation and to examine the implications for managing innovation within this context.

The most revealing conclusion is that successful management of technological innovation in each mode frequently calls for different sets of managerial skills and behavior. In Mode I, the innovation goals are set by the founder or a small group of key individuals. The goal-setting process and communications system tend to be informal, and the options for innovation are circumscribed by the skills and perceptions of the founder and his team of top management. Managerial activity reflects the personal competencies of top managers. The strengths of the Mode I firm are in the unique technological skills of its top management and in its ability to respond quickly and find a solid niche in the marketplace. Many Mode I firms exhibit a tendency to be technology-oriented rather than business-oriented. Such a situation often leads to a neglect of the marketing function and to a lack of ability to deal with the financial issues affecting the firm. Clearly, those managers involved in developing a Mode I innovation should make certain that the marketing and financial aspects of that innovation receive complete attention.

In Mode II, the goal-setting process for innovation becomes relatively more complicated due to the complexities caused by the great variety of existing and potential products and businesses. The top managers are usually unaware of all the options available to them or are unable to evaluate them personally. As a result, top managers have to rely on the knowledge and judgment of lower level executives and specialists who sponsor and help evaluate projects. Top managers must use sophisticated managerial mechanisms, such as formal resource-allocation procedures and control and evaluation systems, to influence a certain correspondence between corporate goals and the corporation's posture regarding technological innovation. The complex Mode II communication system that flows across different units, levels, and functions should be managed with this in mind.

The task of managing Mode II innovations is not merely a question of making sure that the necessary managerial skills are available and that a viable opportunity exists. Mode II corporations have massive and multiple opportunities, and sufficient skills usually exist. One essential task, however, is the surfacing and selection of the innovation(s) best suited to the corporation's overall strategy. Another important management mission is being able to guide the innovation(s) through the complex maze of management systems found in such institutions. Therefore, the managerial skills required for managing Mode II innovations emphasize the ability to deal with complexity and with conflicting signals within a setting where an overall strategic purpose and direction can be set. Such managers must also know how to use the complex, formal Mode II management systems to encourage innovation.

Mode III innovations offer yet another, very different dilemma for managers. In contrast to Mode I or Mode II, innovations in Mode III can take place in a fragmented, politicized, and potentially highly visible setting. The Mode III enterprise is composed of different organizations and frequently has no definable formal boundaries. Organizations or interest groups may enter or leave the goal-setting process, and different groups may have different interests and perform different functions. As the constellation of actors changes, so may the goals of the endeavor.

Thus, Mode III managers must deal with the crucial factors of complexity and fluidity. They must acknowledge that they are involved in a process where no single group has total control over the enterprise and realize that total communication with the organizations involved in a Mode III enterprise is impossible. They must be able to communicate at different times with different cultures and different interest groups. Mastering an established strategy-formulation process and sophisticated management systems (as required in Mode II) is not enough. The successful Mode III manager must be more flexible, adaptive, and political. If a Mode III setting changes from a contained to a highly visible one, the Mode III manager must be able to switch from dealing with a single group (e.g., technical experts) to communicating effectively with the public at large. In order to build a large base of support, such a manager frequently must transcend the formal boundaries of his own organization and of the other organizations formally involved in the Mode III enterprise.

The successful management of technological innovation is a very complex question. One key reason for this is that modern technological innovation comes in diverse forms. Each broad type of innovation requires a somewhat different set of managerial skills. For innovation in Mode I firms, it is suggested that a balance of basic managerial functions combined with a key technological skill is important. For Mode II innovations, managers need to be able to integrate innovation projects into the corporation's overall strategy and to understand and use sophisticated management systems. Mode III innovations, on the other hand, depend more on the adaptive and political ability of their managers. There is, therefore, a danger of thinking that successful managers of one kind of innovation can also successfully manage another kind. In a society where technological innovation is critical, it is important to delineate explicitly the essential requirements for managing successfully each general type of innovation and then to develop different managerial structures to meet these different sets of requirements.

8

The Art of High-Technology Management

Modesto A. Maidique

Robert H. Hayes

The authors argue that, contrary to popular opinion, U.S. firms need not look overseas for models of successfully managed companies. Instead, many U.S. companies can benefit from using well-managed American high-tech firms as their guides. Through their studies of a wide range of high-technology firms, the authors identified those characteristics they believe make a company successful, and grouped them into six themes. Analysis of their findings has led them to conclude that well-managed companies have found ways to resolve a critical dilemma—the ability to manage the conflict between continuity and rapid change. *SMR.*

Over the past fifteen years, the world's perception of the competence of U.S. companies in managing technology has come full circle. In 1967, a Frenchman, J.J. Servan-Schreiber, expressed with alarm in his book *The American Challenge* that U.S. technology was far ahead of the rest of the industrialized world.[1] This "technology gap," he argued, was continually widening because of the *superior ability of Americans to organize and manage technological development.*

Today, the situation is perceived to have changed drastically. The concern now is that the gap is reversing: the onslaught of Japanese and/or European challenges is threatening America's technological leadership. Even such informed Americans as Dr. Simon Ramo express great concern: In *America's Technology Slip,* Dr. Ramo notes the apparent inability of U.S. companies to compete technologically with their foreign counterparts.[2] Moreover, in the bestseller *The Art of Japanese Management,* the authors use as a basis of com-

From *Sloan Management Review,* Winter 1984, Vol. 25, No. 2. Reprinted with permission.

parison two technology-based firms: Matsushita (Japanese) and ITT (American).[3] Here, the Japanese firm is depicted as a model for managers, while the management practices of the U.S. firm are sharply criticized.

Nevertheless, a number of U.S. companies appear to be fending off these foreign challenges successfully. These firms are repeatedly included on lists of "America's best-managed companies." Many of them are competitors in the R&D intensive industries, a sector of our economy that has come under particular criticism. Ironically, some of them have even served as models for highly successful Japanese and European high-tech firms.

For example, of the forty-three companies that Peters and Waterman, Jr., judged to be "excellent" in *In Search of Excellence,* almost half were classified as "high technology," or as containing a substantial high-technology component.[4] Similarly, of the five U.S. organizations that William Ouchi described as best prepared to meet the Japanese challenge, three (IBM, Hewlett-Packard, and Kodak) were high-technology companies.[5] Indeed, high-technology corporations are among the most admired firms in America. In a *Fortune* study that ranked the corporate reputation of the 200 largest U.S. corporations, IBM and Hewlett-Packard (HP) ranked first and second, respectively.[6] And of the top ten firms, nine compete in such high-technology fields as pharmaceuticals, precision instruments, communications, office equipment, computers, jet engines, and electronics.

The above studies reinforce our own findings, which have led us to conclude that U.S. high-technology firms that seek to improve their management practices to succeed against foreign competitors need not look overseas. The firms mentioned above are not unique. On the contrary, they are representative of scores of well-managed small and large U.S. technology-based firms. Moreover, the management practices they have adopted are widely applicable. Thus, perhaps the key to stimulating innovation in our country is not to adopt the managerial practices of the Europeans or the Japanese, but to adapt some of the policies of our own successful high-technology firms.

The Study

Over the past two decades, we have been privileged to work with a host of small and large high-technology firms as participants, advisers, and researchers. We and our assistants interviewed formally and informally over 250 executives, including more than 30 CEOs, from a wide cross section of high-tech industries—biotechnology, semiconductors, computers, pharmaceuticals, and aerospace. About 100 of these executives were interviewed in 1983 as part of a large-scale study of product innovation in the electronics industry (conducted by one of this article's authors and his colleagues).[7] Our research has been guided by a fundamental question: what are the strategies, policies, practices, and decisions that result in successful management of high-technology enterprises? One of our principal findings was that no company has a monopoly on managerial excellence. Even the best run companies make big mistakes, and many smaller, less regarded companies are surprisingly sophisticated about the factors that mediate between success and failure.

It also became apparent from our interviews that the driving force behind the successes of many of these companies was strong leadership. All companies need leaders and visionaries, of course, but leadership is particularly essential when the future is blurry and when the world is changing rapidly. Although few high-tech firms can succeed for long without strong leaders, leadership itself is not the subject of this article. Rather, we accept it as given and seek to understand what strategies and management practices can reinforce strong leadership.

The companies we studied were of different sizes ($10 million to $30 billion in sales); their technologies were at different stages of maturity; their industry growth rates and product mixes were different; and their managers ranged widely in age. But they all had the same unifying thread: a rapid rate of change in the technological base of their products. This common thread, rapid technological change, implies novel products and functions and thus usually rapid growth. But even when growth is slow or moderate, the destruction of the old capital base by new technology results in the need for rapid redeployment of resources to cope with new product designs and new manufacturing processes. Thus, the two dominant characteristics of the high-technology organizations that we focused on were growth and change.

In part because of this split focus (growth and change), the companies we studied often appeared to display contradictory behavior over time. Despite these differences, in important respects, they were remarkably similar because they all confronted the same two-headed dilemma: how to unleash the creativity that promotes growth and change without being fragmented by it, and how to control innovation without stifling it. In dealing with this concern, they tended to adopt strikingly similar managerial approaches.

The Paradox: Continuity and Chaos

When we grouped our findings into general themes of success, a significant paradox gradually emerged: Some of the behavioral patterns that these companies displayed seemed to favor promoting disorder and informality, while others would have us conclude that it was consistency, continuity, integration, and order that were the keys to success. As we grappled with this apparent paradox, we came to realize that continued success in a high-technology envi-

ronment requires periodic shifts between chaos and continuity.[8] Our originally static framework, therefore, was gradually replaced by a dynamic framework within whose ebbs and flows lay the secrets of success.

Six Themes of Success

The six themes that we grouped our findings into were: (1) business focus; (2)
adaptability; (3) organizational cohesion; (4) entrepreneurial culture; (5)
sense of integrity; and (6) "hands-on" top management. No one firm exhibits
excellence in every one of these categories at any one time, nor are the less
successful firms totally lacking in all. Nonetheless, outstanding high-technology firms tend to score high in most of the six categories, while less successful
ones usually score low in several.[9]

1. Business Focus

Even a superficial analysis of the most successful high-technology firms leads
one to conclude that they are highly focused. With few exceptions, the leaders
in high-technology fields, such as computers, aerospace, semiconductors,
biotechnology, chemicals, pharmaceuticals, electronic instruments, and duplicating machines, realize the great bulk of their sales either from a single product line or from a closely related set of product lines.[10] For example, IBM,
Boeing, Intel, and Genentech confine themselves almost entirely to computer
products, commercial aircraft, integrated circuits, and genetic engineering, respectively. Similarly, four-fifths of Kodak's and Xerox's sales come from pho-
tographic products and duplicating machines, respectively. In general, the
smaller the company, the more highly focused it is. Tandon concentrates on
disk drives; Tandem on high-reliability computers; Analog Devices on linear
integrated circuits; and Culinet on software products.

Closely Related Products. This extraordinary concentration does not stop with the
dominant product line. When the company grows and establishes a secondary
product line, it is usually closely related to the first. Hewlett-Packard, for instance, has two product families, each of which accounts for about half of its
sales. Both families—electronic instruments and data processors—are focused
on the same technical, scientific, and process control markets. IBM also
makes two closely related product lines—data processors (approximately 80
percent of sales) and office equipment—both of which emphasize the business
market.

Companies that took the opposite path have not fared well. Two of yesterday's technological leaders, ITT and RCA, have paid dearly for diversifying away from their strengths. Today, both firms are trying to divest themselves of many of what were once highly touted acquisitions. As David Packard, chairman of the board of Hewlett-Packard, once observed, "No company ever died from starvation, but many have died from indigestion."[11]

A communications firm that became the world's largest conglomerate, ITT began to slip in the early 1970s after an acquisition wave orchestrated by Harold Geneen. When Geneen retired in 1977, his successors attempted to redress ITT's lackluster performance through a far-reaching divestment program.[12] So far, forty companies and other assets worth over $1 billion have been sold—and ITT watchers believe the program is just getting started. Some analysts believe that ITT will ultimately be restructured into three groups, with the communications/electronics group and engineered products (home of ITT semiconductors) forming the core of a "new" ITT.

RCA experienced a similar fate to ITT. When RCA's architect and longtime chairman, General David Sarnoff, retired in 1966, RCA was internationally respected for its pioneering work in television, electronic components, communications, and radar. But by 1980, the three CEOs who followed Sarnoff had turned a technological leader into a conglomerate with flat sales, declining earnings, and a $2.9 billion debt. This disappointing performance led RCA's new CEO, Thorton F. Bradshaw, to decide to return RCA to its high-technology origins.[13] Bradshaw's strategy is to now concentrate on RCA's traditional strengths—communications and entertainment—by divesting its other businesses.

Focused R&D.   Another policy that strengthens the focus of leading high-technology firms is concentrating R&D on one or two areas. Such a strategy enables these businesses to dominate the research, particularly the more risky leading-edge explorations. By spending a higher proportion of their sales dollars on R&D than their competitors do, or through their sheer size (as in the case of IBM, Kodak, and Xerox), such companies maintain their technological leadership. It is not unusual for a leading firm's R&D investment to be one and a half to two times the industry's average as a percentage of sales (8–15 percent) and several times more than any individual competitor on an absolute basis.[14]

Moreover, their commitment to R&D is both enduring and consistent, and is maintained through slack periods and recessions, because it is believed to be in the best, long-term interest of the stockholders. As the CEO of Analog Devices, a leading linear integrated-circuit manufacturer, explained in a quarterly report that noted a 30 percent decline in profits, "We are sharply con-

straining the growth of fixed expenses, but we do not feel it is in the best interest of shareholders to cut back further on product development . . . in order
to relieve short-term pressure on earnings."[15] Similarly, when sales flattened
and profit margins plummeted at Intel as the result of a recession, its management invested a record-breaking $130 million in R&D and another $150 million in plant and equipment.[16]

Consistent Priorities.   Still, another way for a company to demonstrate a strong
business focus is through a set of priorities and a pattern of behavior that is
continually reinforced by top management: for example, planned manufacturing improvement at Texas Instruments (TI); customer service at IBM; the concept of the entrepreneurial product champion at 3M; and the new products at
HP. Belief in the competitive effectiveness of their chosen theme runs deep in
each of these companies.

A business focus that is maintained over extended periods of time has fundamental consequences. By concentrating on what it does well, a company develops an intimate knowledge of its markets, competitors, technologies, employees, and of the future needs and opportunities of its customers.[17] The Stanford
Innovation Project recently completed a three-year study of 224 U.S. high-
technology products (half of which were successes, half of which were failures) and concluded that a continuous, in-depth, informal interaction with
leading customers throughout the product-development process was the principal factor behind successful new products. In short, this coupling is the cor-
nerstone of effective high-technology progress. Such an interaction is greatly
facilitated by the longstanding and close customer relationships that are fostered by concentrating on closely related product-market choices.[18] "Customer needs," explains Tom Jones, chairman of Northrop Corporation,
"must be understood *way ahead of time*" (authors' emphasis).[19]

2. Adaptability

Successful firms balance a well-defined business focus with the willingness,
and the will, to undertake major and rapid change when necessary. Concentration, in short, does not mean stagnation. Immobility is the most dangerous behavioral pattern a high-technology firm can develop: technology can change
rapidly, and with it the markets and customers served. Therefore, a high-technology firm must be able to track and exploit the rapid shifts and twists in market boundaries as they are redefined by new technological, market, and competitive developments.

The cost of strategic stagnation can be great, as General Radio (GR) found
out. Once the proud leader of the electronic instruments business, GR almost

single-handedly created many sectors of the market. Its engineering excellence and its progressive human-relations policies were models for the industry. But when its founder, Melville Eastham, retired in 1950, GR's strategy ossified. In the next two decades, the company failed to take advantage of two major opportunities for growth that were closely related to the company's strengths: microwave instruments and minicomputers. Meanwhile, its traditional product line withered away. Now all that remains of GR's once dominant instruments line, which is less than 10 percent of sales, is a small assembly area where a handful of technicians assemble batches of the old instruments.

It wasn't until William Thurston, in the wake of mounting losses, assumed the presidency at the end of 1972 that GR began to refocus its engineering creativity and develop new marketing strategies. Using the failure of the old policies as his mandate, Thurston deemphasized the aging product lines, focused GR's attention on automated test equipment, balanced its traditional engineering excellence with an increased sensitivity to market needs, and gave the firm a new name—GenRad. Since then, GenRad has resumed rapid growth and has won a leadership position in the automatic test-equipment market.[20]

The GenRad story is a classic example of a firm making a strategic change because it perceived that its existing strategy was not working. But even successful high-technology firms sometimes feel the need to be rejuvenated periodically to avoid technological stagnation. In the mid-1960s, for example, IBM appeared to have little reason for major change. The company had a near monopoly in the computer mainframe industry. Its two principal products—the 1401 at the low end of the market and the 7090 at the high end—accounted for over two-thirds of industry sales. Yet, in one move the company obsoleted both product lines (as well as others) and redefined the rules of competition for decades to come by simultaneously introducing six compatible models of the "System 360," based on proprietary hybrid-integrated circuits.[21]

During the same period, GM, whose dominance of the U.S. auto industry approached IBM's dominance of the computer mainframe industry, stoutly resisted such a rejuvenation. Instead, it became more and more centralized and inflexible. Yet, GM was also once a high-technology company. In its early days when Alfred P. Sloan ran the company, engines were viewed as high-technology products. One day, Charles F. Kettering told Sloan he believed the high efficiency of the diesel engine could be engineered into a compact power plant. Sloan's response was: "Very well—we are now in the diesel engine business. You tell us how the engine should run, and I will . . . capitalize the program."[22] Two years later, Kettering achieved a major breakthrough in diesel technology. This paved the way for a revolution in the railroad industry and led to GM's preeminence in the diesel locomotive markets.

Organizational Flexibility. To undertake such wrenching shifts in direction requires both agility and daring. Organizational agility seems to be associated
with organizational flexibility: frequent realignments of people and responsibilities as the firm attempts to maintain its balance on shifting competitive
sands. The daring and the willingness to take you-bet-your-company kind of
risks is a product of both the inner confidence of its members and a powerful
top management—one that either has effective shareholder control or the full
support of its board.

3. Organizational Cohesion

The key to success for a high-tech firm is not simply periodic renewal. There
must also be cooperation in the translation of new ideas into new products and
processes. As Ken Fisher, the architect of Prime Computer's extraordinary
growth, puts it, "If you have the driving function, the most important success
factor is the ability to integrate. It's also the most difficult part of the task."[23]

To succeed, the energy and creativity of the whole organization must be
tapped. Anything that restricts the flow of ideas, or undermines the trust, respect, and sense of a commonality of purpose among individuals is a potential
danger. This is why high-tech firms fight so vigorously against the usual organizational accoutrements of seniority, rank, and functional specialization. Little
attention is given to organizational charts: often they don't exist.

Younger people in a rapidly evolving technological field are often as
good—and sometimes even better—a source of new ideas as older ones. In
some high-tech firms, in fact, the notion of a "halflife of knowledge" is used;
that is, the amount of time that has to elapse before half of what one knows is
obsolete. In semiconductor engineering, for example, it is estimated that the
halflife of a newly minted Ph.D. is about seven years. Therefore, any practice
that relegates younger engineers to secondary nonpartnership roles is considered counterproductive.

Similarly, product design, marketing, and manufacturing personnel must
collaborate in a common cause rather than compete with one another, as happens in many organizations. Any policies that appear to elevate one of these
functions above the others—either in prestige or in rewards—can poison the
atmosphere for collaboration and cooperation.

A source of division, and one that distracts the attention of people from the
needs of the firm to their own aggrandizement, are the executive "perks" that
are found in many mature organizations: Pretentious job titles, separate dining
rooms and restrooms for executives, larger and more luxurious offices (often
separated in some way from the rest of the organization), and even separate or
reserved places in the company parking lot all tend to establish "distance" be-

tween managers and doers and substitute artificial goals for the crucial real ones of creating successful new products and customers. The appearance of an executive dining room, in fact, is one of the clearest danger signals.

Good Communication.   One way to combat the development of such distance is by making top executives more visible and accessible. IBM, for instance, has an open-door policy that encourages managers at different levels of the organization to talk to department heads and vice-presidents. According to senior IBM executives, it was not unusual for a project manager to drop in and talk to Frank Cary (IBM's chairman) or John Opel (IBM's president). Likewise, an office with transparent walls and no door, such as that of John Young, CEO at HP, encourages communication. In fact, open-style offices are common in many high-tech firms.

A regular feature of 3M's management process is the monthly "technical forum" where technical staff members from the firm exchange views on their respective projects. This emphasis on communication is not restricted to internal operations. Such a firm supports and often sponsors industry-wide technical conferences, sabbaticals for staff members, and cooperative projects with technical universities.

Such forums serve to compensate partially for the loss of visibility that technologists usually experience when an organization becomes more complex and when production, marketing, and finance staffs swell. So does the concept of the dual-career ladder that is used in most of these firms: that is, a job hierarchy through which technical personnel can attain the status, compensation, and recognition accorded to a division general manager or a corporate vice-president. By using this strategy, companies try to retain the spirit of the early days of the industry, when scientists played a dominant role, often even serving as members of the board of directors.[24]

Again, a strategic business focus contributes to organizational cohesion. Managers of firms that have a strong theme/culture and that concentrate on closely related markets and technologies generally display a sophisticated understanding of their businesses. Someone who understands where the firm is going and why is more likely to be willing to subordinate the interests of his or her own unit or function in the interest of promoting the common goal.

Job Rotation.   A policy of conscious job rotation also facilitates this sense of communality. In the small firm, everyone is involved in everyone else's job, but specialization tends to creep in as size increases and boundary lines between functions appear. If left unchecked, these boundaries can become rigid and impermeable. Rotating managers in temporary assignments across these boundaries helps keep the lines fluid and informal, however. When a new process is developed at TI, for example, the process developers are sent to the production unit where the process will be implemented. They are allowed to return to their usual posts only after that unit's operations manager is convinced that the process is working properly.

Integration of Roles.   Other ways that high-tech companies try to prevent organizational, and particularly hierarchical, barriers from arising is through multidisciplinary project teams, "special venture groups," and matrixlike organizational structures. Such structures, which require functional specialists and product/market managers to interact in a variety of relatively short-term problem-solving assignments, both inject a certain ambiguity into organizational relationships and require each individual to play a variety of organizational roles.

For example, AT&T uses a combination of organizational and physical mechanisms to promote integration. The Advanced Development sections of Bell Labs are physically located on the sites of the Western Electric plants. This location creates an organizational bond between Development and Bell's basic research and an equally important spatial bond between Development and the manufacturing engineering groups at the plants. In this way, communication is encouraged among Development and the other two groups.[25]

Long-term Employment.   Long-term employment and intensive training are also important integrative mechanisms. Managers and technologists are more likely to develop satisfactory working relationships if they know they will be harnessed to each other for a good part of their working lives. Moreover, their loyalty and commitment to the firm is increased if they know the firm is continuously investing in upgrading their capabilities.

At Tandem, technologists regularly train administrators on the performance and function of the firm's products and, in turn, administrators train the technologists on personnel policies and financial operations.[26] Such a firm also tends to select college graduates who have excellent academic records, which suggest self-discipline and stability, and then encourages them to stay with the firm for most, if not all, of their careers.

4. Entrepreneurial Culture

While continuously striving to pull the organization together, successful high-tech firms also display fierce activism in promoting internal agents of change. Indeed, it has long been recognized that one of the most important characteristics of a successful high-technology firm is an entrepreneurial culture.[27]

Indeed, the ease with which small entrepreneurial firms innovate has always inspired a mixture of puzzlement and jealousy in larger firms. When new ventures and small firms fail, they usually do so because of capital shortages and managerial errors.[28] Nonetheless, time and again they develop remarkably innovative products, processes, and services with a speed and efficiency that baffle the managers of large companies. The success of the Apple II, which created a new industry, and Genentech's genetically engineered insulin are of this genre. The explanation for a small entrepreneurial firm's innovativeness is straightforward, yet it is difficult for a large firm to replicate its spirit.

Entrepreneurial Characteristics.   First, the small firm is typically blessed with excellent communication. Its technical people are in continuous contact (and often in cramped quarters). They have lunch together, and they call each other outside of working hours. Thus, they come to understand and appreciate the difficulties and challenges facing one another. Sometimes they will change jobs or double up to break a critical bottleneck; often the same person plays multiple roles. This overlapping of responsibilities results in a second blessing: a dissolving of the classic organizational barriers that are major impediments to the innovating process. Third, key decisions can be made immediately by the people who first recognize a problem, not later by top management or by someone who barely understands the issue. Fourth, the concentration of power in the leader/entrepreneurs makes it possible to deploy the firm's resources very rapidly. Last, the small firm has access to multiple funding channels, from the family dentist to a formal public offering. In contrast, the manager of an R&D project in a large firm has effectively only one source, the "corporate bank."

Small Divisions.   In order to recreate the entrepreneurial climate of the small firm, successful large high-technology firms often employ a variety of organizational devices and personnel policies. First, they divide and subdivide. Hewlett-Packard, for example, is subdivided into fifty divisions: The company has a policy of splitting divisions soon after they exceed 1,000 employees. Texas Instruments is subdivided into more than thirty divisions and 250 "tactical action programs." Until recently, 3M's business was split into forty divisions. Although these divisions sometimes reach $100 million or more in sales, by Fortune 500 standards they are still relatively small companies.

Variety of Funding Channels.   Second, such high-tech firms employ a variety of funding channels to encourage risk taking. At Texas Instruments managers have three distinct options in funding a new R&D project. If their proposal is rejected by the centralized Strategic Planning (OST) System because it is not expected to yield acceptable economic gains, they can seek a "Wild Hare Grant." The Wild Hare program was instituted by Patrick Haggerty, while he was TI's chairman, to ensure that good ideas with long-term potential were not systematically turned down. Alternatively, if the project is outside the mainstream of the OST System, managers or engineers can contact one of dozens of individuals who hold "IDEA" grant purse strings and who can authorize up to $25,000 for prototype development. It was an IDEA grant that resulted in TI's highly successful "Speak and Spell" learning aid.

3M managers also have three choices: They can request funds from their own division, corporate R&D, or the new ventures division.[29] This willingness to allow a variety of funding channels has an important consequence: It encourages the pursuit of alternative technological approaches, particularly during the early stages of a technology's development, when no one can be sure of the best course to follow.

IBM, for instance, has found that rebellion can be good business. Arthur K. Watson, the founder's son and a longtime senior manager, once described the way the disk memory, a core element of modern computers, was developed:

> [It was] not the logical outcome of a decision made by IBM management. [Because of budget difficulties] it was developed in one of our laboratories as a bootleg project. A handful of men . . . broke the rules. They risked their jobs to work on a project they believed in.[30]

At Northrop the head of aircraft design usually has at any one time several projects in progress without the awareness of top management. A lot can happen before the decision reaches even a couple of levels below the chairman. "We like it that way," explains Northrop Chairman Tom Jones.[31]

Tolerance of Failure.   Moreover, the successful high-technology firms tend to be very tolerant of technological failure. "At HP," Bob Hungate, general manager of the Medical Supplies Division, explains, "it's understood that when you try something new you will sometimes fail."[32] Similarly, at 3M, those who fail to turn their pet project into a commercial success almost always get another chance. Richard Frankel, the president of the Kevex Corporation, a $20 million instrument manufacturer, puts it this way, "You need to encourage people to make mistakes. You have to let them fly in spite of aerodynamic limitations."[33]

Opportunity to Pursue Outside Projects.   Finally, these firms provide ample time to pursue speculative projects. Typically, as much as 20 percent of a productive scientist's or engineer's time is "unprogrammed," during which he or she is free to pursue interests that may not lie in the mainstream of the firm. IBM

Technical Fellows are given up to five years to work on projects of their own choosing, from high-speed memories to astronomy.

5. Sense of Integrity

While committed to individualism and entrepreneurship, at the same time successful high-tech firms tend to exhibit a commitment to long-term relationships. The firms view themselves as part of an enduring community that includes employees, stockholders, customers, suppliers, and local communities: Their objective is to maintain stable associations with all of these interest groups.

Although these firms have clearcut business objectives, such as growth, profits, and market share, they consider them subordinate to higher order ethical values. Honesty, fairness, and openness—that is, integrity—are not to be sacrificed for short-term gain. Such companies don't knowingly promise what they can't deliver to customers, stockholders, or employees. They don't misrepresent company plans and performance. They tend to be tough but forthright competitors. As Herb Dwight, president of Spectra-Physics, one of the world's leading laser manufacturers, says, "The managers that succeed here go *out of their way* to be ethical."[34] And Alexander d'Arbeloff, cofounder and president of Teradyne, states bluntly, "Integrity comes first. If you don't have that, nothing else matters."[35]

These policies may seem utopian, even puritanical, but in a high-tech firm they also make good business sense. Technological change can be dazzlingly rapid; therefore, uncertainty is high, risks are difficult to assess, and market opportunities and profits are hard to predict. It is almost impossible to get a complex product into production, for example, without solid trust between functions, between workers and managers, and between managers and stockholders (who must be willing to see the company through the possible dips in sales growth and earnings that often accompany major technological shifts). Without integrity the risks multiply and the probability of failure (in an already difficult enterprise) rises unacceptably. In such a context, Ray Stata, cofounder of the Massachusetts High Technology Council, states categorically, "You need an environment of mutual trust."[36]

This commitment to ethical values must start at the top, otherwise it is ineffective. Most of the CEOs we interviewed consider it to be a cardinal dimension of their role. As Bernie Gordon, president of Analogic, explains, "The things that make leaders are their philosophy, ethics, and psychology."[37] Nowhere is this dimension more important than in dealing with the company's employees. Paul Rizzo, IBM's vice-chairman, puts it this way, "At IBM we have a fundamental respect for the individual. . . . People must be free to disagree and to be heard. Then, even if they lose, you can still marshall them behind you."[38]

Self-understanding.   This sense of integrity manifests itself in a second, not unrelated way: self-understanding. The pride, almost arrogance, of these firms in their ability to compete in their chosen fields is tempered by a surprising acknowledgment of their limitations. One has only to read Hewlett-Packard's corporate objectives or interview one of its top managers to sense this extraordinary blend of strength and humility. Successful high-tech companies are able to reconcile their "dream" with what they can realistically achieve. This is one of the reasons why they are extremely reluctant to diversify into unknown territories.

6. *"Hands-on" Top Management*

Notwithstanding their deep sense of respect and trust for individuals, CEOs of successful high-technology firms are usually actively involved in the innovation process to such an extent that they are sometimes accused of meddling. Tom McAvoy, Corning's president, sifts through hundreds of project proposals each year trying to identify those that can have a "significant strategic impact on the company"—the potential to restructure the company's business. Not surprisingly, most of these projects deal with new technologies. For one or two of the most salient ones, he adopts the role of "field general," frequently visiting the line operations, receiving direct updates from those working on the project, and assuring himself that the required resources are being provided.[39]

The direct involvement of the top executive at Corning sounds more characteristic of vibrant entrepreneurial firms, such as Tandon, Activision, and Seagate, but Corning is far from unique. Similar patterns can be identified in many larger high-technology firms. Milt Greenberg, president of GCA, a $180 million semiconductor process-equipment manufacturer, stated: "Sometimes you just have to short-circuit the organization to achieve major change."[40] Tom Watson, Jr. (IBM's chairman), and Vince Learson (IBM's president) were doing just that when they met with programmers and designers and other executives in Watson's ski cabin in Vermont to finalize software design concepts for the System 360—at a point when IBM was already a $4 billion firm.[41]

Good high-tech managers not only understand how organizations, and in particular engineers, work; they understand the fundamentals of their technology and can interact directly with their people about it. This does not imply that it is necessary for the senior managers of such firms to be technologists (although they usually are, in the early stages of growth). Neither Watson nor Learson was a technologist. What appears to be more important is the ability to ask lots of questions, even "dumb" questions, and dogged patience in order to understand, in depth, such core questions as: (1) how the technology works; (2) its limits, as well as its potential (together with the limits and potential of competitors' technologies); (3) what these various technologies require in terms of technical and economic resources; (4) the direction and speed of change; and (5) the available technological options, their cost, probability of failure, and potential benefits if they prove successful.

This depth of understanding is difficult enough to achieve for one set of related technologies and markets; it is virtually impossible for one person to master many different sets. This is another reason why business focus appears to be so important in high-tech firms. It matters little if one or more perceptive scientists or technologists foresees the impact of new technologies on the firm's markets, if its top management doesn't internalize these risks and make the major changes in organization and resource allocation that are usually necessitated by a technological transition.

The Paradox of High-Technology Management

The six themes around which we arranged our findings can be organized into two apparently paradoxical groupings: Business focus, organizational cohesion, and a sense of integrity fall into one group; adaptability, entrepreneurial culture, and hands-on management fall into the other group. On the one hand, business focus, organizational cohesion, and integrity imply stability and conservatism. On the other hand, adaptability, entrepreneurial culture, and hands-on top management are synonymous with rapid, sometimes precipitous change. The fundamental tension is between order and disorder. Half of the success factors pull in one direction; the other half tug the other way.

This paradox has frustrated many academicians who seek to identify rational processes and stable cause-effect relationships in high-tech firms and managers. Such relationships are not easily observable unless a certain constancy exists. But in most high-tech firms, the only constant is continual change. As one insightful student of the innovation process phrased it, "Advanced technology requires the collaboration of diverse professions and organizations, often with ambiguous or highly interdependent jurisdictions. In such situations, many of our highly touted rational management techniques break down."[42] One recent researcher, however, proposed a new model of the firm that attempts to rationalize the conflict between stability and change by splitting the strategic process into two loops, one that extends the past, the other that periodically attempts to break with it.[43]

Established organizations are, by their very nature, innovation resisting. By defining jobs and responsibilities and arranging them in serial reporting relationships, organizations encourage the performance of a restricted set of tasks in a programmed, predictable way. Not only do formal organizations resist innovation, they often act in ways that stamp it out. Overcoming such behavior—in much the way the human body mobilizes antibodies to overcome foreign cells—is, therefore, a core job of high-tech management.

The Paradoxical Challenge.   High-tech firms deal with this challenge in different ways. Texas Instruments, long renowned for the complex, interdependent matrix structure it used in managing dozens of product-consumer centers (PCCs), recently consolidated groups of PCCs and made them into more autonomous units. "The manager of a PCC controls the resources and operations for his entire family . . . in the simplest terms, the PCC manager is to be an entrepreneur," explained Fred Bucy, TI's president.[44]

Meanwhile, a different trend is evident at 3M, where entrepreneurs have been given a free rein for decades. A recent major reorganization was designed to arrest snowballing diversity by concentrating the company's sprawling structure of autonomous divisions into four market groups. "We were becoming too fragmented," explained Vincent Ruane, vice-president of 3M's electronics division.[45]

Similarly, HP recently reorganized into five groups, each with its own strategic responsibilities. Although this simply changes some of its reporting relationships, it does give HP, for the first time, a means for integrating product and market development across generally autonomous units.[46]

These reorganizations do not mean that organizational integration is dead at Texas Instruments, or that 3M's and HP's entrepreneurial cultures are being dismantled. Rather, they signify first, that these firms recognize that both organizational integration and entrepreneurial cultures are important, and second, that periodic change is required for environmental adaptability. These three firms are demonstrating remarkable adaptability by reorganizing from a position of relative strength—not, as is far more common, in response to financial difficulties. As Lewis Lehr, 3M's president, explained, "We can change now because we're not in trouble."[47]

Such reversals are essentially antibureaucratic, in the same spirit as Mao's admonition to "let a hundred flowers blossom and a hundred schools of thought contend."[48] At IBM, in 1963, Tom Watson, Jr., temporarily abolished the corporate management committee in an attempt to push decisions downward and thus facilitate the changes necessary for IBM's great leap forward to the System 360.[49] Disorder, slack, and ambiguity are necessary for innovation, since they provide the porosity that facilitates entrepreneurial behavior, just as do geographically separated, relatively autonomous organizational subunits.

But the corporate management committee is alive and well at IBM today. As it should be. The process of innovation, once begun, is both self-perpetuating and potentially self-destructive: Although the top managers of high-tech firms must sometimes espouse organizational disorder, for the most part they must preserve order.

Winnowing Old Products.   Not all new product ideas can be pursued. As Charles Ames, former president of Reliance Electric, states, "An enthusiastic inventor is a menace to practical businessmen."[50] Older products, upon which the current success of the firm was built, at some point have to be abandoned. Just as the long-term success of the firm requires the planting and nurturing of new products, it also requires the conscious, even ruthless, pruning of other products, so that the resources they consume can be used elsewhere.

This attitude demands hard-nosed managers who are continually managing the functional and divisional interfaces of their firms. They cannot be swayed by nostalgia, or by the fear of disappointing the many committed people who are involved in the development and production of discontinued products. They must also overcome the natural resistance of their subordinates, and even their peers, who often have a vested interest in the products that brought them early personal success in the organization.

Yet firms also need a certain amount of continuity, because major change often emerges from the accretion of a number of smaller, less visible improvements. Studies of petroleum refining, rayon, and rail transportation, for example, show that half or more of the productivity gains ultimately achieved within these technologies were the result of the accumulation of minor improvements.[51] Indeed, most engineers, managers, technologists, and manufacturing and marketing specialists work on what Thomas Kuhn might have called "normal innovation,"[52] the little steps that improve or extend existing product lines and processes.

Managing Ambivalently.   The successful high-technology firm, then, must be managed ambivalently. A steady commitment to order and organization will produce one-color Model T Fords. Continuous revolution will bar incremental productivity gains. Many companies have found that alternating periods of relaxation and control appear to meet this dual need. Surprisingly, such ambiguity does not necessarily lead to frustration and discontent.[53] In fact, interspersing periods of tension, action, and excitement with periods of reflection, evaluation, and revitalization is the same sort of irregular rhythm that characterizes many favorite pastimes—including sailing, which has been described as "long periods of total boredom punctuated with moments of stark terror."

Knowing when and where to change from one stance to the other, and having the power to make the shift, is the core of the art of high-technology management. James E. Webb, administrator of the National Aeronautics and Space Administration during the successful Apollo ("man on the moon") program, recalled that "we were required to fly our administrative machine in a turbulent environment, and . . . a certain level of *organizational instability was essential if NASA was not to lose control*" (authors' emphasis).[54]

In summary, the central dilemma of the high-technology firm is that it must succeed in managing two conflicting trends: continuity and rapid change. There are two ways to resolve this dilemma. One is an old idea: managing different parts of the firm differently—some business units for innovation, others for efficiency.

A second way—a way we believe is more powerful and pervasive—is to manage differently at different times in the evolutionary cycle of the firm. The successful high-technology firm *alternates* periods of consolidation and continuity with sharp reorientations that can lead to dramatic changes in the firm's strategies, structure, controls, and distribution of power, followed by a period of consolidation.[55] Thomas Jefferson knew this secret when he wrote 200 years ago, "A little revolution now and then is a good thing."

9

Defining the Charter for Product Innovation

C. Merle Crawford

Strategic planning techniques have provided direction for established business functions such as marketing, production, and finance. Today, many companies are using these techniques to guide new product development. The author reports on a study of new product planning in 125 American firms. Based on the information obtained from both the business press and personal interviews, he identifies a key element in this planning—the product innovation charter. The author outlines a composite charter and uses numerous examples from the companies studied to illustrate its various components. The charter, says the author, can provide a comprehensive activity and directional mandate for managers and can ensure a coordinated and integrated plan for any new product function. *SMR.*

Few businesses of any economic, social, or political significance can be optimally managed today without strategic planning.[1] Perhaps the groups most appreciative of the advent of strategic planning are those engaged in producing new products. These groups, being multifunctional in nature, lack the organizational unity of purpose and direction enjoyed by, say, a typical sales force or factory. Informal planning styles have had a tendency to leave many of their multifunctional processes unplanned. Indeed, "back-of-the-envelope" planning styles were the bane of new product developers until recent years.[2] There have been exceptions, of course. For instance, when the chief executive or operations officer has been de facto head of development (as was Land at Polaroid, Wilson at Xerox, Iacocca at Ford, and Sarnoff at RCA), sound processes have been possible without formal strategic planning. Other exceptions have included small firms or the really independent profit centers of such compa-

From *Sloan Management Review*, Fall 1980, Vol. 22, No. 1. Reprinted with permission.

Table 9.1   Firms in the Sample

	Number	Percentage
Markets:		
Primarily industrial	57	45.6%
Primarily consumer	68	54.4
Total	125	100.0%
Size:		
Large firms or closely integrated divisions of large firms	72	57.6%
Medium, small, or independent divisions	53	42.4
Total	125	100.0%
Output:		
Products	116	92.8%
Services	9	7.2
Total	125	100.0%

All are in the United States and are profit-making organizations.

nies as 3M. In general, though, informal planning styles have been inadequate to guide new product development in a comprehensive way.

Today's strategic planning techniques enable any firm to give its product development function an integrated, goals-oriented character. The key element in accomplishing this orientation is a spin-off of the strategic planning process. It consists of a set of policies and objectives designed to guide new product development. This set of policies and objectives, which has not yet had a name, will here be called the *product innovation charter*. The purpose of this article is to report on a study of product-innovation charters and to describe the various dimensions these charters have assumed within companies.

The Study

The research for this study was of two types. First, over 500 business press reports of companies' new product strategies were studied. Although most were quite incomplete, seventy-one reports were thought to yield enough detail for inclusion here.[3] Second, fifty-four field interviews were conducted between 1976 and 1979 by the author and various research assistants. Altogether, this research yielded partial charters for 125 firms. Characteristics of these firms are summarized in Table 9.1.

Although all 125 firms included in this study are profit-making companies, many nonprofit organizations (e.g., state lotteries and business schools) have also reported on similar new service planning. However, these reports have not occurred with sufficient frequency to indicate solid patterns—perhaps because not enough nonprofit organizations have yet adopted overall strategic planning. Thus, nonprofit organizations were excluded from this study.

It should be noted that despite the increasing frequency and comprehensiveness of reports on companies' new product strategies, there is probably much information still undisclosed. Firms generally keep their new product strategies confidential, since they feel constrained from revealing too much to their competitors. Thus, published press reports—and to a lesser degree, field interviews—may be presumed to be incomplete or even deliberately misleading.

It should also be noted that the sample consists only of firms willing to discuss publicly the new product portion of their strategic planning. Because this sample, therefore, is not random, the discussion to follow may not necessarily reflect the current state of new product planning in American industry. However, it presents a composite outline of the product-innovation charter, based on what firms were willing to say they were doing. Its main purpose is to delineate the concept and content of product-innovation charters, rather than to quantify their use.

The most significant finding of this study is that one document can give comprehensive direction to *all* of a business unit's new product activities. In the past, a policy might have cited only a market to be served ("Babies are our business"), the organizational mode (P&G's brand system), or commitment to technical innovation (Corning, IBM). But now it appears that companies are pulling all of these elements together. Firms' policies include every strategy dimension deemed necessary to produce the particular flow of product innovation that will optimize profits.

Outline of the Product-Innovation Charter

The product-innovation charter, which most larger firms and better-managed medium and smaller firms now use, contains the following sections.

A. *The target business arenas* that product innovation is to take the firm into or keep it in. These arenas are defined in four ways:[4]

    1. By product type (e.g., specialty chemicals or passenger cars);

2. By end-user activity or function (e.g., data processing or food);
3. By technology (e.g., fluidics or xerography); and
4. By intermediate or end-user customer group (e.g., service stations, state lotteries, younger men).

B. *The goals or objectives* of object innovation activities. These goals or objectives may be expressed in terms of:

1. *The quantitative results* to be achieved by the product innovation. Examples include:
    a. Market share or position of leadership;[5]
    b. Sales volume (usually expressed in dollars and typically with growth goals); or
    c. Profit level (e.g., total dollars, ROI, payback, or percent on sales, considered on a short- or long-term basis).

2. *Special qualitative goals or objectives* peculiar to the firm's unique situation. Examples are:
    a. To create a sense of urgency or crisis;
    b. To diversify;
    c. To fill out a product line;
    d. To maintain or seek an image;
    e. To protect a position; or
    f. To smooth out various irregularities.

C. *The program of activities* (policies) chosen to achieve the goals in Section B above. The program typically will discuss:

1. *Strengths the program is to exploit.* These strengths are usually one or more of three types:
    a. An *R&D* skill or capability (e.g., glass technology);
    b. A *manufacturing* facility, process, skill, or material (e.g., food processing or wood chips); or
    c. A *marketing* advantage (e.g., a strong sales force, an image, or a trade franchise).

2. *Weaknesses to avoid.* These weaknesses are usually of the same three types as noted above. For instance, a firm may wish to avoid investing in a particular R&D project, building a particular facility, or marketing to the government.

3. *The source of the innovation.* The new product's points of differentiation can be developed in the following ways:
   a. *Internally* (by R&D, marketing, etc.);
   b. *Externally* (by licensing or by acquiring companies, products, or processes); or
   c. By a special *combination* of both, one variation of which is the joint venture.

4. *The degree of innovativeness sought.* In terms of Ansoff and Stewart's paradigm, which was developed over ten years ago, the degrees of innovativeness sought by firms can be characterized as:[6]
   a. *Inventive.* The firm seeks technological leadership vis-à-vis product packaging, positioning, etc. It tries to be the "first to market" with the product.
   b. *Adaptive.* The firm chooses to wait and let others lead, then to quickly adapt or modify the product. By means of "innovative imitation," it seeks to be "second but best."
   c. *Economic.* The firm builds strength by producing what others have created, but by doing so more economically. It tries to be the low-cost producer, particularly in the early maturity phase of the life cycle.
   d. *Innovative applications.* The firm utilizes established technology, but applies it creatively to new uses—e.g., adhesives or MOS technology.

5. *Special conditions, restrictions, or mandates.* These conditions are highly situational, but not miscellaneous or casual. For example, special instructions to the innovation team may specify:
   a. *The product-quality level*—usually to protect or improve an image;
   b. *The level of risk* that is acceptable;
   c. Seeking low-volume *niches* for "quiet" intrusions;
   d. Serving only *"real"* or *"genuine" needs*;
   e. *The size or growth trends* in markets being considered;
   f. Either specifically avoiding or confronting particular *competitors*;
   g. Low-cost *repeat-buying* product categories;
   h. Avoiding *regulatory* or *social* problems;
   i. *Patentability;*
   j. *Keying to systems* of products or of products and services; or
   k. *Avoiding systems* of products.

A Hypothetical Example

Although many examples will be given later to illustrate these outline items, it is desirable to show how these ideas fit into a complete PIC. The power of the charter lies in its integration of otherwise isolated decisions. The following is a hypothetical product-innovation charter in highly abbreviated form:

◇ The XYZ Company is committed to a program of innovation in specialty chemicals as utilized in the automobile and other metal-finishing businesses. Our goal is to become the market-share leader in this market. We also intend to achieve at least 35 percent ROI from our program on a three-year payout basis. We seek recognition as the most technically competent company in metal finishing.

   These goals will be achieved by building on our current R&D skills and by embellishing them as necessary. We will produce in-house, with only emergency reliance on outside sources, new items that are technically superior to competitors' products. The company is willing to invest funds as necessary to achieve these technical breakthroughs, even though IATs may suffer in the first year. Care will be taken to establish patent-protected positions in these new developments and to increase the safety of customer company personnel.

The PIC versus Scoring Models or Checklists

Several of the PIC items are similar to those found in many scoring models or checklists that are used to screen new product ideas. This similarity is not surprising, since scoring models should result directly from PICs. However, firms often rely upon scoring models in the absence of PICs. A typical checklist is the following one used by a chemical company:[7]

1. Do we have marketplace skills?
2. Is there patent protection?
3. Does it match our manufacturing capability?
4. Do we have the raw material?
5. Is the market large enough?

These are passive or reactive criteria: They do not stipulate positive direction. They clearly offer managers much less direction than does a PIC. A product-innovation charter charts a course. It says: "Go this way, and do these things. They offer the best bet for optimizing profits from new products."

Components of the Product-Innovation Charter

Target Business Arenas

Of the firms studied, about one-third defined their new product-activity arenas in terms of products. Planning specialists have argued against this kind of definition, but apparently the practice has become highly institutionalized in such industries as cars, chemicals, banking services (albeit constrained by law), pharmaceuticals, women's wear, appliances, beer, and tape labels. Some definitions that seemed to be keyed to products were actually based on activities (e.g., food, cosmetics, and cutting tools), and have been so classified here.

The most common *nonproduct* definition, by far, was that of the end user's function or activity. Terms, such as data processing, measuring electricity, preparing coal, controlling machine tools, and law enforcement, were typical.

Surprisingly, only about 10 percent of the firms said they used a definition based on technology. This low result may be more a function of the firms' reluctance to disclose too many details to their competitors than of their actual strategies. Several of the firms' definitions, however, combined technology with function (e.g., electronic games, electromechanical devices for cardiovascular treatment, or xerography in education).

Equally surprising was the small number of firms who said they found a specific customer or customer orientation helpful. Actually, four of them were oriented to trade groups (e.g., beauty and barber shops and company-owned service stations), and two used unique groups (outdoor people and operators of state lotteries). One is no longer operative (Gerber's babies), and one is new (Winchester gun owners).

Goals to be Achieved by the New Products Program

It was apparent, particularly from the personal interviews, that managements differed on the question of how to state goals for the product innovation function. Their stated goals took several forms:

1. The traditional *sales gap goal.* Closing the gap between planning objectives and an extension of current sales lines was often more a concept than a specific dollar target.
2. Some expression of *profit.* This goal could be stated in many ways, though most often it was expressed as a gap concept.
3. *A first-level surrogate for profit.* This goal was usually stated in terms of achieving some combination of "large or growing markets" and a "large or

leading share." Profit was then presumed to follow as a natural consequence. Loctite, Sarns (medical devices), Iroquois Brands, Keithley (measuring instruments), Jovan, Rucker, Stauffer, Texas Instruments, and Gould are examples of firms that stated goals in this manner.

4. *A second-level surrogate.* By far the most commonly stated goal was to exploit some company strength. The premise was that working from a strength should yield a good market share, which in turn should yield good profits. Firms using this approach actually avoided setting goals in the form of results or output.

5. Special *situation goals.* There was no end to the variety of these goals, but common ones were:

- Urgency. Some firms faced situations where new products were urgently essential—for example, to avoid a takeover.
- Diversification away from a high-risk or limiting situation. For example, Hoover Universal and Midland Adhesive both sought new products that would relieve them from dependence on the automobile.
- Offering a complete line. Frito-Lay, a large NYC bank, and Digital Equipment are examples of firms having this goal. NCR built its turn-around on this idea.
- Altering, holding, or strengthening an image. Waterford Glass, Texas Instruments, and Cincinnati Milacron stated such goals.
- Being defensive. Often firms sought to protect a profitable market position or to add a seasonal pattern to complement existing ones. Hallmark had the latter goal.

Program of Activities: Strengths to Exploit

Managements increasingly use the term "technology" to mean any system or set of operations, skills, or activities that constitutes a capability. For instance, Rockwell's engineering skill, a technology in the traditional sense, has been a strength that Rockwell clearly has planned to exploit. Similarly, GE's Carboloy Division has sought to exploit tungsten carbide technology; Hallmark, its creative processes and skills; Gelman, membrane filtration; Potlatch, high graphics; Rucker, oil-well technology; Helena Rubenstein, the science of cosmetology; and Remington, powdered-metals technology. Most firms in the sample favored the R&D technology. Those having no exploitable R&D technology often moved to acquire one. A chemical firm, a computer firm, and a small bank, for instance, said they were doing so.

About a third of the companies cited manufacturing skills as exploitable strengths, and slightly less cited marketing capabilities. For example, Pillsbury has a strong supermarket franchise; a dental sundries firm has a strong sales force; and P&G has high-volume TV purchasing discounts. Tressler Oil owns a chain of service stations; Chelsea Milling has a unique franchise as a push-marketer on its line of Jiffy Mixes; and Standard Brands uses its Planters brand to seek a stronger position in snacks.

In sum, most of the firms in this study felt they had exploitable strengths of one sort or another. Assuming that the firms were somewhat reticent, owing to their reluctance to reveal too much to their competitors, it is entirely possible that their cleverest strategies remain undisclosed.

Weaknesses to Avoid

Managements similarly were reluctant to discuss the weakness dimension, but examples were found. An engineering firm knew it had a weak marketing operation, so it listed "no strong marketing required" as a key criterion. A bank decided it really had no exploitable creative skills, so it adopted a strategy of selecting new services from those introduced by other banks. Several firms that had acute dollar shortages stipulated a low R&D cost requirement.

Degree of Innovation

New product strategists have recognized the importance of defining the degree of product innovativeness they wish to use. In this study, fifty-seven firms claimed to be invention-oriented, sixty-eight adaptive, and twenty economic (low cost). Twenty-eight were in a unique situation: they could avoid the risks of invention by sticking to a known technology and seeking new applications for it. Loctite, the adhesive producer, was the classic example of a firm using the "innovative applications" strategy. This strategy was also used by chemical firms such as Dow and by mineral firms such as Climax-Molybdenum. Because data on slightly over half of the firms were taken from the business press, however, there may be some bias in the results. A firm is likely to find it more gratifying to discuss its exciting policy of technical excellence than to comment on its commitment to being a low-cost imitator.

As the numbers indicate, most firms planned to follow more than one route. Inventiveness and adaptive innovation constituted the most typical combination. In terms of the new products that were actually developed and marketed, most firms ended up with at least two levels of innovativeness. Although there is a disparity here between the planned and actual strategies, it should be remembered that the charter reflects strategic *intention;* it is not meant to prevent the firm from exercising some flexibility. An indication that product-innovation charters are subject to change was that most of the firms referred to pasts or presents where commitments had been or would be different. Many Japanese firms (though not examined specifically in this study) have dramatized this point. They adopted economic strategies during the 1950s, progressed into adaptive strategies as resources permitted or as labor costs required, and now use inventive strategies, especially in markets where they have become volume leaders. Many United States firms probably have followed the same progression, though some that started out with inventive strategies either kept them (Hewlett-Packard) or else gradually became adaptive (Sycor, computer peripherals). Of course, changes caused by the firm's life cycle should not be confused with the effect of the life cycle of a product category.

Source of Innovation

Most of the firms studied decided to seek new products only internally; most of the others combined the internal and external routes. Personal discussions with managers revealed several alternative strategies regarding the source of innovation.

- *New products, but no innovation.* Betty Dain (women's clothing), most local banks, Tressler Oil, a food company, and an auto-parts firm all wanted products that were new to *them,* but which would have no innovative element. This approach related to the economic strategy of low-cost production or to that of serving the needs of a narrow captive market.
- *Innovative products developed totally inside.* This strategy called for a strong R&D program with no interest in outside sources. Some highly technical firms such as Hewlett-Packard used this approach, as did such consumer firms as Revlon and Pillsbury.
- *A general policy of seeking internal innovations, but with a willingness to take advantage of outside opportunities,* particularly licensing. Du Pont, Sybron, and Upjohn followed this approach.
- *A policy of limited inside technical or marketing innovative skills, with principal reliance on outside sources.* A large technical machinery firm, having a small engineering department, mainly licensed developments found in Europe.

Special Conditions, Restrictions, and Mandates

Many special provisos came up in this investigation; the most common ones were related to some definition of product-quality level. Only one company, a well-known, high-quality firm, actually indicated a desire for low quality in its new products. Its purpose was to tap the low end of its market. However, twenty-six others specifically said their charters called for products of high quality. Trademarks, such as Campbell, Parke-Davis, Gerber, and Hallmark, had powerful consumer franchises, and their owners did not desire to trade down. Industrial firms frequently felt the same, e.g., Sperry Univac, Allen-Bradley, Brown & Sharpe, and McNally-Pittsburgh. Black & Decker (not included in this study) demonstrated the profitability of a lower-quality approach when it developed a line of low-priced electrical tools for home use. Items, such as the eight-hour, ¼-inch electric drill, opened a whole new market many times the size of the traditional professional market.

Another special proviso, mentioned by twenty firms, was the mandate of low risk or conservatism in the product-innovation function. Expressed in many different ways (e.g., "no failures," "evolutionary only," and "minimal R&D dollar investment"), this mandate nevertheless clearly differentiated such a program from one of high-risk, chance-taking innovation. Paramount Pictures (in its refusal to bankroll high-budget movies), National Semiconductor, Milton Bradley, and General Foods (with its "measured introduction" and "orderly manner") were a few firms that included clearly restrictive policies in at least portions of their PICs. In contrast, Intel, Gould, Merck, and Bendix were firms that had no apparent risk-avoidance mandate.

Other special directions included that of seeking market "niches," an approach cited by the managements of American Motors, Iroquois Brands, and others. Another was the mandate to serve "real needs." In Merck's Charter, for instance, "real needs" could easily be translated as the "need for new pharmaceuticals." This kind of mandate was also prominent with a large bank and with the industrial leader, Gould.

Gillette, P&G, and Dean Foods told their developers to seek opportunities only in markets that were large or rapidly growing. Some managers were willing to say openly that their charters led their new-products teams away from markets where certain competitors were strong. IBM and P&G were often named as firms to avoid, but there were others. For example, cosmetics firm A wanted to avoid Avon, and cosmetics firm B wanted to avoid both Avon and firm A. American Motors wanted to avoid all three of its automotive competitors' key segments.

Finally, there was a potpourri of unique situations. Fetterolf and Merck would not touch unpatentable products; a chemical company specifically stipulated that new product decisions would be made "without sentiment"; and a computer peripherals firm said "no systems." These considerations may seem almost incidental, but they were clearly not incidental to the firms citing them. In several cases the special proviso was the key factor in the strategy.

Multiple Charters Within a Firm

Small firms and nondivisionalized medium-sized firms often operate only one strategic business unit and need, therefore, only one product-innovation charter. Most organizations, however, have multiple plans and multiple charters. One such firm is Texas Instruments.[8] TI has at least one "business," MOS memories, in which its strategy is highly innovative: internal only, inventive only, keyed to TI technologies, high risk, and probably having some very high ROI goals. A second TI business, toys, represents mostly innovative application. Its strategy calls for internal innovation with strong marketing involvement and for creation of new markets for technologies already developed. TI's success with Speak 'n Spell demonstrates both the creativity demanded and the potential reward from this particular strategy. A third business, watches and calculators, is geared to the experience curve. It is a classic example of the economic strategy. TI, apparently familiar with all of the basic alternatives, has developed a steadily changing mix of business arenas and activity modes according to existing conditions.

Contrasts Within an Industry

Several recent reports have given us the chance to compare different firms within a common industry setting, as these firms have developed their respective product-innovation charters.

Intel Versus National Semiconductor

These two firms illustrate the contrasts between the inventive and economic strategies.[9] Robert N. Noyce, chairman of Intel Corporation, is known as a "brilliant and outgoing scientist-entrepreneur whose reputation is built on technical breakthroughs." He has tried to find new niches in the semiconductor market by applying highly advanced technologies. Using an inventive strategy, for example, he raised R&D spending during the 1975 recession. His strategy, in short, carries high risks, but has a potential for high returns. Charles E. Spork, on the other hand, has generated a sales-and-profit bonanza at National Semiconductor with precisely the opposite approach. His goal, "achieved in almost every major line of semiconductor products, was to make National a super-efficient manufacturer of high-volume products." Although neither firm intends its strategy to be totally restrictive of the other approach (indeed, National has recently emphasized a plan to change), the difference has been dramatic for many years.

Frito-Lay Versus Nabisco Versus Standard Brands

Frito-Lay has long dominated the snack market, but Standard Brands and Nabisco are now challenging the traditional Frito-Lay position.[10] Nabisco, for instance, has been "experimenting with multigrain products and new textures and shapes." In addition, it has repackaged in bags such items as Mister Salty pretzels and moved them from the cookie section to the snack section. In the short term, it is following both an adaptive strategy (by improving some standard items) and an innovative applications path (by repackaging). In the long term, it has an inventive strategy. These strategies are being carried out internally, and they carry reasonably high risks.

Standard Brands is also applying some available packaging technology (the canister approach used by P&G's Pringles), and applying the Planter's name to some new products (obtained by acquisition) that it claims to be superior. Its strategy is adaptive, not inventive.

While Nabisco is in the lab and Standard Brands is acquiring, Frito-Lay is developing new items of its own. Its strategy is not inventive, however, since it regards snack inventiveness as having run its course. It is also expanding production, planning on an economic strategy if necessary, and strengthening its distribution.

The Firearms Business

The firearms business is a business "with tired blood." It is expected to have "slow or no growth" or even to decline in the future.[11] As a result, the product-innovation charters of five firms have had to be altered. Colt has chosen not to innovate, but rather to raise prices and to continue its line of high-quality commemorative firearms. Remington is trying to apply its powdered metal and abrasives technologies to other business arenas. Winchester, defining an arena in consumer terms, is running a gun book club and franchising gun clubs. Smith & Wesson is also taking a consumer approach. Its particular arena, however, is law-enforcement agencies. It is now developing handcuffs, holsters, police car lights, and other products for these agencies. Sturm Ruger is trying to exploit its manufacturing facility, especially its foundry, by offering to produce for other (nongun) manufacturers. In the meantime, small firms and foreign firms are not idle in the industry. One, using the inventive approach, has developed do-it-yourself, muzzle-loading firearm kits. Another firm is following an economic strategy. It uses its plants in the South to assemble guns at the lowest possible cost.

Summary

This article has reported on a study of the strategic plans of 125 firms. Such plans are usually quite confidential, but managements often have occasion to reveal, or even to expound at length on, selected aspects of their new product strategies. This study relied upon unusually complete business press reports and on personal interviews. It has resulted in the description of a strategic concept—termed here the product-innovation charter.

The product-innovation charter is a recent spin-off of the strategic planning process. From the strategic planning process have come approved directions for the established functions—marketing plans, production schedules, financing requirements, and budgets for specific R&D projects. The PIC, a more recent development, is designed to guide the organization's crossfunctional subset of activities charged with developing new products, and to give clear direction to the diverse personnel involved in new products.

The outline of a composite charter presented in this article can be used by any management planning product or service innovation. It will enable the management to test the comprehensiveness of its own decision set, or to scan its strategic planning process to identify missing elements. Use of the product-innovation charter in new product planning can help managers to develop coordinated and integrated plans, and ultimately to achieve their overall profit goals.

10

Entering New Businesses:
Selecting Strategies for Success

Edward B. Roberts

Charles A. Berry

Selective use of the alternative strategies available for entering new businesses is a key issue for diversifying corporations. The approaches include internal development, acquisition, licensing, joint ventures, and minority venture-capital investments. Using the existing literature, the authors devise a matrix of company "familiarity" with relevant market and technological experiences. Through a case study of a successful diversified technological firm, they demonstrate how the familiarity matrix can be applied to help a company select optimum entry strategies. *SMR.*

Entry into new product markets, which represents diversification for the existing firm, may provide an important source of future growth and profitability. Typically, such new businesses are initiated with low-market share in high-growth markets and require large cash inflows to finance growth. In addition, many new product-market entries fail, draining additional cash resources and incurring high opportunity costs to the firm. Two strategic questions are thus posed: (1) Which product markets should a corporation enter? and (2) How should the company enter these product markets to avoid failure and maximize gain?

Although these questions are fundamentally different, they should not be answered independently of one another. Entering a new business may be achieved by a variety of mechanisms, such as internal development, acquisition, joint ventures, and minority investments of venture capital. As Roberts indicates, each of these mechanisms makes different demands upon the corporation.[1] Some, such as internal development, require a high level of commit-

From *Sloan Management Review,* Spring 1985, Vol. 26, No. 3. Reprinted with permission.

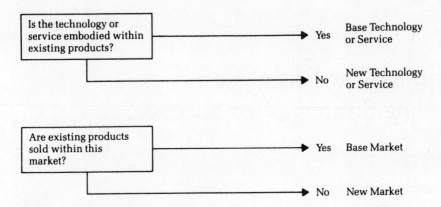

Figure 10.1 Tests of Newness

ment and involvement. Others, such as venture-capital investment, require much lower levels of involvement. What are the relative benefits and costs of each of these entry mechanisms? When should each be used?

This article attempts to analyze and answer these questions, first by proposing a framework for considering entry issues, second by a review of relevant literature, third by application of this literature to the creation of a matrix that suggests optimum entry strategies, and finally by a test of the matrix through a case analysis of business development decisions by a successful diversified corporation.

Entry Strategy: A New Selection Framework

New business development may address new markets, new products, or both. In addition, these new areas may be ones that are familiar or unfamiliar to a company. Let us first define "newness" and "familiarity":

● Newness of a Technology or Service: the degree to which that technology or service has not formerly been embodied within the products of the company.
● Newness of a Market: the degree to which the products of the company have not formerly been targeted at that particular market.
● Familiarity with a Technology: the degree to which knowledge of the tech-

Table 10.1   Tests of Technological Familiarity

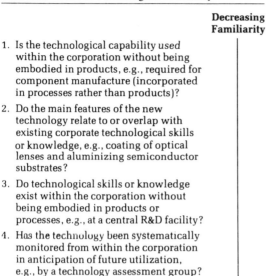

	Decreasing Familiarity
1. Is the technological capability used within the corporation without being embodied in products, e.g., required for component manufacture (incorporated in processes rather than products)?	
2. Do the main features of the new technology relate to or overlap with existing corporate technological skills or knowledge, e.g., coating of optical lenses and aluminizing semiconductor substrates?	
3. Do technological skills or knowledge exist within the corporation without being embodied in products or processes, e.g., at a central R&D facility?	
4. Has the technology been systematically monitored from within the corporation in anticipation of future utilization, e.g., by a technology assessment group?	
5. Is relevant and reliable advice available from external consultants?	

nology exists within the company, but is not necessarily embodied in the products.

• Familiarity with a Market: the degree to which the characteristics and business patterns of a market are understood within the company, but not necessarily as a result of participation in the market.

If the businesses in which a company currently competes are its *base* businesses, then market factors associated with the new business area may be characterized as *base, new familiar,* or *new unfamiliar.* Here, "market factors" refers not only to particular characteristics of the market and the participating competitors, but also includes the appropriate pattern of doing business that may lead to competitive advantage. Two alternative patterns are performance-premium price and lowest-cost producer. Similarly, the technologies or service embodied in the product for the new business area may be characterized on the same basis. Figure 10.1 illustrates some tests that may be used to distinguish between "base" and "new" areas. Table 10.1 lists questions that may be used to distinguish between familiar and unfamiliar technologies. (Equivalent tests may be applied to services.) Questions to distinguish between familiar and unfamiliar markets are given in Table 10.2.

The application of these tests to any new business development opportunity

Table 10.2 Tests of Market Familiarity

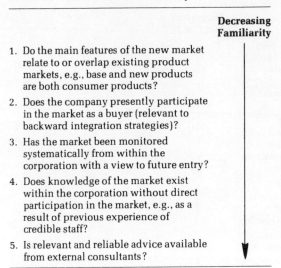

Decreasing Familiarity

1. Do the main features of the new market relate to or overlap existing product markets, e.g., base and new products are both consumer products?

2. Does the company presently participate in the market as a buyer (relevant to backward integration strategies)?

3. Has the market been monitored systematically from within the corporation with a view to future entry?

4. Does knowledge of the market exist within the corporation without direct participation in the market, e.g., as a result of previous experience of credible staff?

5. Is relevant and reliable advice available from external consultants?

enables it to be located conceptually on a 3 × 3 technology/market *familiarity matrix* as illustrated in Figure 10.2. The nine sectors of this matrix may be grouped into three regions, with the three sectors that comprise any one region possessing broadly similar levels of familiarity.

Literature Review: Alternative Strategies

Extensive writings have focused on new business development and the various mechanisms by which it may be achieved. Much of this literature concentrates on diversification, the most demanding approach to new business development, in which both the product and market dimensions of the business area may be new to a company. Our review of the literature supports and provides details for the framework shown in Figure 10.2, finding that familiarity of a company with the technology and market being addressed is the critical variable that explains much of the success or failure in new business development approaches.

Rumelt's pioneering 1974 study of diversification analyzed company performance against a measure of the relatedness of the various businesses forming the company.[2] Rumelt identified nine types of diversified companies, clustered into three categories: dominant business companies, related business companies, and unrelated business companies. From extensive analysis Ru-

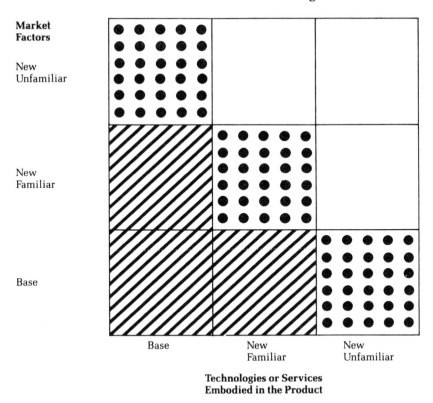

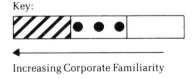

Increasing Corporate Familiarity

Figure 10.2 The Familiarity Matrix

melt concluded that related business companies outperformed the averages on five accounting-based performance measures over the period 1949 to 1969.

Rumelt recently updated his analysis to include Fortune 500 companies' performances through 1974 and drew similar conclusions: The related constrained group of companies was the most profitable, building on single strengths or resources associated with their original businesses.[3] Rumelt, as well as Christensen and Montgomery, also found, however, that the performance in part reflected effects of concentrations in certain categories of industrial market clusters.[4] While some (e.g., Bettis and Hall)[5] have questioned Rumelt's earlier conclusions, others (e.g., Holzmann, Copeland, and Hayya)[6] have supported the findings of lower returns by unrelated business firms and highest profitability for the related constrained group of firms.

Peters supports Rumelt's general conclusions on the superior performance of related business companies.[7] In his study of thirty-seven "well-managed" organizations, he found that they had all been able to define their strengths and build upon them: They had not moved into potentially attractive new business areas that required skills they did not possess. In their recent book Peters and Waterman termed this "sticking to the knitting."[8]

Even in small high-technology firms similar effects can be noted. Recent research by Meyer and Roberts on ten such firms revealed that the most successful in terms of growth had concentrated on one key technological area and introduced product enhancements related to that area.[9] In contrast, the poorest performers had tackled "unrelated" new technologies in attempts to enter new product-market areas.

The research discussed above indicates that in order to ensure highest performance, new business development should be constrained within areas related to a company's *base* business—a very limiting constraint. However, no account was taken of how new businesses were in fact entered and the effect that the entry mechanism had on subsequent corporate performance. As summarized in Table 10.3, the literature identifies a wide range of approaches that are available for entering new business areas, and highlights various advantages and disadvantages.

New Business Development Mechanisms

Internal Developments.   Companies have traditionally approached new business development via two routes: internal development and acquisition. Internal development exploits internal resources as a basis for establishing a business new to the company. Biggadike studied Fortune 500 companies that had used this approach in corporate diversification.[10] He found that, typically, eight years were needed to generate a positive return on investment, and performance did not match that of a mature business until a period of ten to twelve years had elapsed. However, Weiss asserts that this need not be the case.[11] He compared the performance of internal corporate developments with comparable businesses newly started by individuals and found that the new independent businesses reached profitability in half the time of corporate effort—approximately four years versus eight years. Although Weiss attributes this to the more ambitious targets established by independent operations, indeed the opposite may be true. Large companies' overhead-allocation charges or their

Table 10.3 Entry Mechanisms: Advantages and Disadvantages

New Business Development Mechanisms	Major Advantages	Major Disadvantages
Internal Developments	Use existing resources	Time lag to break even tends to be long (on average eight years) Unfamiliarity with new markets may lead to errors
Acquisitions	Rapid market entry	New business area may be unfamiliar to parent
Licensing	Rapid access to proven technology Reduced financial exposure	Not a substitute for internal technical competence Not proprietary technology Dependent upon licensor
Internal Ventures	Use existing resources May enable a company to hold a talented entrepreneur	Mixed record of success Corporation's internal climate often unsuitable
Joint Ventures or Alliances	Technological/marketing unions can exploit small/large company synergies Distribute risk	Potential for conflict between partners
Venture Capital and Nurturing	Can provide window on new technology or market	Unlikely alone to be a major stimulus of corporate growth
Educational Acquisitions	Provide window and initial staff	Higher initial financial commitment than venture capital Risk of departure of entrepreneurs

attempts at large-scale entry and other objectives that preclude early profitability may be more correct explanations for the delayed profitability of these ventures.

Miller indicates that forcing established attitudes and procedures upon a new business may severely handicap it, and he suggests that success may not come until the technology has been adapted, new facilities established, or familiarity with the new markets developed.[12] Miller stresses this last factor. Gilmore and Coddington also believe that lack of familiarity with new markets often leads to major errors.[13]

Acquisitions. In contrast to internal development, acquisition can take weeks rather than years to execute. This approach may be attractive not only because of its speed, but because it offers a much lower initial cost of entry into a new business or industry. Salter and Weinhold point out that this is particularly true if the key parameters for success in the new business field are intangibles, such as patents, product image, or R&D skills, which may be difficult to duplicate via internal developments within reasonable costs and time scales.[14]

Miller believes that a diversifying company cannot step in immediately after acquisition to manage a business it knows nothing about.[15] It must set up a communication system that will permit it to understand the new business gradually. Before this understanding develops, incompatibility may exist between the managerial judgment appropriate for the parent and that required for the new subsidiary.

Licensing. Acquiring technology through licensing represents an alternative to acquiring a complete company. J. P. Killing has pointed out that licensing avoids the risks of product development by exploiting the experience of firms who have already developed and marketed the product.[16]

Internal Ventures. Roberts indicates that many corporations are now adopting new venture strategies in order to meet ambitious plans for diversification growth.[17] Internal ventures share some similarities with internal development, which has already been discussed. In this venture strategy, a firm attempts to enter different markets or develop substantially different products from those of its existing base business by setting up a separate entity within the existing corporate body. Overall, the strategy has had a mixed record, but some companies such as 3M have exploited it with considerable success. This was due in large part to their ability to harness and nurture entrepreneurial behavior within the corporation. More recently, IBM's Independent Business Units (especially its PC venture) and Du Pont's new electronic-materials division demonstrate the effectiveness of internal ventures for market expansion and/or diversification. Burgelman has suggested that corporations need to "develop greater flexibility between new venture projects and the corporation," using external as well as internal ventures.[18]

The difficulty in successfully diversifying via internal ventures is not a new one. Citing Chandler,[19] Morecroft comments on Du Pont's failure in moving from explosive powders to varnishes and paints in 1917:

[C]ompeting firms, though much smaller and therefore lacking large economies of scale and production, were nonetheless profitable. . . . Their sole advantage lay in the fact that they specialized in the manufacture, distribution, and sale of varnishes and paints. This focus provided them with clearer responsibilities and clearer standards for administering sales and distribution.[20]

Joint Ventures or Alliances. Despite the great potential for conflict, many companies successfully diversify and grow via joint ventures. As Killing points out, when projects get larger, technology more expensive, and the cost of failure too large to be borne alone, joint venturing becomes increasingly important.[21] Shifts in national policy in the United States are now encouraging the formation of several large research-based joint ventures involving many companies. But the traditional forms of joint ventures, involving creation of third corporations, seem to have limited life and/or growth potential.

Hlavacek et al. and Roberts believe one class of joint venture to be of particular interest—"new style" joint ventures in which large and small companies join forces to create a new entry in the market place.[22] In these efforts of "mutual pursuit," usually without the formality of a joint-venture company, the small company provides the technology, the large company provides marketing capability, and the venture is synergistic for both parties. Recent articles have indicated how these large company/small company "alliances," frequently forged through the creative use of corporate venture capital, are growing in strategic importance.[23]

Venture Capital and Nurturing. The venture strategy that permits some degree of entry, but the lowest level of required corporate commitment, is that associated with external venture-capital investment. Major corporations have exploited this approach in order to become involved with the growth and development of small companies as investors, participants, or even eventual acquirers. Roberts points out that this approach was popular as early as the mid-to-late 1960s with many large corporations, such as Du Pont, Exxon, Ford, General Electric, Singer, and Union Carbide.[24] Their motivation was the so-called window on technology, the opportunity to secure closeness to and possibly later entry into new technologies by making minority investments in young and growing high-technology enterprises. However, few companies in the 1960s were able to make this approach alone an important stimulus of corporate growth or profitability. Despite this, ever-increasing numbers of companies today are experimenting with venture capital, and many are showing important financial and informational benefits.

Studies carried out by Greenthal and Larson[25] show that venture capital investments can indeed provide satisfactory and perhaps highly attractive returns, if they are properly managed, although Hardymon et al.[26] essentially disagree. Rind distinguishes between direct venture investments and investment into pooled funds of venture-capital partnerships.[27] He points out that although direct venture investments can be carried out from within a corporation by appropriate planning and organization, difficulties are often encountered because of a lack of appropriately skilled people, contradictory rationales between the investee company and parent, legal problems, and an inadequate time horizon. Investment in a partnership may remove some of these problems, but if the investor's motives are something other than simply maximizing financial return, it may be important to select a partnership concentrating investments in areas of interest. Increasingly, corporations are trying to use pooled funds to provide the "windows" on new technologies and new markets that are more readily afforded by direct investment, but special linkages with the investment-fund managers are needed to implement a "window" strategy. Fast cites 3M and Corning as companies that have invested as limited partners in venture-capital partnerships.[28] This involvement in business-development financing can keep the company in touch with new technologies and emerging industries as well as provide the guidance and understanding of the venture-development process necessary for more effective internal corporate venturing.

In situations where the investing company provides managerial assistance to the recipient of the venture capital, the strategy is classed "venture nurturing" rather than pure venture capital. This seems to be a more sensible entry toward diversification objectives as opposed to a simple provision of funds, but it also needs to be tied to other company diversification efforts.

Educational Acquisitions.   Although not discussed in the management literature, targeted small acquisitions can fulfill a role similar to that of a venture-capital minority investment and, in some circumstances, may offer significant advantages. In an acquisition of this type, the acquiring firm immediately obtains people familiar with the new business area, whereas in a minority investment, the parent relies upon its existing staff to build familiarity by interacting with the investee. Acquisitions for educational purposes may therefore represent a faster route to familiarity than the venture capital "window" approach. Staff acquired in this manner may even be used by the parent as a basis for redirecting a corporation's primary product-market thrust. Harris Corporation (formerly Harris-Intertype) entered the computer and communication-systems industry using precisely this mechanism: It acquired internal skills and knowledge through its acquisition of Radiation Dynamics, Inc. Procter & Gamble recently demonstrated similar behavior in citing its acquisition of the Tender Leaf Tea brand as an "initial learning opportunity in a growing category of the beverage business."[29]

One potential drawback to this acquisition approach is that it usually requires a higher level of financial commitment than minority investment and

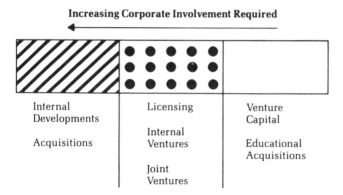

Figure 10.3 Spectrum of Entry Strategies

therefore increases risk. In addition, it is necessary to ensure that key people do not leave soon after the acquisition as a result of the removal of entrepreneurial incentives. A carefully designed acquisition deal may be necessary to ensure that incentives remain. When Xerox acquired Versatec, for example, the founder and key employees were given the opportunity to double their "sellout" price by meeting performance targets over the next five years.

Though not without controversy, major previous research work on large U.S. corporations indicated that the highest performers had diversified to some extent but had constrained the development of new business within areas related to the company's base business. The range of mechanisms employed for entering new businesses, previously displayed in Table 10.3, is divided in Figure 10.3 into three regions, each requiring a different level of corporate involvement and commitment. No one mechanism is ideal for all new business development. It may be possible, therefore, that selective use of entry mechanisms can yield substantial benefits over concentration on one particular approach. If this presumption is valid, then careful strategy selection can reduce the risk associated with new business development in unrelated areas.

Determining Optimum Entry Strategies

How can the entry strategies in Figure 10.3 be combined with the conceptual framework in Figure 10.2? Which entry strategies are appropriate in the various regions of the familiarity matrix? The literature provides some useful guides.

In his discussion of the management problems of diversification, Miller proposes that acquisitive diversifiers are frequently required to participate in the strategic and operating decisions of the new subsidiary before they are properly oriented to the new business.[30] In this situation the parent is "unfamiliar" with the new business area. It is logical to conclude that if the new business is unfamiliar *after* acquisition, it must also have been unfamiliar *before* acquisition. How then could the parent have carried out comprehensive screening of the new company before executing the acquisition? In a situation in which familiarity was low or absent, preacquisition screening most probably overlooked many factors, turning the acquisition into something of a gamble from a portfolio standpoint. Similar arguments can be applied to internal development in unfamiliar areas, and Gilmore and Coddington specifically stress the dangers associated with entry into unfamiliar markets.[31]

This leads to the rather logical conclusion that entry strategies requiring high corporate involvement should be reserved for new businesses with familiar market and technological characteristics. Similarly, entry mechanisms requiring low corporate input seem best for unfamiliar sectors. A recent discussion meeting with a number of chief executive officers suggested that, at most, 50 percent of major U.S. corporations practice even this simple advice.

The three sections of the Entry Strategy Spectrum in Figure 10.3 can now be aligned with the three regions of the familiarity matrix in Figure 10.2. Let us analyze this alignment for each region of the matrix, with particular regard for the main factors identified in the literature.

Region 1: Base/Familiar Sectors

Within the base/familiar sector combinations illustrated in Figure 10.4, a corporation is fully equipped to undertake all aspects of new business development. Consequently, the full range of entry strategies may be considered, including internal development, joint venturing, licensing, acquisition, or minority investment of venture capital. However, although all of these are valid from a corporate familiarity standpoint, other factors suggest what may be the optimum entry approach.

The potential of conflict between partners may reduce the appeal of a joint venture, and minority investments offer little benefit, since the investee would do nothing that could not be done internally.

The most attractive entry mechanisms in these sectors probably include internal development, licensing, and acquisition. Internal development may be appropriate in each of these sectors, since the required expertise already exists within the corporation. Licensing may be a useful alternative in the base market/new familiar technology sector, since it offers fast access to proven products. Acquisition may be attractive in each sector but, as indicated by

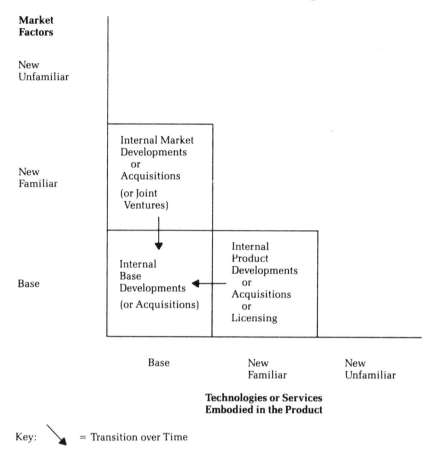

Market Factors

New
Unfamiliar

New
Familiar

Base

Internal Market
Developments
or
Acquisitions
(or Joint
 Ventures)

Internal
Base
Developments
(or Acquisitions)

Internal
Product
Developments
or
Acquisitions
or
Licensing

Base   New
              Familiar

New
Unfamiliar

**Technologies or Services
Embodied in the Product**

Key: = Transition over Time

Figure 10.4   Preferred Entry Mechanisms in Base/Familiar Sectors

Shanklin, may not be feasible for some companies in the base/base sector as a result of antitrust legislation.[32] For example, although IBM was permitted to acquire ROLM Corporation, the Justice Department did require that IBM divest ROLM's MIL-SPECS Division because of concern for concentration in the area of military computers.

It may therefore be concluded that in these base/familiar sectors, the optimum-entry strategy range may be limited to internal development, licensing, and acquisition as illustrated in Figure 10.4. In all cases a new business developed in each of these sectors is immediately required to fulfill a conventional sales/profit role within the corporate business portfolio.

Finally, since new businesses within the base market/new familiar technology and new familiar market/base technology sectors immediately enter the portfolio of ongoing business activities, they transfer rapidly into the base/base sector. These expected transitions are illustrated by the arrows in Figure 10.4.

Region 2: Familiar/Unfamiliar Sectors

Figure 10.5 illustrates the sectors of lowest familiarity from a corporate standpoint. It has already been proposed that a company is potentially competent to carry out totally appropriate analyses only on those new business opportunities that lie within its own sphere of familiarity. Large-scale entry decisions outside this sphere are liable to miss important characteristics of the technology or market, reducing the probability of success. This situation frequently generates unhappy and costly surprises. Furthermore, if the unfamiliar parent attempts to exert strong influence on the new business, the probability of success will be reduced still further.

These factors suggest that a two-stage approach may be best when a company desires to enter unfamiliar new business areas. The first stage should be devoted to building corporate familiarity with the new area. Once this has been achieved, the parent is then in a position to decide whether to allocate more substantial resources to the opportunity and, if appropriate, select a mechanism for developing the business.

As indicated earlier, venture capital provides one possible vehicle for building corporate familiarity with an unfamiliar area. With active nurturing of a venture-capital minority investment, the corporation can monitor, firsthand, new technologies and markets. If the investment is to prove worthwhile, it is essential for the investee to be totally familiar with the technology/market being monitored by the investor. The technology and market must therefore be the investee's base business. Over time active involvement with the new investment can help the investor move into a more familiar market/technology region, as illustrated in Figure 10.5, from which the parent can exercise appropriate judgment on the commitment of more substantial resources.

Similarly, educational acquisitions of small young firms may provide a more transparent window on a new technology or market, and even on the initial key employees, who can assist the transition toward higher familiarity. It is important, however, that the performance of acquisitions of this type be measured according to criteria different from those used to assess the "portfolio" acquisitions discussed earlier. These educational acquisitions should be measured initially on their ability to provide increased corporate familiarity with a new technology or market, and not on their ability to perform immediately a conventional business-unit role of sales and profits contributions.

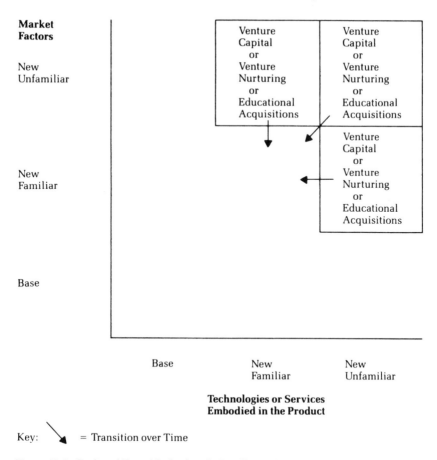

Market Factors

New Unfamiliar

New Familiar

Base

Base

New Familiar

New Unfamiliar

Technologies or Services Embodied in the Product

Key: = Transition over Time

Figure 10.5   Preferred Entry Mechanisms in Familiar/Unfamiliar Sectors

Region 3: Marginal Sectors

The marginal sectors of the matrix are the two base/new unfamiliar combinations plus the new familiar market/new familiar technology area, as illustrated in Figure 10.6. In each of the base/new unfamiliar sectors, the company has a strong familiarity with either markets or technologies, but is totally unfamiliar with the other dimension of the new business. In these situations joint venturing may be very attractive to the company and prospective partners can see that the company may have something to offer. However, in the new familiar technology/market region the company's base business strengths do not communicate obvious familiarity with that new technology or market. Hence, pro-

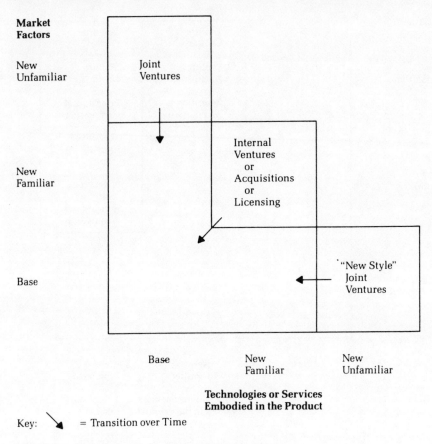

Figure 10.6   Preferred Entry Mechanisms in Marginal Sectors

spective partners may not perceive that a joint-venture relationship would yield any benefit for them.

In the base market/new unfamiliar technology sector the "new style" joint venture or alliance seems appropriate. The large firm provides the marketing channels, and the small company provides the technological capability, forming a union that can result in a very powerful team.[33] The complement of this situation may be equally attractive in the new unfamiliar market/base technology sector, although small companies less frequently have strong marketing/distribution capabilities to offer a larger ally.

The various forms of joint ventures not only provide a means of fast entry into a new business sector, but offer increased corporate familiarity over time, as illustrated in Figure 10.6. Consequently, although a joint venture may be the optimum entry mechanism into the new business area, future development of that business may be best achieved by internal development or acquisition, as discussed in the earlier base/familiar sectors section of this article.

In the new familiar market/new familiar technology sector, the company may be in an ideal spot to undertake an internal venture. Alternatively, licensing may provide a useful means of obtaining rapid access to a proven product embodying the new technology. Minority investments can also succeed in this sector but, since familiarity already exists, a higher level of corporate involvement and control may be justifiable.

Acquisitions may be potentially attractive in all marginal sectors. However, in the base/new unfamiliar areas this is dangerous, since the company's lack of familiarity with the technology or market prevents it from carrying out comprehensive screening of candidates. In contrast, the region of new familiar market/new familiar technologies does provide adequate familiarity to ensure that screening of candidates covers most significant factors. In this instance an acquisitive strategy is reasonable.

Sector Integration: Optimum Entry Strategies

The above discussion has proposed optimum entry strategies for attractive new business opportunities based on their position in the familiarity matrix. Figure 10.7 integrates these proposals to form a tool for selecting entry strategies based on corporate familiarity.

Testing the Proposals

In testing the proposed entry strategies, Berry studied fourteen new business development episodes that had been undertaken within one highly successful diversified technological corporation.[34] These episodes were all initiated within the period 1971 to 1977, thus representing relatively recent activity, while still ensuring that sufficient time had elapsed for performance to be measurable.

The sample comprised six internal developments (three successful, three unsuccessful); six acquisitions (three successful, three incompatible); and two successful minority investments of venture capital. These were analyzed in order to identify factors that differentiated successful from unsuccessful episodes, measured in terms of meeting very high corporate standards of growth, profitability, and return on investment. Failures had not achieved these standards and had been discontinued or divested. The scatter of these episodes on the familiarity matrix is illustrated in Figure 10.8. Internal developments are

Market Factors	Base	New Familiar	New Unfamiliar
New Unfamiliar	Joint Ventures	Venture Capital or Venture Nurturing or Educational Acquisitions	Venture Capital or Venture Nurturing or Educational Acquisitions
New Familiar	Internal Market Developments or Acquisitions (or Joint Ventures)	Internal Ventures or Acquisitions or Licensing	Venture Capital or Venture Nurturing or Educational Acquisitions
Base	Internal Base Developments (or Acquisitions)	Internal Product Developments or Acquisitions or Licensing	"New Style" Joint Ventures

**Technologies or Services
Embodied in the Product**

Figure 10.7   Optimum Entry Strategies

represented by symbols A to F, acquisitions by symbols G to L, with symbols M and N showing the location of the minority investments.

The distribution of success and failure on the matrix gives support to the entry strategy proposals that have been made in this article. All high corporate-involvement mechanisms (internal development and regular "portfolio" acquisitions) in familiar sectors were successful. However, in unfamiliar areas, only one of this category of entry mechanism, acquisition G, succeeded. This acquisition was a thirty-year-old private company with about 1,000 employees, producing components for the electronics and computer industries. Company G was believed to offer opportunities for high growth, although it was unrelated to any area of the parent's existing business. The deal was completed after an unusually long period of two years of candidate evaluation carried out from within the parent company. The only constraint imposed upon Company G

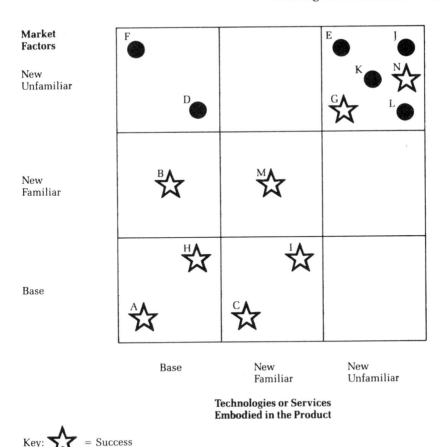

Market Factors

New Unfamiliar

New Familiar

Base

Base   New Familiar   New Unfamiliar

Technologies or Services Embodied in the Product

Key: ☆ = Success

● = Failure

Figure 10.8   Episode Scatter on the Familiarity Matrix

following acquisition was the parent's planning and control system, and in fact the acquired company was highly receptive to the introduction of this system. This indicated that Company G was not tightly integrated with the parent and that any constraints imposed did not severely disrupt the established operating procedures of the company.

All factors surrounding the acquisition of Company G—its size, growth market, low level of constraints, and low disruption by the parent—suggest that Company G might have continued to be successful even if it had not been acquired. Representatives of the parent agreed that this might be the case, although they pointed out that the levels of performance obtained following acquisition might not have occurred if Company G had remained independent. Hence, if an acquired company is big enough to stand alone and is *not* tightly integrated with the parent, its degree of operational success is probably independently determined.

It is important to point out that despite the success that occurred in instance G, an acquisition of this type in unfamiliar areas must carry some degree of risk. The parent is liable to overlook many subtle details while screening candidates. Furthermore, when an established company is acquired and continues to operate with a high degree of independence, identification of synergy becomes difficult. Synergy must exist in any acquisitive development, if economic value is to be created by the move.[35] Consequently, an acquisition of this type not only carries risk, but may also be of questionable benefit to shareholders, especially if a high price was required because of an earlier good performance record.

The other success in an unfamiliar area, episode N, is a minority investment of venture capital. By the very nature of minority investments, corporate involvement is limited to a low level. Although some influence may be exerted via participation on the board of directors of the investee, again, the investee is not tightly bound to the parent. Consequently, the success of the investee tends to be determined to a large extent by its own actions.

Detailed examination of episodes G and N suggests a good reason for the subject companies' success despite their location in unfamiliar sectors: The companies did not require significant input from the unfamiliar parent in the decision-making process. This suggests that new-business-development success rates in unfamiliar areas may be increased by limiting corporate input to the decision-making process to low levels until corporate familiarity with the new area has developed. These experiences support the entry proposals already outlined in this article.

Some companies have already adopted entry strategies that seem to fit the proposals of this article, and Monsanto represents one of the best examples. Monsanto is now committed to significant corporate venturing in the emerging field of biotechnology. Its first involvement in this field was achieved with the aid of its venture-capital partnership, Innoven, which invested in several small biotechnology firms, including Genentech. During this phase Monsanto interacted closely with the investees, inviting them in-house to give seminars to senior management on their biotechnology research and opportunities. Once some internal familiarity with the emerging field had developed, Monsanto decided to commit substantial resources to internal research-based ventures. Monsanto used venture capital to move from an unfamiliar region to an area of more familiar technology and market and is currently continuing those venture-capital activities to seek new opportunities in Europe. Joint ventures with Harvard Medical School and Washington University of St. Louis are further enhancing its familiarity with biotechnology, while producing technologies that Monsanto hopes to market. Contract research leading to licenses from small companies, primarily those in which it holds minority investments, is another strategy Monsanto is employing. Although the outcome is far from determined, Monsanto seems to be effectively entering biotechnology by moving from top right to bottom left across the familiarity matrix of Figure 10.7.

Conclusion

A spectrum of entry strategies was presented in this article, ranging from those that require high corporate involvement, such as internal development or acquisition, to those that require only low involvement, such as venture capital. These were incorporated into a new conceptual framework designed to assist in selecting entry strategies into potentially attractive new business areas. The framework concentrates on the concept of a corporation's "familiarity" with the technology and market aspects of a new business area, and a matrix was used to relate familiarity to optimum entry strategy.

In this concept, no one strategy is ideal. Within familiar sectors virtually any strategy may be adopted; internal development or acquisition is probably most appropriate. However, in unfamiliar areas these two high involvement approaches are very risky, and greater familiarity should be built *before* they are attempted. Minority investments and small targeted educational acquisitions form ideal vehicles for building familiarity and are therefore the preferred entry strategies in unfamiliar sectors.

Early in this article, research results from the literature were outlined that indicated that, in order to ensure highest performance, new business development should be constrained within areas related to a company's base business. However, this research did not account for alternative entry mechanisms. This article proposes that a multifaceted approach, encompassing internal developments, acquisitions, joint ventures, and venture-capital minority investments, can make available a much broader range of business development opportunities, at lower risk than would otherwise be possible.

11

Managing the Internal Corporate Venturing Process

Robert A. Burgelman

The strategic management of internal corporate venturing (ICV) presents a major challenge for many large established firms. The author's conceptualization of ICV suggests that vicious circles and managerial dilemmas typically emerge in the development of new ventures. These problems are exacerbated by the indeterminateness of the strategic context for ICV in the corporation, and by perverse selective pressures exerted by its structural context. This article presents four major recommendations for improving the effectiveness of a firm's ICV strategy. *SMR.*

Many large established firms currently seem to be trying hard to improve their capacity for managing internal entrepreneurship and new ventures. Companies like Du Pont and General Electric have appointed CEOs with a deep understanding of the innovation process.[1] IBM has generated much interest with its concept of "independent business units."[2] To head its new ventures division, Allied Corporation has attracted the person who ran 3M's new ventures group for many years.[3] These are only some of the better publicized cases.

Most managers in large established firms will probably agree that internal corporate venturing (ICV) is an important avenue for corporate growth and diversification. However, they will also probably observe that it is a hazardous one, and will be ready to give examples of new ventures (and managerial careers) gone for naught.

Systematic research suggests that such apprehension is not unfounded. In a large sample study of firms attempting to diversify through internal development, Ralph Biggadike found that it takes on the average about eight years for a venture to reach profitability, and about ten to twelve years before its

From *Sloan Management Review*, Winter 1984, Vol. 25, No. 2. Reprinted with permission.

ROI equals that of mainstream business activities.[4] He concludes his study with the caveat that new business development is "not an activity for the impatient or for the fainthearted." Norman Fast did a study of firms that had created a separate new venture division to facilitate internally developed ventures.[5] He found that the position of such new venture divisions was precarious. Many of these were short-lived, and most others suffered rather dramatic changes as a result of often erratic alterations in the corporate strategy and/or in political position. An overview of earlier studies on new ventures is provided by Eric von Hippel, who observed a great diversity of new venture practices.[6] He also identified some key factors associated with the success and failure of new ventures, but did not document how the ICV process takes shape.

The purpose of this article is to shed additional light on some of the more deep-rooted problems inherent in the ICV process and to suggest recommendations for making a firm's ICV strategy more effective. This article presents a new model capable of capturing the intricacies of managerial activities involved in the ICV process. By using this model, which provides a fairly complete picture of the organizational dynamics of the ICV process, we can identify and discuss key problems and their interrelationships and then suggest some ideas for alleviating, if not eliminating, these deep-rooted problems.

A New Model of the ICV Process

The hazards facing internal corporate ventures are similar in many ways to those confronting new businesses developed by external entrepreneurs. Not surprisingly, the ICV process has typically been conceptualized in terms of a "stages model" that describes the evolution and organization development of a venture as a *separate* new business. Such a model emphasizes the sequential aspects of the development process and focuses on problems within the various stages and on issues pertaining to the transitions between stages. For example, Jay Galbraith has recently proposed a model of new venture development that encompasses five generic stages: (1) proof of principle, prototype; (2) model shop; (3) start-up volume production; (4) natural growth; (5) strategic maneuvering.[7] He discusses the different requirements of these five stages in terms of tasks, people, rewards, processes, structures, and leadership.

A stages model is useful for helping managers to organize their experiences and to anticipate problems of fledgling businesses. However, it does not really address the problems of growing a new business in a corporate context. Many difficult problems generated and encountered by ICV result from the fact that related strategic activities take place at multiple levels of corporate management. These must be considered simultaneously as well as sequentially in order to understand the special problems associated with ICV.

A Process Model of ICV

The work of Joseph Bower and his associates has laid the foundation for a "process model" approach that depicts the simultaneous as well as sequential managerial activities involved in strategic decision making in large complex firms.[8] Recently, I proposed an extension of this approach that has generated a new model of the ICV process.[9] This new model is based on the findings of an in-depth study of the complete development process of six ICV projects in the context of the new venture division of one large diversified firm. These ICV projects purported to develop new businesses based on new technologies, and constituted radical innovation efforts from the corporation's viewpoint. The Appendix provides a brief description of the methodology used in the study. Figure 11.1 shows the new model of ICV.

Figure 11.1 shows the *core* processes of an ICV project and the *overlaying* processes (the corporate context) in which the core processes take shape. The core processes of ICV comprise the activities through which a new business becomes defined (definition process) and its development gains momentum in the corporation (impetus process). The overlaying processes comprise the activities through which the current corporate strategy is extended to accommodate the new business thrusts resulting from ICV (strategic context determination), and the activities involved in establishing the administrative mechanisms to implement corporate strategy (structural context determination).

The model shows how each of the processes is constituted by activities of managers at different levels in the organization. Some of these activities were found to be more important for the ICV process than others. These key activities are indicated by the shaded areas. They represent new concepts which are useful to provide a more complete description of the complexities of the ICV process. Because they allow us to refer to these complexities in a concise way, they also serve to keep the discussion manageable. The process model shown in Figure 11.1 is *descriptive*. It does *not* suggest that the pattern of activities is optimal from a managerial viewpoint. In fact, many of the problems discussed below result from this particular pattern that the ICV process seems to take on naturally.

Levels	Core Processes: Definition	Core Processes: Impetus	Overlaying Processes: Strategic Context	Overlaying Processes: Structural Context
Corporate Management	Monitoring	Authorizing	Rationalizing	Structuring
NVD Management	Coaching Stewardship	Strategic Building; Organizational Championing	Selecting; Delineating	Negotiating
Group Leader Venture Leader	Technical & Need Linking	Product Championing; Strategic Forcing	Gatekeeping Idea Generating Bootlegging	Questioning

☐ = Key Activities

Figure 11.1 Key and Peripheral Activities in a Process Model of ICV. (Reprinted from R.A. Burgelman, "A Process Model of Internal Corporate Venturing in the Diversified Major Firm," *Administrative Science Quarterly*, June 1983, by permission of the *Administrative Science Quarterly*. Copyright 1983 Cornell University.)

Major Problems in the ICV Process

The process model provides a framework for elucidating four important problem areas observed in my study:

- Vicious circles in the definition process
- Managerial dilemmas in the impetus process
- Indeterminateness of the strategic context of ICV development, and
- Perverse selective pressures exerted by the structural context on ICV development.

Table 11.1 serves as a road map for discussing each of these problem areas.

Vicious Circles in the Definition Process

The ICV projects in my study typically started with opportunistic search activities at the group-leader level (first-level supervisor) in the firm's research function. Technical linking activities led to the assembling of external and/or internal pieces of technological knowledge to create solutions for new or known, but unsolved, technical problems. Need-linking activities involved the matching of new technical solutions to new or poorly served market needs. Both types of linking activities took place in an iterative fashion. Initiators of ICV projects perceived their initiatives to fall outside of the current strategy of the

Table 11.1 Major Problems in the ICV Process

Levels	Core Processes		Overlaying Processes	
	Definition	**Impetus**	**Strategic Context**	**Structural Context**
Corporate Management	Top management lacks capacity to assess merits of specific new venture proposals for corporate development.	Top management relies on purely quantitative growth results to continue support for new venture.	Top management considers ICV as insurance against mainstream business going badly. ICV objectives are ambiguous & shift erratically.	Top management relies on reactive structural changes to deal with problems related to ICV.
NVD Management	Middle-level managers in corporate R&D are not capable of coaching ICV project initiators.	Middle-level managers in new business development find it difficult to balance strategic building efforts with efforts to coach venture managers.	Middle-level managers struggle to delineate boundaries of new business field. They spend significant amounts of time on political activities to maintain corporate support.	Middle-level managers struggle with unanticipated structural impediments to new venture activities. There is little incentive for star performers to engage in ICV activities.
Group Leader Venture Leader	Project initiators cannot convincingly demonstrate in advance that resources will be used effectively. They need to engage in scavenging to get resources.	Venture managers find it difficult to balance strategic forcing efforts with efforts to develop administrative framework of emerging ventures.	Project initiators do not have clear idea of which kind of ICV projects will be viable in corporate context. Bootlegging is necessary to get new idea tested.	Venture managers do not have clear idea of what type of performance will be rewarded, except fast growth.

firm, but felt that there was a good chance they would be included in future strategic development if they proved to be successful.

At the outset, however, project initiators typically encountered resistance and found it difficult to obtain resources from their managers to demonstrate the feasibility of their project. Hence, the emergence of vicious circles: Resources could be obtained if technical feasibility was demonstrated, but such a demonstration required resources. Similar problems arose with efforts to demonstrate commercial feasibility. Even when a technically demonstrated product, process, or system existed, corporate management was often reluctant to start commercialization efforts, because they were unsure about the firm's capabilities to do this effectively.

Product championing activities, which have been well documented in the literature, served to break through these vicious circles.[10] Using bootlegging and scavenging tactics, the successful product champion was able to provide positive information that reassured middle-level management and provided them with a basis for claiming support for ICV projects in their formal plans. As the product initiator of a medical-equipment venture explained:

When we proposed to sell the ANA product by our own selling force, there was a lot of resistance, out of ignorance. Management did numerous studies, had outside consultants on which they spent tens of thousands of dollars; they looked at ZYZ Company for a possible partnership. Management was just very unsure about its marketing capability. I proposed to have a test marketing phase with twenty to twenty-five installations in the field. We built our own service group; we pulled ourselves up by the "bootstrap." I guess we had more guts than sense.

Why Do Vicious Circles Exist?   The process model provides some insight about this by showing the connection between the activities of the different levels of management involved in the definition process (see Table 11.1). Operational-level managers typically struggled to conceptualize their somewhat nebulous (at least to outsiders) business ideas, which made communication with management difficult. Their proposals often went against conventional corporate wisdom. They could not clearly specify the development path of their projects, and they could not demonstrate in advance that the resources needed would be used effectively in uncharted domains.

Middle-level managers in corporate R&D (where new ventures usually originated) were most concerned about maintaining the integrity of the R&D work environment, which is quite different from a business-oriented work environment. They were comfortable with managing relatively slow-moving exploratory research projects and well-defined development projects. However, they were reluctant to commit significant amounts of resources (especially people) to suddenly fast-moving areas of new development activity that fell outside of the scope of their current plans and that did not yet have demonstrated technical and commercial feasibility. In fact, the middle-level manager often seemed to encourage, not just tolerate, the sub-rosa activities of a project's champion. As one such manager said, "I encourage them to do 'bootleg' research; tell them to come back [for support] when they have results."

At the corporate level, managers seemed to have a highly reliable frame of reference to evaluate business strategies and resource-allocation proposals pertaining to the main lines of the corporation's business. However, their capacity to deal with substantive issues of new business opportunities was limited, and their expectations concerning what could be accomplished in a short time frame were often somewhat unrealistic. Also, ICV proposals competed for scarce top management time. Their relatively small size combined with the difficulty in assessing their merit made it at the outset seem uneconomical for top management to allocate much time to them.

The process model shows the lack of articulation between the activities of different levels of management; this may, to a large extent, account for the vicious circles encountered in the definition process.

Managerial Dilemmas in the Impetus Process

Successful efforts at product championing demonstrated that the technical and commercial potential of a new product, process, or system was sufficient to result in a sizable new business. This, in turn, allowed an ICV project to receive "venture" status: to become a quasi-independent, embryonic new business organization with its own budget and general manager. From then on, continued impetus for its development seemed entirely dependent on achieving fast growth in order to convince top management that it could grow to a $50 to $100 million business within a five- to ten-year period.

My findings suggest that this created a *dilemmatic* situation for the venture manager: maximizing growth with the one product, process, or system available versus building the functional capabilities of the embryonic business organization. Similarly, the middle-level manager was confronted with a *dilemmatic* situation: focusing on expanding the scope of the new business versus spending time coaching the (often recalcitrant) venture manager.

Ironically, my study indicates that new product development was likely to be a major problem of new ventures.[11] Lacking the carefully evolved relationships between R&D, engineering, marketing, and manufacturing typical for the mainstream operations of the firm, the venture's new product development schedules tended to be delayed, and completed products often showed serious flaws. This was exacerbated by the tendency of the venture's emerging R&D group to isolate itself from the corporate R&D department, partly in order to establish its own "identity." A related and somewhat disturbing finding was that new venture managers seemed to become the victims of their own success at maintaining impetus for the venture's development. Here are some examples from my study:

- In an environmental systems venture, the perceived need to grow very fast led to premature emphasis on commercialization. Instead of working on the technical improvement of the new system, the venture's resources were wasted on (very costly) remedial work on systems already sold. After a quick rise, stagnation set in and the venture collapsed.
- In a medical equipment venture, growth with one new system was very fast and could be sustained. However, after about five years, the new products needed for sustaining the growth rate turned out to be flawed. As one manager in the venture commented: "Every ounce of effort with Dr. S. [the venture manager] was spent on the short run. There was no strategizing. New product development was delayed, was put to corporate R&D. Every year we had doubled in size, but things never got any simpler."

In both cases the venture manager was eventually removed.

How Do These Dilemmas Arise?   The process model shows how the strategic situation at each level of management in the impetus process is different, with fast growth being the only shared interest (see Table 11.1).

At the venture-manager level, continued impetus depended on strategic forcing efforts: attaining a significant sales volume and market-share position centered on the original product, process, or system within a limited time horizon.[12] To implement a strategy of fast growth, the venture manager attracted generalists who could cover a number of different functional areas reasonably well. Efficiency considerations became increasingly important with the growth of the venture organization and with competitive pressures due to product maturation. New functional managers were brought in to replace the generalists. They emphasized the development of routines, standard operating procedures, and the establishment of an administrative framework for the venture. This, however, was time-consuming and detracted from the all-out efforts to grow fast. Growth concerns tended to win out, and organization building was more or less purposefully neglected.

While the venture manager created a "beachhead" for the new business, the middle-level manager engaged in strategic building efforts to sustain the impetus process. Such efforts involved the conceptualization of a master strategy for the broader new field within which the venture could fit. They also involved the integration of projects that existed elsewhere in the corporation, and/or of small firms that could be acquired with the burgeoning venture.

These efforts became increasingly important as the strategic forcing activities of the venture manager reached their limit, and major discontinuities in new product development put more stress on the middle-level manager to find supplementary products elsewhere to help maintain the growth rate. At the same time, the administrative problems created by the strategic forcing efforts increasingly required the attention of the venture manager's manager. Given the overwhelming importance of growth, however, the coaching activities and organization building were more or less purposefully neglected.

The decision by corporate-level management to authorize further resource allocations to a new venture was, to a large extent, dependent on the credibility of the managers involved. Credibility, in turn, depended primarily on the quantitative results produced. Corporate management seemed to have somewhat unrealistic expectations about new ventures. They sent strong signals concerning the importance of making an impact on the overall corporate position soon. This, not surprisingly, reinforced the emphasis to achieve growth on the part of the middle and operational levels of management. One manager in a very successful venture said, "Even in the face of the extraordinary growth rate of the ME venture, the questions corporate management raised when they came here concerned our impact on the overall position of GAMMA, rather than the performance of the venture per se."

Indeterminateness of the Strategic Context of ICV

The problems encountered in the core process of ICV are more readily understood when examining the nature of the overlaying processes (the corporate context) within which ICV projects took shape. My findings indicated a high level of indeterminateness in the strategic context of ICV. Strategic guidance on the part of top management was limited to declaring corporate interest in broadly defined fields like "health" or "energy." Also, there seemed to be a tendency for severe oscillations in top management's interest in ICV—a "now we do it, now we don't" approach. It looked very much as if new ventures were viewed by top management as insurance against mainstream business going badly, rather than as a corporate objective per se.[13] As one experienced middle-level manager said:

They are going into new areas because they are not sure that we will be able to stay in the current mainstream businesses. That is also the reason why the time of maturity of a new venture is never right. If current business goes OK, then it is always too early, but when current business is not going too well, then we will just jump into anything!

In other words, corporate management's interest in new ventures seemed to be activated primarily by the expectation of a relatively poor performance record with mainstream business activities—a legacy most top managers want to avoid. Treating ICV as "insurance" against such an undesirable situation, however, implies the unrealistic assumption that new ventures can be developed at will within a relatively short time frame, and plays down the importance of crafting a corporate development strategy in substantive terms. Lacking an understanding of substantive issues and problems in particular new venture developments, top management is likely to become disenchanted when progress is slower than desired. Perhaps not surprisingly, venture managers in my study seemed to prefer less rather than more top-management attention until the strategic context of their activities was more clearly defined.

Why This Indeterminateness?   In determining the strategic context (even more than the impetus process), the strategies of the various levels of management showed a lack of articulation with each other. The process model in Table 11.1 allows us to depict this.

Corporate management's objectives concerning ICV seemed to be ambiguous. Top management did not really know which specific new businesses they wanted until those businesses had taken some concrete form and size, and decisions had to be made about whether to integrate them into the corporate portfolio through a process of retroactive rationalizing. Top management's actual (as opposed to declared) time horizon was typically limited to three to five years, even though new ventures take between eight and twelve years on the average to become mature and profitable.

Middle managers were aware that they had to take advantage of the short-term windows for corporate acceptance. They struggled with delineating the boundaries of a new business field. They were aware that it was only through their strategic building efforts and the concomitant articulation of a master strategy for the ongoing venture initiatives that the new business fields could be concretely delineated and possible new strategic directions determined. This indeterminateness of the strategic context of ICV required middle-level managers to engage in organizational championing activities.[14] Such activities were of a political nature and time-consuming. As one venture manager explained, these activities required an "upward" orientation that is very different from the venture manager's substantive and downward (hands-on) orientation. One person who had been general manager of the new venture division said: "It is always difficult to get endorsement from the management committee for ventures which require significant amounts of resources but where they cannot clearly see what is going to be done with these resources. It is a matter of proportion on the one hand, but it is also a matter of educating the management committee which is very difficult to do."

The middle-level manager also had to spend time working out frictions with the operating system that were created when the strategies of the venture and mainstream businesses interfered with each other. The need for these activities further reduced the amount of time and effort the middle-level manager spent coaching the venture manager.

At the operational level, managers engaged in opportunistic search activities that led to the definition of ICV projects in new areas. These activities were basically independent of the current strategy of the firm. The rate at which mutant ideas were pursued seemed to depend on the amount of slack resources available at the operational level. Many of these autonomous efforts were started as "bootlegged" projects.

Perverse Selective Pressures of the Structural Context

Previous research indicates that reaching high market share fast has survival value for new ventures.[15] Hence, the efforts to grow fast that I found pervading the core processes correspond to the managers' correct assessment of the external strategic situation.

My study, however, suggests that the firm's structural context exerted perverse selective pressures to grow fast that exacerbated the external ones. This seemed in part due to the incompleteness of the structural context in relation to the special nature of the ICV process. Establishing a separate new venture division was useful for nurturing and developing new businesses that fell outside of the current corporate strategy. (It was also convenient to have a separate "address" for projects that were "misfits" or "orphans" in the operating divisions.) However, because the managerial work involved in these was very different from that of the mainstream business, the corporate measurement and reward systems were not adequate, and yet they remained in effect, mostly, in the new venture division (NVD).

Another part of the structural context problems resulted from the widely shared perception that the position of the NVD was precarious.[16] This, in turn, created an "it's now or never" attitude on the part of the participants in the NVD, adding to the pressures to grow fast.

How Do These Selective Pressures Arise?   Table 11.1 shows the situation at each of the management levels. Corporate management did not seem to have a clear purpose or strong commitment to new ventures. It seemed that, when ICV activities expanded beyond a level that corporate management found opportune to support in light of their assessment of the prospects of mainstream business activities, changes were effected in the structural context to "consolidate" ICV activities. These changes seemed reactive and indicative of the lack of a clear strategy for diversification in the firm. One high-level manager charged with making a number of changes in which the NVD would operate in the future said:

> To be frank, I don't feel corporate management has a clear idea. Recently, we had a meeting with the management committee, and there are now new directives. Basically, it de-emphasizes diversification for the moment. The emphasis is on consolidation, with the recognition that diversification will be important in the future. . . . The point is that we will not continue in four or five different areas anymore.

At the middle level, the incompleteness of the structural context also manifested itself in the lack of integration between the ICV activities and the mainstream businesses. Middle-level managers of the new venture division experienced resistance from managers in the operating divisions when their activities had the potential to overlap. Ad hoc negotiations and reliance on political savvy substituted for long-term joint optimization arrangements.[17] This also created the perception that there was not much to gain for middle-level star performers by participating directly in the ICV activities. In addition, the lack of adequate reward systems also made middle-level managers reluctant to remove venture managers who were in trouble. One middle-level manager talked about the case of a venture manager in trouble who had grown a project from zero to about $30 million in a few years:

> When the business reached, say, $10 million, they should have talked to him; have given him a free trip around the world, $50 thousand, and six months off; and then have persuaded him to take on a new assignment. But that's not the way it happened. For almost two years, we knew that there were problems, but no one would touch the problem until it was too late and he had put himself in a real bind. We lost some good people during this period, and we lost an entrepreneur.

At the operational level, managers felt that the only reward available was to become general manager of a sizable new business in the corporate structure. This "lure of the big office" affected the way in which they searched for new opportunities. One high-level manager observed, "People are looking around to find a program to latch onto, and that could be developed into a demonstration plan. Business research always stops after one week, so to speak."

Making the ICV Strategy Work Better

Having identified major problem areas with the help of the process model, we can now propose recommendations for improving the strategic management of ICV. They serve to alleviate, if not eliminate, the problems by making the corporate context more hospitable to ICV. This could allow management to focus more effectively on the problems inherent in the core processes.

Four "themes" for the recommendations correspond to the four major problem areas already discussed:

- Facilitating the definition process,
- Moderating the impetus process,
- Elaborating the strategic context of ICV, and
- Refining the structural context of ICV.

Each of these themes encompasses more specific action items for management. Table 11.2 summarizes the various recommendations and their expected effects on the ICV process.

Facilitating the Definition Process

Timely assessment of the true potential of an ICV project remains a difficult problem. This follows from the very nature of such projects: the many uncertainties around the technical and marketing aspects of the new business, and the fact that each case is significantly different from all others. These factors make it difficult to develop standardized evaluation procedures and development programs, without screening to death truly innovative projects.

Managing the definition process effectively poses serious challenges for middle-level managers in the corporate R&D department. They must facilitate the integration of technical and business perspectives, and they must maintain a lifeline to the technology developed in corporate R&D as the project takes off. As stated earlier, the need for product championing efforts, if excessive, may cut that lifeline early on and lead to severe discontinuities in new product development after the project has reached the venture stage. The middle-level manager's efforts must facilitate both product championing and the continued development of the technology base by putting the former in perspective and by making sure that the interface between R&D and businesspeople works smoothly.

Facilitating the Integration of R&D-Business Perspectives.   To facilitate the integration of technical and business perspectives, the middle manager must understand the operating logic of both groups. He or she must avoid getting bogged down in technical details, yet have sufficient technical depth to be respected by the R&D people. Such managers must be able to motivate the R&D people to collaborate with the businesspeople toward the formulation of business objectives against which progress can be measured. Formulating adequate business objectives is especially important if corporate management becomes more actively involved in ICV and develops a greater capacity to evaluate the fit of new projects with the corporate development strategy.

Table 11.2 Recommendations for Making ICV Strategy Work Better

Levels	Core Processes		Overlaying Processes	
	Definition	Impetus	Strategic Context	Structural Context
Corporate Management	ICV proposals are evaluated in light of corporate development strategy. Conscious efforts are made to avoid subjecting them to conventional corporate wisdom.	New venture progress is evaluated in substantive terms by top managers who have experience in organizational championing.	A process is in place for developing long-term corporate development strategy. This strategy takes shape as result of ongoing interactive learning process involving top & middle levels of management.	Managers with successful ICV experience are appointed to top management. Top management is rewarded financially & symbolically for long-term corporate development success.
NVD Management	Middle-level managers in corporate R&D are selected who have both technical depth & business knowledge necessary to determine minimum amount of resources for project, & who can coach star players.	Middle-level managers are responsible for use & development of venture managers as scarce resources of corporation, & they facilitate intrafirm project transfers if new business strategy warrants it.	Substantive interaction between corporate & middle-level management leads to clarifying merits of new business field in light of corporate development strategy.	Star performers at middle level are attracted to ICV activities. Collaboration of mainstream middle level with ICV activities is rewarded. Integrating mechanisms can easily be mobilized.
Group Leader Venture Leader	Project initiators are encouraged to integrate technical & business perspectives. They are provided access to resources. Project initiators can be rewarded by means other than promotion to venture manager.	Venture managers are responsible for developing functional capabilities of emerging venture organizations, & for codification of what has been learned in terms of required functional capabilities while pursuing new business opportunity.	Slack resources determine level of emergence of mutant ideas. Existence of substantive corporate development strategy provides preliminary self-selection of mutant ideas.	A wide array of venture structures & supporting measurement & reward systems clarifies expected performance for ICV personnel.

213

Middle-level managers in R&D must be capable of facilitating give-and-take between the two groups in a process of mutual adjustment toward the common goal of advancing the progress of the new business project. It is crucial to create mutual respect between technical and businesspeople. If the R&D manager shows respect for the contribution of the businesspeople, this is likely to affect the attitudes of the other R&D people. Efforts will probably be better integrated if regular meetings are held with both groups to evaluate, as peers, the contribution of different team members.

The Middle Manager as Coach.   Such meetings also provide a vehicle to better coach the product champion, who is really the motor of the ICV project in this stage of development. There are some similarities between this role and that of the star player on a sports team. Product champions are often viewed in either/or terms: Either they can do their thing, and chances are the project will succeed (although there may be discontinuities and not fully exploited ancillary opportunities), or we harness them but they will not play.

A more balanced approach is for the middle-level manager to use a process that recognizes the product champion as the star player, but that, at times, challenges him or her to maintain breadth by having to respond to queries:

- How is the team benefiting more from this particular action than from others that the team may think to be important?
- How will the continuity of the team's efforts be preserved?
- What will the next step be?

To support this approach, the middle manager should be able to reward team members differently. This, of course, refers back to the determination of the structural context, and reemphasizes the importance of recognizing, at the corporate level, that different reward systems are necessary for different business activities.

Moderating the Impetus Process

The recommendations for improving the corporate context (the overlaying processes) of ICV, have implications for the way in which the impetus process is allowed to take shape. Corporate management should expect the middle-level managers to think and act as corporate strategists and the operational-level managers to view themselves as organization builders.

The Middle-Level Managers as Corporate Strategists.   Strategy making in new ventures depends, to a very great extent, on the middle-level managers. Because new ventures often intersect with multiple parts of mainstream businesses, middle managers learn what the corporate capabilities and skills—and shortcomings—are, and they learn to articulate new strategies and build new businesses based on new combinations of these capabilities and skills. This, in turn, also creates possibilities to enhance the realization of new operational synergies existing in the firm. Middle-level managers can thus serve as crucial integrating and technology transfer mechanisms in the corporation, and corporate management should expect them to perform this role as they develop a strategy for a new venture.

The Venture Managers as Organization Builders.   Pursuing fast growth and the administrative development of the venture simultaneously is a major challenge during the impetus process. This challenge, which exists for any start-up business, is especially treacherous for one in the context of an established firm. This is because managers in ICV typically have less control over the selection of key venture personnel, yet, at the same time, have access to a variety of corporate resources. There seems to be less pressure on the venture manager and the middle-level manager to show progress in building the organization than there is to show growth.

The recommendations concerning measurement and reward systems should encourage the venture manager to balance the two concerns better. The venture manager should have leeway in hiring and firing decisions, but should also be held responsible for the development of new functional capabilities and the administrative framework of the venture. This would reduce the probability of major discontinuities in new product development mentioned earlier. In addition, it would provide the corporation with codified know-how and information that can be transferred to other parts of the firm or to other new ventures, even if the one from which it is derived ultimately fails as a business. Know-how and information, as well as sales and profit, become important outputs of the ICV process.

Often the product champion or venture manager will not have the required capabilities to achieve these additional objectives. The availability of compensatory rewards and of avenues for recycling the product champion or venture manager would make it possible for middle management to tackle deteriorating managerial conditions to the new business organization. Furthermore, the availability of a competent replacement (after systematic corporate search) may induce the product champion or venture manager to relinquish his or her position, rather than see the venture go under.

Elaborating the Strategic Context of ICV

Determining the strategic context of ICV is a subtle and somewhat elusive process involving corporate and middle-level managers. More effort should be spent on developing a long-term corporate-development strategy explicitly encompassing ICV. At the same time measures should be taken to increase corporate management's capacity to assess venture strategies in substantive terms as well as in terms of projected quantitative results.

The Need for a Corporate Development Strategy. Top management should recognize that ICV is an important source of strategic renewal for the firm and that it is unlikely to work well if treated as insurance against poor mainstream business prospects. ICV should, therefore, be considered an integral and continuous part of the strategy-making process. To dampen the oscillations in corporate support for ICV, top management should create a process for developing an explicit long-term (ten to twelve years) strategy for corporate development, supported by a strategy for resource generation and allocation. Both should be based on ongoing efforts to determine the remaining growth opportunities in the current mainstream businesses and the resource levels necessary to exploit them. Given the corporate objectives of growth and profitability, a resource pool should be reserved for activities outside the mainstream business. This pool should not be affected by short-term fluctuations in current mainstream activities. The existence of this pool of "slack" (or perhaps better, "uncommitted") resources would allow top management to affect the rate at which new venture initiatives will emerge (if not their particular content). This approach reflects a broader concept of strategy making than maintaining corporate R&D at a certain percentage of sales.

Substantive Assessment of Venture Strategies. To determine more effectively the strategic context of ICV and to reduce the political emphasis in organizational championing activities, top management should increase their capacity to make substantive assessments of the merits of new ventures for corporate development. Top management should learn to assess better the strategic importance of ICV projects to corporate development and their degree of relatedness to core corporate capabilities. One way to achieve this capacity is to include in top management people with significant experience in new business development. In addition, top management should require middle-level organizational champions to explain how a new field of business would further the corporate development objectives in substantive rather than purely numerical terms and how they expect to create value from the corporate viewpoint with a new business field. Operational-level managers would then be able to assess better which of the possible directions their envisaged projects could take and would be more likely to receive corporate support.

Refining the Structural Context of ICV

Refining the structural context requires corporate management to use the new venture division design in a more deliberate fashion, and to complement the organization design effort with supporting measurement and reward systems.

More Deliberate Use of the New Venture Division Design.   Corporate management should develop greater flexibility in structuring the relationships between new venture projects and the corporation. In some instances, greater efforts would seem to be in order to integrate new venture projects directly into the mainstream businesses, rather than transferring them to the NVD because of lack of support in the operating division where they originated. In other cases, projects should be developed using external venture arrangements. Where and how a new venture project is developed should depend on top management's assessment of its strategic importance for the firm, and of the degree to which the required capabilities are related to the firm's core capabilities. Such assessments should be easier to implement by having a wide range of available structures for venture-corporation relationships.[18]

Also, the NVD is a mechanism for decoupling the activities of new ventures and those of mainstream businesses. However, because this decoupling usually cannot be perfect, integrative mechanisms should be established to deal constructively with conflicts that will unavoidably and unpredictably arise. One such mechanism is a "steering committee" involving managers from operating divisions and the NVD.

Finally, top management should facilitate greater acceptance of differences between the management processes of the NVD and the mainstream businesses. This may lead to more careful personnel assignment policies and to greater flexibility in hiring and firing policies in the NVD to reflect the special needs of emerging businesses.

Measurement and Reward Systems in Support of ICV.   Perhaps the most difficult aspect concerns how to provide incentives for top management to seriously and continuously support ICV as part of corporate strategy making. Corporate history writing might be an effective mechanism to achieve this. This would involve the careful tracing and periodical publication (e.g., a special section in annual reports) of decisions whose positive or negative results may become clear only after ten or more years. Corporate leaders (like political ones) would, presumably, make efforts to preserve their position in corporate history.[19] Another mechanism is to attract "top performers" from the mainstream businesses of the corporation to ICV activities. To do this, at least a few spots on the top management team should always be filled with managers who have had significant experience in new business development. This will also eliminate the perception that NVD participants are not part of the real world and, therefore, have little chance to advance in the corporation as a result of ICV experience.

The measurement and reward systems should be used to alleviate some of the more destructive consequences of the necessary emphasis on fast growth in venture development. This would mean, for instance, rewarding accomplishments in the areas of problem finding, problem solving, and know-how development. Success in developing the administrative aspects of the emerging venture organization should also be included, as well as effectiveness in managing the interfaces with the operating division.

At the operational level where some managerial failures are virtually unavoidable, top management should create a reasonably foolproof safety net. Product champions at this level should not have to feel that running the business is the only possible reward for getting it started. Systematic search for and screening of potential venture managers should make it easier to provide a successor for the product champion in time. Avenues for recycling product champions and venture managers should be developed and/or their reentry into the mainstream businesses facilitated.

Finally, more flexible systems for measuring and rewarding performance should accompany the greater flexibility in structuring the venture-corporate relations mentioned earlier. This would mean greater reliance on negotiation processes between the firm and its entrepreneurial actors. In general, the higher the degree of relatedness (the more dependent the new venture is on the firm's resources) and the lower the expected strategic importance for corporate development, the lower the rewards the internal entrepreneurs would be able to negotiate. As the venture evolves, milestone points could be agreed upon to revise the negotiations. To make such processes symmetrical (and more acceptable to the nonentrepreneurial participants in the organization), the internal entrepreneurs should be required to substitute negotiated for regular membership awards and benefits.[20]

Conclusion: No Panaceas

This article proposes that managers can make ICV strategy work better if they increase their capacity to conceptualize the managerial activities involved in ICV in process-model terms. This is because the process-model approach allows the managers involved to think through how their strategic situation relates to the strategic situation of managers at different levels who are simultaneously involved in the process. Understanding the interplay of these different strategic situations allows managers to see the relationships between problems that otherwise remain unanticipated and seemingly disparate. This may help them perform better as individual strategists while also enhancing the corporate strategy-making process.

Of course, by focusing on the embedded, nested problems and internal organizational dynamics of ICV strategy making, this article has not addressed other important problems. I believe, however, that the vicious circles, managerial dilemmas, indeterminateness of the strategic context, and perverse selective pressures of the structural context are problem areas that have received the least systematic attention.

The recommendations (based on this viewpoint) should result in a somewhat better use of the individual entrepreneurial resources of the corporation and, therefore, in an improvement of the corporate entrepreneurial capability. Yet, the implication is not that this process can or should become a planned one, or that the discontinuities associated with entrepreneurial activity can be avoided. ICV is likely to remain an uncomfortable process for the large complex organization. This is because ICV upsets carefully evolved routines and planning mechanisms, threatens the internal equilibrium of interests, and requires revising a firm's self-image. The success of radical innovations, however, is ultimately dependent on whether they can become institutionalized. This may pose the most important challenge for managers of large established firms in the eighties.

Appendix: A Field Study of ICV

A qualitative method was chosen as the best way to arrive at an encompassing view of the ICV process.

Research Setting

The research was carried out in one large, diversified, U.S.-based, high-technology firm, which I shall refer to as GAMMA. GAMMA had traditionally produced and sold various commodities in large volume, but it had also tried to diversify through the internal development of new products, processes, and systems in order to get closer to the final user or consumer and to catch a greater portion of the total value added in the chain from raw materials to end products. During the 1960s, diversification efforts were carried out within existing operating divisions, but in the early 1970s, the company established a separate new venture division (NVD).

Data Collection

Data were obtained on the functioning of the NVD. The charters of its various departments, the job descriptions of the major positions in the division, the reporting relationships and mechanisms of coordination, and the reward system were studied. Data were also obtained on the relationships between the NVD and the rest of the corporation. In particular, the collaboration between the corporate R&D department and divisional R&D groups was studied. Finally, data were also obtained on the role of the NVD in the implementation of the corporate strategy of unrelated diversification. These data describe the historical evolution of the structural context of ICV development at GAMMA before and during the research period.

The bulk of the data was collected by studying the six major ICV projects in progress at GAMMA at the time of the research. These ranged from a case where the business objectives were still being defined to one where the venture had reached a sales volume of $35 million.

In addition to the participants in the six ICV projects, I interviewed NVD administrators, people from several operating divisions, and one person from corporate management. A total of sixty-one people were interviewed. The interviews were unstructured and took from 1½ to 4½ hours. Tape recordings were not made, but the interviewer took notes in shorthand. The interviewer usually began with an open-ended invitation to discuss work-related activities and then directed the interview toward three major aspects of the ICV development process: the evolution over time of a project, the involvement of different functional groups in the development process, and the involvement of different hierarchical levels in the development process. Respondents were asked to link particular statements they made to statements of other respondents on the same issues or problems and to give examples where appropriate. After completing an interview, the interviewer made a typewritten copy of the conversation. About 435 legal-size pages of typewritten field notes resulted from these interviews.

The research also involved the study of documents. As it might be expected, the ICV project participants relied little on written procedures in their day-to-day working relationships with other participants. One key set of documents, however, were the corporate long-range plans concerning the NVD and each of the ICV projects. These official descriptions of the evolution of each project between 1973 and 1977 were compared with the interview data.

Finally, occasional behavioral observations were made when other people would call or stop by during an interview, for example, or in informal discussions during lunch at the research site. These observations, though not systematic, led to the formulation of new questions for further interviews.

Conceptualization

The field notes were used to write a case history for each of the venture projects that put together the data obtained from all participants on each of the three major aspects of venture development. The comparative analysis of the six ICV cases allowed the construction of a stages model that described the sequence of stages and their key activities. The process model resulted from combining the analysis at the project level with the data obtained at the corporate level.

12

Government Intervention and Innovation in Industry: A Policy Framework

William J. Abernathy

Balaji S. Chakravarthy

Government intervention in industrial activity has become more intense in the last decade. Unfortunately, the term *intervention* is often used in its narrower sense and equated with regulation. This article argues that there are at least two other dimensions to government intervention: technology-creation action and market-modification action. A framework relating combinations of the above actions to their joint consequences for technological innovation is developed, and its general applicability is then tested using other known examples of technological significance. *SMR*.

There is a mounting national concern over what is termed the "innovation recession" in the United States.[1] Elaborating on this concern, a White House statement contends that "In recent years, private-sector research and development has concentrated on low-risk, short-term projects directed at improving existing products. Emphasis on the longer-term research that could lead to new products and processes has decreased."[2] The Commerce Department has recently initiated a massive inquiry to spot existing government policies that may be to blame for this trend and new ones that may help reverse it.

The balance and intensity of government intervention in industrial activity have shifted decisively over the past decade.[3] This change in the nature of government action is of vital importance to technological progress and economic development in the United States, since government policy sets the context for industrial development.[4] Some contend that recent changes in the nature

From *Sloan Management Review*, Spring 1979, Vol. 20, No. 3. Reprinted with permission.

of government intervention have begun to retard our capability for technological innovation and productivity improvement. The problem is too complex, and the ramifications of recent changes are not sufficiently understood to support sweeping generalizations, but the implications are of such importance as to warrant careful inquiry.

One important form of intervention, federal investment in research and development (R&D), has declined in real dollar terms both relative to prior years and relative to the investment ratios of other major developed countries.[5] Even though the decline is rather modest, it is significant because of the role that federal R&D investments play in stimulating innovation in the U.S. economy.

Over the same time period regulatory intervention has increased dramatically. Traditionally, intervention in this form has arisen from public concern about the effectiveness of a free market in producing certain kinds of goods and services efficiently and equitably. The thrust of regulatory intervention now seems to have extended far beyond this narrow focus, however, to become a pervasive factor in broadly shaping industrial performance.

A comparative study of regulated industries provides a perspective on possible implications of this change in the mix of federal initiatives. The Brookings Institution examined technological change in four important regulated sectors: electric power, telecommunications, civil air transport, and surface transport.[6] The study concluded that

Regulation in railroad and truck transport almost certainly slowed and distorted the pace and pattern of technological change. . . . In contrast, the net impact of regulation on the pace and pattern of technological change in telephonic communication has probably been positive, or at worst neutral. The structure of the industry, completely dominated by a single firm (AT&T), that is both horizontally and (more significantly in this context) vertically integrated, is the most important factor in explaining this.[7]

In the case of electric utilities and civil aviation, the study concludes that the strong federal support for R&D has helped in sustaining a rapid pace of technological change. While the electric power industry had done almost no R&D, it had "relied on the equipment industry and other suppliers and on the federal government to support R&D."[8] In the case of civil aviation, "Major technical advances have usually come from efforts supported by the military to improve military aircraft capabilities."[9]

The findings of this study reinforce the notion that regulatory intervention plays a vital role in shaping technological progress, but one that defies simple generalizations. The efforts apparently depend on several conspicuous factors, such as the type of regulation and the industry's technology base and structure. Perhaps of equal if not greater interest, however, is the subtle interplay between federal intervention in the form of R&D investment and intervention in the form of regulation. These interrelationships suggest that it may be useful to view these two forms of intervention as interdependent rather than as separate policy instruments through which different national goals might be pursued.

At a time when the mix and intensity of federal intervention have shifted dramatically, there is a need to better understand the joint effects on technological progress. The purpose of this article is to explore this question in greater depth. A framework is developed and illustrated that shows promise in clarifying a few interactions with potential implications for policy formulation. Alternate intervention options that the government has for influencing innovation in industry can be explored using the proposed framework.

A Framework for Understanding Government Intervention

Options for government intervention can be grouped into three broad categories that seek to initiate change in one of two ways: by directly creating new technology, or by changing requirements so that new technology will be developed indirectly to meet these requirements.

Technology Push Actions

1. *Technology Creation Actions* involve the government directly in supporting the development of new technology or the modification of existing technology.

Technology Pull Actions

2. *Product Characteristic Interventions* shape product innovation either directly or indirectly through a variety of actions ranging from persuasion (jawboning) to regulating product standards.

3. *Market Modification Actions* induce innovation by market incentives through changes in price, the indirect effects of regulation in related industries, modifications in the market structure, or direct government purchases.

The second and third categories rely on designing market mechanisms or incentives to induce producers to create new products[10] or modify existing ones. We refer to such a process of induced change as "technology pull." R&D programs that seek to induce change through the creation of superior new technologies are designated as "technology push" initiatives.

Technology Creation Actions. The costs, timing, or payoff and implications of the outcome are distinctly unique for different types of technology-creation actions. At one extreme basic research is undertaken to support the creation of new knowledge. As Kenneth Arrow and Richard Nelson have concluded, the ultimate payoff to society from such work is very high relative to cost.[11] On the other hand, the payoff is uncertain and long in coming. A recent National Science Foundation study of ten highly beneficial innovations, including products like the Heart Pacemaker, Hybrid Corn, and Magnetic Ferrites, successfully traced the essential underlying research events.[12] The results show the vital contribution of such work, but they also highlight the long gestation period. On the 533 significant events (or breakthroughs) underlying the ten innovations, 72 percent were the fruits of research (dividing 34 percent for nonmission-related work and 38 percent for mission-related work), while only 26 percent arose from development. At the same time the period for innovation alone, from first product conception to commercial application, averaged over nineteen years, and half of the essential nonmission research events dated back thirty years prior to commercialization. These and other related studies show the enormous importance of basic research, but they also graphically point out the uncertainty as well as the difficulty in analytically justifying such investments and in relating the ultimate contribution of any given basic research project to a previously identified product objective.

The other extreme includes programs that involve direct government expenditures for the development or production of a product that will be placed into immediate use. The best example of this is in equipment or ordnance production for the Department of Defense or for NASA. Even for products destined to serve the private sector (like nuclear fuels or satellite communications), there are instances of direct "technology push" investment in "close-to-market" technology-creation activities.

The majority of federal expenditures in the technology-push category, however, fall between these two extremes. Demonstration programs, mission-oriented R&D programs leading to prototypes, etc., are the types of actions that are most frequently encountered in practice.

Figure 12.1 lists six different types of technology-creation actions, arranged in an order that suggests differences in their characteristics. Six different types of actions from research for criteria and needs definition to direct production are described along the left-hand side of the figure. The rank order of each action is intended to roughly suggest the increasing extent to which the characteristics of the final product are determined by the specified type of R&D program. Stated another way, the order concerns how far the action takes the product concept toward "reduction to practice."

Basic research is shown as the most removed from product application,

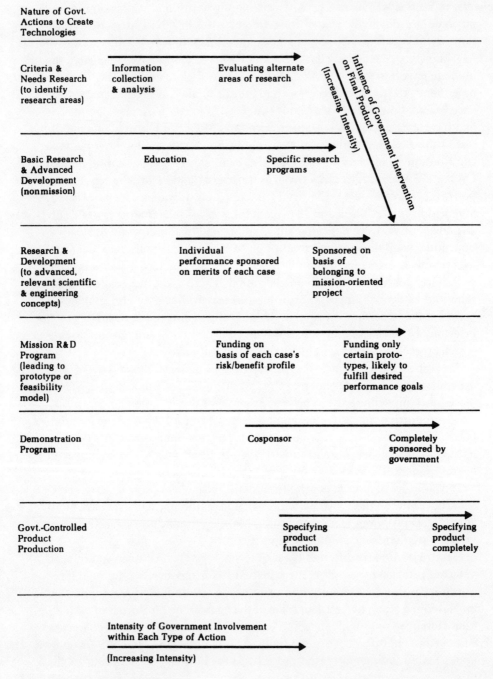

Nature of Govt.
Actions to Create
Technologies

Criteria &
Needs Research
(to identify
research areas)

Information
collection
& analysis

Evaluating alternate
areas of research

Influence of Government Intervention
on Final Product
(Increasing Intensity)

Basic Research
& Advanced
Development
(non mission)

Education

Specific research
programs

Research &
Development
(to advanced,
relevant scientific
& engineering
concepts)

Individual
performance sponsored
on merits of each case

Sponsored on
basis of
belonging to
mission-oriented
project

Mission R&D
Program
(leading to
prototype or
feasibility
model)

Funding on
basis of each case's
risk/benefit profile

Funding only
certain proto-
types, likely to
fulfill desired
performance goals

Demonstration
Program

Cosponsor

Completely
sponsored by
government

Govt.-Controlled
Product
Production

Specifying
product
function

Specifying
product
completely

Intensity of Government Involvement
within Each Type of Action

(Increasing Intensity)

Figure 12.1 Technology Creation Actions

226

while production or control over production obviously takes the concept closest to practice. The scale going across the figure, on the other hand, shows the increasing intensity of government involvement within a specific type of R&D program. For example, a demonstration program with a minor percentage of government funding or control may still not greatly influence the product, since the outcome will be shaped significantly by normal economic and market incentives. On the other hand, a demonstration program that is completely funded by the government, as depicted by the right-hand extreme on the scale, represents a high degree of government control over the new product.

The criteria for rank ordering each possible government action and the intensity scale within each activity are obviously closely related. The stepped arrows in Figure 12.1 illustrate this relationship. For different types of government action along a left-to-right downward sloping diagonal (down the vertical scale and toward the right on the horizontal scale), there is increasing governmental influence in shaping the final product.

Other changes will also typically accompany the movement down the diagonal. When the action's influence on the product becomes more immediate and visible, the cost per program also grows significantly. In a sense moving down the diagonal from the upper left to the lower right of Figure 12.1 involves increasing government support for immediate technological change.

Product Characteristic Interventions. The array of possible government regulatory actions (Figure 12.2) ranges from relatively weak persuasion to the fine detail of controlling the specific technology of a product through regulation. While the latter is potentially the most powerful option for immediately influencing product technology, its long-run effects on technological progress are still controversial.

Rubenstein and Ettlie's recent study of thirty-two innovations by automotive suppliers shows that federal laws or regulations affected innovation at the detailed component level, both as the most important barrier and as the most important stimulant of change.[13] They acted as a barrier in 47 percent of the cases and as a stimulant in 44 percent (multiple response possible). If this pattern is generalizable now when regulations are recent, there may be reason to question what their effect may be if standards are not constantly updated. A plethora of specific standards might well impair future technological progress in industry.

As in Figure 12.1, the movement along the diagonal represents increasing government control over changes in product characteristics.

Market Modification Actions. The several government actions that may be used to influence or direct technological change through market incentives are sug-

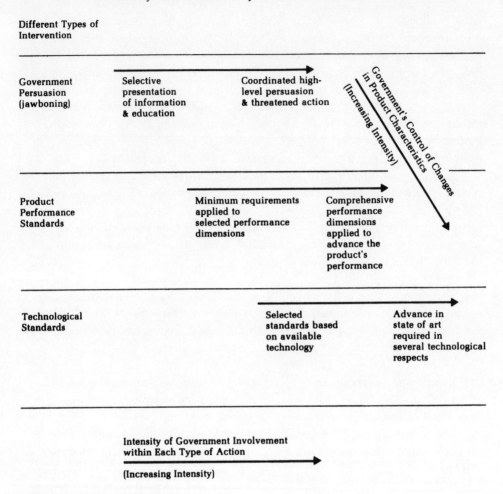

Figure 12.2   Product Intervention

gested in Figure 12.3. As with the prior category, this figure is arranged so that the diagonal suggests increasing direct government influence over the final product.

Rigorous enforcement of restraint-of-trade legislation (shown as the first type of action in the upper left-hand corner of Figure 12.3) is expected to bring about product change through increased competition. It is shown to offer the least control, because this form of action would not normally provide a mechanism for use by the government to shape the form of the technological outcome. A more competitive industry structure would place more control in the hands of traditional market mechanisms. On the other hand, actions that

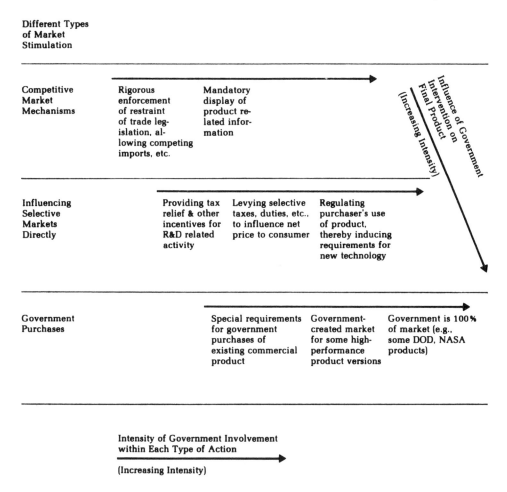

Different Types
of Market
Stimulation

Figure 12.3   Market Modification

encourage more competition in selected areas may increase the degree of government control. Procedures that establish selective information bases for use by the market (for example, publishing miles-per-gallon ratings for cars) may create incentives that can shape technologies in intended directions.

Clearly the greatest potential for market modification is realized when the government itself represents 100 percent of the market. In their study of Department of Defense influences on innovation in the electronics industry, Utterback and Murray describe the important role of procurement as follows: "Defense demands have strongly focused and have tended to be the pacing element of change in the industry as a whole."[14] Their findings suggest that the government's purchases of high-performance products supported innovation and contributed significantly to the initial leading-edge entry of highly significant products such as jet aircraft, computers, advanced semiconductors, and even polyethylene film.

The Building Blocks for a Conceptual Framework

Three types of federal initiatives that can provide impetus for technological change have been described above, each represented by the diagonal in one of the three figures. Taken collectively, these three forces may be used as dimensions in a conceptual scheme that can be applied to explore the effects of federal actions in influencing technological change. Though ideally the influence of all three forces should be considered, some major interactions are revealed when we reduce them to two, which is more practical for further representation on a two-dimensional scale. Technology-creation action represents the federal government's direct participation in R&D. However, market-modification and product-intervention actions both require that firms perform the R&D in response to government action—a technology pull response. We group the three types of federal initiatives into two categories:

1. Direct technology push actions (DTP), comprising technology creation action;
2. Indirect technology pull action (ITP), comprising both market-modification action and product-characteristic interventions.

The roles of both DTP and ITP categories are more apparent when their implications are considered in an industrial context. The impetus for change within a particular industry can be described aggregately for a particular product in terms of the two dimensions discussed above, the degree of direct technology push (DTP) and indirect technology pull (ITP). The more urgent the national goal and the longer the time span of normal industry response, then the greater the political pressure for increased intensity of federal action. The intensity of action relevant to a given product is illustrated in Figure 12.4.

Development of the Framework Using Past Federal Projects

Judgments may vary widely about the effect of the two different categories of government action. Some objectivity about this can be gained by applying the present framework to recast results from a set of prior federal projects whose circumstances are documented and whose outcomes have already been evaluated. The RAND Corporation's recent study of federally funded demonstration projects provides a useful source of data for such a purpose.[15]

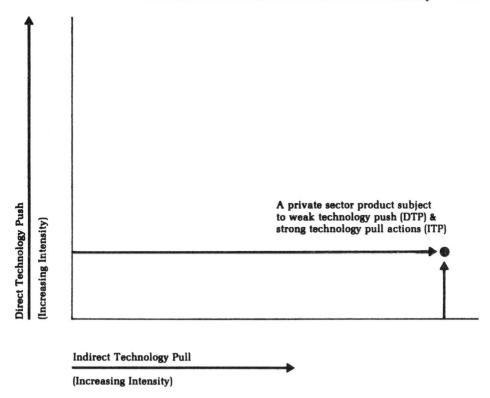

Figure 12.4   Illustration of Technology Push and Pull Through Government Action

A rather distinct pattern of interaction is apparent between the two major categories of government action when the characteristics and outcomes of ten prior federal demonstration projects from this study are viewed from the perspective of Figure 12.4. The ten projects that were selected are listed in Table 12.1.

The projects were selected to represent a range of predemonstration technological uncertainty, defined as the " . . . uncertainty about the feasibility of a technology for a particular use."[16] The demonstration projects were by and large successful in reducing technological uncertainty in all of the ten cases. In fact, RAND assessed their application success to be moderate to high. Whereas application success—which "measures the extent to which the local adopters are satisfied with the reliability of the system and quality of goods or services"—was pleasing, the diffusion success of the projects varied (see Table 12.2).[17] Diffusion success measures "the extent to which the technology has consequently passed into general use."[18] This is the measure of success

Table 12.1   Ten Select Demonstration Projects*

Title	Identifying Abbreviation	Approximate Cost to Federal Agencies ($ Million)	Predemonstration Technological Uncertainty
1. Nuclear Ship *Savannah*	SAVANA	100	High
2. Morgantown, WV's Personal Rapid Transit	P.R.T.	61	Medium to High
3. Haddonfield, NJ's Dial-A-Ride	D.A.R.	10	High
4. Commercial Maritime Satellite	MARSAT	8.2	Medium
5. Yankee Nuclear Power Reactor	YANK NR	8.3	Medium
6. St. Louis's Refuse Firing Demonstration	RFSE F	2.6	Medium
7. Point Loma Saline Water Conversion Plant	SALT WP	2.3	Medium
8. Scottsdale, AZ's Mechanized Refuse Collection	RFSE C	0.18	Low
9. Poultry Waste Processing	PLTRY WP	0.2	Low
10. Chicago's Expressway Surveillance and Control	XPRS SC	5.7	Low

*The Appendix provides a brief description of the projects.

meaningful from a policy standpoint. We shall attempt to explain the discrepancy between application success and diffusion success using the framework developed earlier.

From judgments based on project histories and their analyses as reported by RAND, each project can be generally positioned along the two major dimensions of government action described in Figure 12.4. Figure 12.5 illustrates graphically the pattern that results when the projects are cast in such a framework. It must be emphasized that Figure 12.5 is judgmental, since neither the data nor the definition of the scales is sufficiently precise to support analytic treatment. Despite this imprecision, the positioning of projects within the four quadrants supports a few interesting if speculative propositions.

With reference to Figure 12.5, it is important to note that first, it was suggested earlier in this article that participating in a demonstration program per se constitutes a moderate intensity of government involvement in direct technology push (see Figure 12.1); consequently even those demonstration projects that received low impetus from the federal government must be represented as projects of medium direct technology push. And second, no project in our sample really had a high intensity of indirect technology pull, though four of them that had moderate ITP have been classified as such. The positioning of projects in Figure 12.5 attempts to recognize the above qualifications.

Table 12.2   A Contrast of Application Success and Diffusion Success

Project	Technological Uncertainty		Application Success	Diffusion Success
	Pre	Post		
1. SAVANA	High	Medium	High	Little or None
2. P.R.T.	High	Medium	Medium	Little or None
3. D.A.R.—Manual	Medium	Low	High	Little or None
D.A.R.—Computer	High	Medium	Low	Little or None
4. MARSAT	Medium	Low	Moderate	Some
5. YANK NR	Medium	Low	High	Significant
6. RFSE F	Medium	Low	High	Significant
7. SALT WP	Medium	Low	Medium	Significant
8. RFSE C	Low	Low	High	Some
9. PLTRY WP	Low	Low	High	Significant
10. XPRS SC	Low	Low	High	Significant

The Interaction of Federal Initiatives

A definite pattern of interaction between the two categories of government action is apparent in Figure 12.5. Considering the top half alone, representing projects with stronger technology push, the presence or absence of corresponding technology pull actions would seem to be critical.

Failure is the predominant outcome in the upper left cell, where there is intense direct technology push action, but no corresponding technology pull action. This cell includes the Nuclear Ship *Savannah,* Dial-a-Ride, and Personal Rapid Transit. These projects uniformly represent situations where there were few or no changes in market incentives to encourage and support the adoption of a new technology. On the other hand, for the upper right cell (high/high), the government actually supported the market for many of these projects through procurement, creating a strong modification action whether intended as such or not. The Commercial Maritime Satellite was supported through the Navy's purchases of navigational satellite services, and the Point Loma Saline Water Conversion Plant was actually acquired by the Department of Defense for use at a Navy base during the demonstration project.

The successful Yankee Nuclear Power Reactor appears to be the one exception to the pattern that is otherwise so apparent in the upper cells. Actually even in this case, from a historical perspective, the same generalization also

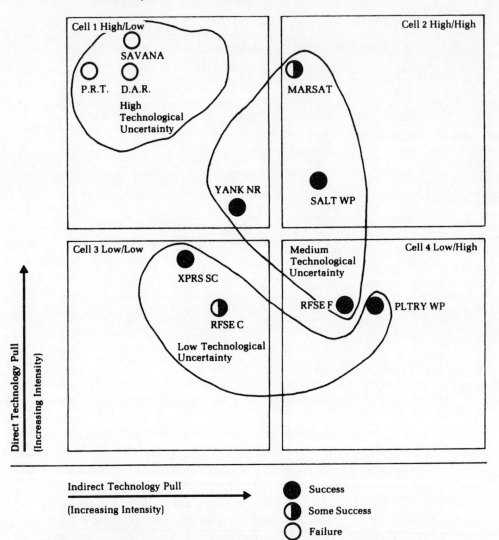

Figure 12.5   Project Success and Failure Pattern (Degree of Technology Push/Technology Pull)

applies. Although the market for nuclear-generated electric power had not been altered through government intervention at the time of this project, the market for nuclear products in general had indeed been created earlier through purchases by the Atomic Energy Commission and the Department of Defense. As in the other cases, the government modified or created the initial market through purchases for its own use. Beyond the issue of success or failure, a second distinctive characteristic of the two upper cells is that they are populated by radical products. If successful, they led to major innovations. These projects suggested major changes in practice within the industry where they were to apply. In doing so, new organizations were stimulated to enter the field. The demonstration projects here may be characterized as big gambles to introduce major changes.

The two lower cells represent situations where the government has been less venturesome in a technology-push sense. The ratio of success appears much higher. From the case data it would seem, however, that the innovations that result are much more incremental than for the upper cells.

Cell four, representing low-intensity technology push but strong technology pull (low/high), includes two projects. The Poultry Waste Processing and the Refuse Firing Demonstration projects both represent successful attempts to solve waste-disposal problems under conditions of tightening environmental controls and concerns. The regulatory action by the federal government forced regulatees to collaborate with research organizations in exploring innovative ways of waste disposal. The impetus was not toward a major new technology but more toward an incremental development of available technologies. Since the demonstration projects addressed the concerns of many such regulated organizations, it is not surprising that diffusion success was significant once the application success of the projects was demonstrated.

Cell three (low/low in Figure 12.5) has two projects: the Chicago Expressway Surveillance and Control System and Scottsdale's Mechanized Refuse Collection. The two projects were not sponsored in response to either a regulatory threat or an indirect market inducement. They had very low indirect technology pull and received low direct technology push as well from the federal government. Their diffusion success is attributable to the favorable benefit/cost information that the projects provided. There were other projects in the RAND study that would have fallen into this quadrant, but that had poor diffusion success despite high application success because of their adverse benefit/cost ratio. Here the role of the federal government seems to be to provide some technology-creation help and to let the economics of the experiment determine diffusion of the innovation in a natural fashion. The government merely acts as a catalyst to encourage the normal process of innovation. Diffusion success is not guaranteed. In fact, the Scottsdale project, despite its great application success and favorable benefit/cost characteristic, was only a moderate diffusion success. The innovation's diffusion suffered because of the inadequate industrial infrastructure to successfully refine and adapt the innovation to the needs of other cities.

Table 12.3   Interaction of Federal Actions

| | | Indirect Federal Technology Pull | |
		LOW	HIGH
		1	2
Direct Federal Technology Push	HIGH	Extreme Risk (High Failure Rate)	Radical Innovation (High Risk/High Payoff When Successful)
		3	4
	LOW	Normal Process of Industrial Innovation—Enabled (Low Risk and Varying Success)	Incremental Innovation— Accelerated (Low Risk and Moderate Success)

The Framework Generalized

The joint effects of direct government technology push and indirect technology pull, as discussed above, are illustrated by the two-by-two matrix in Table 12.3. Each cell is summarized in turn.

1. Intense Technology Push/Weak Technology Pull

The troublesome failure-to-success pattern that is so apparent in the high/low cell is not just an artifact of the particular sample of cases that has been used to illustrate the present framework. Earlier experiences with other programs, like the Eisenhower Administration's Atomic Aircraft program, the Breeder Reactor, or the Supersonic Transport, are suggestive of the present pattern. This does not imply that all federal programs that undertake a technology-based initiative are failures. From a broad perspective the space program might be characterized as a federal action of this type, and on a different level so might TVA and the original Atomic Energy Program. The outcome of these programs has certainly been important, but even so, successful industrial diffusion has come very slowly. The programs where technology push alone has been successful seem to have involved funding levels measured in fractions of the Gross National Product.

On balance it seems appropriate to characterize normal projects within this category as extremely risky. This does not mean they should all be shunned.

The benefits to society may greatly outweigh the cost even when adjusted for risk.

2. High Technology Push/High Technology Pull

This cell is perhaps the most interesting. Beyond the present sample this category represents the environment of origin for many major innovations that have strengthened the U.S. economy in the post-World War II era. For such products as the computer, the jet engine, and advanced semiconductor devices, as well as the present cases, the federal government has been a major factor in the innovation process through its joint initiatives in market modification and direct investments in technology.[19] In particular, within the market-modification category, government procurement seems to have been critically important in creating a market for advanced technologies at a time early in their life cycles when prices were very high vis-à-vis competitive technologies, and the range of applications was limited. Such support during a technology's infancy stage helps to nurture evolutionary development to the point that broad-based commercial applications are economically justified.

Government action within this category was apparently a factor in major innovations not only in the 1950s and 1960s, but it also seems to have influenced many less well-known innovations in the distant past as well as in the present. In his classic study of the radio industry, McLaurin reports that government support was critical in the early development of that industry at the turn of the century.[20]

Today we find evidence of innovative stimulation through the combination of government investment in technology and procurement even in a relatively mature industry like motor vehicles. A particular example of this is the FMC Corporation's New Choker Arch High Speed Logger, which has recently increased productivity in commercial logging operations. This equipment is claimed to operate at twice the speed of conventional tracked loggers through the use of a torsion-bar suspension system that was originally developed by FMC for the U.S. Army's MII3 Armored Personal Carrier. Data concerning this innovation suggest that both military and commercial customers have benefited from technology transfers within the divisions of FMC. A factor that seems to be important to innovation and successful technology transfer in this case is that the firm that undertook government R&D for the Department of Defense also had the capability to serve industrial markets.

3. Weak Technology Push/Weak Technology Pull

The effect of federal initiatives in the third cell would seem to enable the normal process of industrial innovation in industrial environments where it is otherwise retarded. In terms of government policy goals, this may be an important achievement. In some industries, notably segments of electronics or high-technology segments of the medical-equipment industry, existing competitive conditions already induce a high rate of innovation. In other industries that are highly fragmented or technologically stagnant, such stimulus may be needed to encourage innovation. In such cases, intense regulatory or market-modification actions would probably not have a favorable effect. It is encouraging to note that moderate policies in these cases acted to stimulate innovation.

4. Weak Technology Push/Strong Technology Pull

The effect of federal initiatives that induce strong technology pull relative to technology push would seem to be an acceleration of technological change, but through incremental innovation. The emphasis in this mode is on perfecting and refining established technologies rather than innovating with new ones.

The innovations in this cell that were analyzed earlier acted to perfect and refine approaches and equipment that had already been introduced. This pattern of response would seem to be more pervasive than might be suggested by just the few cases that have been considered. Solutions required by safety, water, and air pollution regulations have frequently been sought by capital-equipment manufacturers through add-on components, minor adaptions, and incremental changes. The effect is most pronounced in mass-production industries where the cost of change is very high.[21]

Recent shifts toward performance regulation as in the case of the auto or drug industries show a governmental bias toward steady evolutionary progress. Jacoby and Steinbruner argue that this intense pressure for constant progress can cause entrenchment in established technologies, since undertaking new approaches involves high risks.[22] As a case in point, the Ford Motor Company recently announced its withdrawal from major R&D effort on the Stirling engine, which some federal energy officials think could become an alternative to the current internal-combustion engine. Instead, Ford announced the stepping up of its development of a more conventional stratified-charge internal combustion engine to try to meet the short-term fuel economy targets set by the government.

Conclusions

The matrix presented in Table 12.3 constitutes a framework that focuses attention on the joint effect on innovation of two major categories of federal intervention. The framework is by no means precise, since scales and measurements for assessing various government actions are needed. Furthermore, product-characteristic intervention actions of the government need to be separated out from market-modification actions in order to better appreciate the scope for technology pull. Nevertheless, the patterns revealed by the framework provide useful guidelines for shaping federal intervention policy for stimulating innovation.

A predominantly technology push orientation is likely to be a failure. It is useful to reassess in this context the potential benefits of the basic research institutes that the government is proposing to organize for various industries. Such an action will yield poor results unless the technology-creation action of the government is intensified by giving it more of a mission orientation, complemented by appropriate technology-pull actions.

Conversely, a predominantly technology pull orientation is likely to induce a rapid, successful, but incremental innovation in industry. Entrenchment in existing technologies is a distinct possibility. There need be no presumption that radical change is better; only the intervention options for the federal government are different depending on whether it seeks a steady evolutionary progress or long-range radical progress in the technologies of the various industries.

Appendix—Case Study Descriptions[23]

Nuclear Ship Savannah

The *Savannah,* the world's first civilian nuclear-powered ship, was authorized in 1956 as a key aspect of President Eisenhower's Atoms for Peace program. The project was managed jointly by the Atomic Energy Commission and the Maritime Administration. The *Savannah* was intended to demonstrate the peaceful application of nuclear power and the technical and economic feasibility of a nuclear-powered merchant ship. Operating from 1962 until 1970, it fulfilled its Atoms for Peace mission well, but was not successful as a commercial prototype.

Personal Rapid Transit System

Personal Rapid Transit (PRT) is a system of public transport using a large number of remotely controlled small cars on an extensive grid of automated guideways. According to the PRT concept, an individual can obtain a vehicle on demand at a nearby station that will take him very close to his ultimate destination. In 1970 the Urban Mass Transit Administration of the Department of Transportation supported a demonstration of the PRT concept for connecting three campuses of West Virginia University in Morgantown, West Virginia. Under severe time constraints, the Morgantown designers were forced to compromise from their original PRT proposal. The system now comprises vehicles capable of carrying twenty people over 3.3 miles of track connecting three stations. The system was formally dedicated in 1972 and began carrying students in October, 1975.

Dial-a-Ride Transportation System

The Dial-a-Ride concept involves the use of small buses to provide door-to-door public transport service in response to individual telephone requests. In 1971 the Urban Mass Transportation Administration of the Department of Transportation sponsored a demonstration of Dial-a-Ride in Haddonfield, New Jersey, a suburb of Philadelphia. The project demonstrated two technologies for vehicle routing and control—one manual, the other computer-based. The manually controlled system attracted substantial ridership, although large operating subsidies were required. The system ceased operations in 1975. Reliable operation of the computer-based system was not achieved until near the very end of the demonstration.

Maritime Satellite Program

Since 1970 the Maritime Administration has sponsored a multiphase program to demonstrate the use of communication satellites for ship-to-ship and ship-to-shore communications. The first three phases of the program through 1975 used NASA experimental satellites; Phase IV beginning in 1976 operates with the MARISAT satellite developed expressly for maritime users. Commercial adoption of maritime satellite communications is proceeding in parallel with Phase IV.

Yankee Nuclear Power Reactor

The Yankee reactor was one of the first civilian nuclear-power reactors built under the Power Demonstration Reactor Program announced by the Atomic Energy Commission (AEC) in 1955. The project involved construction of a pressurized light-water reactor on a scale larger than any other power reactor then supported by the AEC. Yankee was owned and managed by the Yankee Atomic Electric Company, a consortium of ten private electric utilities in the Northeast. It first produced power for the New England grid in November, 1960, and continues in operation today.

Refuse Firing Demonstration (Solid-Waste-to-Fuel Conversion Plant)

The Refuse Firing Demonstration (RFD) is one of several projects supported by the Environmental Protection Agency to demonstrate the recovery of energy, metals, and other materials from municipal refuse. The RFD process involves dry shredding of municipal refuse into small particles, and separation of the lighter particles for burning in a modified coal boiler. Beginning in 1970, the process was demonstrated by the City of St. Louis, in conjunction with the Horner-Shifrin Engineering Company and Union Electric Power Company. As a result, Union Electric has announced plans to build a solid-waste fuel and resource-recovery system for the entire metropolitan region, and the RFD concept is rapidly spreading to other cities.

Saline Water Conversion Plant, Point Loma, California

Another of the desalination demonstrations sponsored by the Office of Saline Water tested the multistage flash (MSF) distillation process in Point Loma, California. In this process, sea water is heated and introduced into a succession of reduced pressure chambers where some of the water boils off into steam. The steam is then condensed into fresh water. The Point Loma plant began operations in 1962 and demonstrated the technical feasibility of the MSF process for salt-water conversion at a rate greater than one million gallons per day. After two years of operation in California, the plant was dismantled and shipped to Guantanamo Naval Base in Cuba to supply the base with fresh water after the Cuban government cut off normal supplies. It remains in operation today.

Mechanized Refuse Collection (Godzilla)

The City of Scottsdale, Arizona, received a federal grant in 1969 to develop and demonstrate a new mechanized system for collecting refuse. Conventional garbage trucks were modified by adding a hydraulic arm that could pick up, dump, and return a refuse container automatically without requiring anyone to leave the truck. The first of these modified trucks was affectionately known as "Godzilla." By the end of the demonstration in 1972, a family of mechanized vehicles had been put into service. The service subsequently has been extended to cover the entire city, and other cities are adopting similar systems.

Poultry Waste Processing

Under its program to improve waste-water management, the Federal Water Pollution Control Administration (now part of the Environmental Protection Agency) supported a demonstration to reduce water usage and improve waste treatment in a large poultry-processing plant in North Carolina. The project ran from 1969 to 1971 and demonstrated a number of improvements in equipment and procedures for water use and treatment. These new processes have subsequently spread throughout the poultry-processing industry.

Expressway Surveillance and Control

Since 1961 the Federal Highway Administration (now part of the Department of Transportation) has supported a development and demonstration project in the Chicago metropolitan area to improve traffic flow on expressways by controlling ramp access. The system includes auto detectors installed in the pavement at entrance ramps and along expressways to continuously monitor traffic operations. Data from the roadway detectors are transmitted to a central computer, which then controls traffic signals at each ramp. The project is currently in operation, and metered ramp control is being adopted by other cities.

13

Managing Innovation: Lessons from the Cardiac-Pacing Industry

David H. Gobeli

William Rudelius

In this article, the authors argue that innovation is a surefire way for a firm to increase its sales and market share. This, in turn, can stimulate American industries and make American firms more competitive in international markets. Through their study of the cardiac-pacing industry, they draw conclusions about what factors contribute to a successful innovation in other industries besides medical electronics. They identify general patterns and stages of the innovation process, key roles top management must fill in an organization, and effective policies that foster important innovations. *SMR.*

Reports of the death of American innovation have been greatly exaggerated. In particular, the cardiac-pacing industry is an example of American innovation that has become the world's standard of excellence. In fact, newspapers have reported that both Western and Eastern bloc leaders Helmut Schmidt and Yuri Andropov wear American-designed heart pacemakers.

Still, as measured by the loss of the U.S. share of many world markets, a lack of innovation in American business poses problems for the nation, entire industries, and individual firms. Both common sense and research studies show that innovation can lead to increased sales and market share for a firm. This, in turn, can stimulate an industry and make American firms more competitive in international markets.[1] The pacing industry illustrates how this can happen.

A testimonial to innovativeness in the pacing industry is that in early 1984 the National Society of Professional Engineers cited the implantable heart

From *Sloan Management Review*, Summer 1985, Vol. 26, No. 4. Reprinted with permission.

pacemaker as one of the ten outstanding engineering achivements of the last fifty years, putting it in the same league with the electronic computer and the Apollo 11 moon landing. Through our study of five major cardiac-pacing firms, Intermedics, Cordis, Cardiac Pacemakers (CPI), Medtronic, and General Electric (GE), we are able to draw conclusions about what contributes to successful innovations in other high-technology industries. The pacing industry is also suited for studying innovation because the limited number of firms in the industry makes it possible to identify in detail the successes and failures of a particular firm. Successful innovations can then be related to subsequent impacts on the firm and its market share.

Stages of the Innovation Process

Fundamentally, an innovation is *something new* to an organization, an industry, or a market. A successful, competitive innovation within an industry, such as the pacing industry, is something new that contributes to the innovating firm's competitive position. Growth in market share is one way to enhance a firm's competitive position. To provide such an advantage, each stage of the innovation process must be properly managed.

A simple but useful model of the innovation process includes three stages: discovery, decision, and development.[2] *Discovery,* the first stage, involves creating a new business concept either inside or outside of the firm. This stage is completed when someone within the organization champions the idea until it is formally recognized by management. The second stage, *decision,* involves analysis and a formal review of the idea and is completed when management makes a formal decision to provide funding. Then the third stage, *development,* begins. It covers the final design, production, and marketing of the new concept.

Discovery

Figure 13.1 shows how executives in the five firms rated their firms' performances at each stage of the innovation process. All firms except General Electric rated the discovery stage high. Performance at this stage is measured by the quantity and quality of ideas available in the firm. Because these two vari-

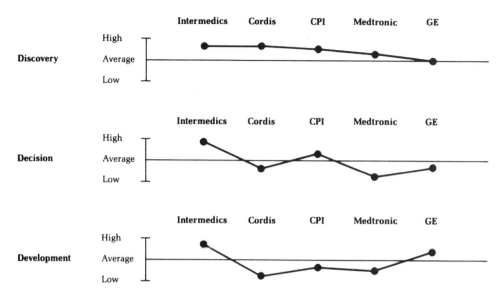

Figure 13.1   Ratings by Executives of Their Firms' Performances at Each Stage of the Innovation Process

ables are highly correlated, they are averaged in Figure 13.1. Those interviewed from GE felt that rumors about selling the pacing operation decreased the quantity and quality of new ideas.

Decision

In the decision stage, executives were asked to evaluate the timeliness and quality (also averaged in Figure 13.1) of their firms' decisions on new concepts. The executives at Intermedics and CPI, the smaller firms, felt they made quick and appropriate strategic decisions. Indeed, the executives at these two companies said the decision stage averaged less than three months. In contrast, the executives at the larger companies often required a year or more to make similar key decisions, and they did not believe that they made as many prudent strategic choices. The conservatism of the larger firms seemed to hamper innovation at the decision stage.

Development

At the development stage, timeliness and quality (again averaged in Figure 13.1) were rated as at least marginal by all firms except Cordis. Although

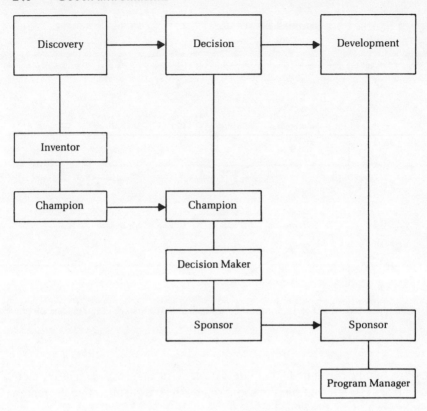

Figure 13.2   Key Roles for Innovation

Cordis has improved dramatically in recent years, in 1981 it was plagued with product advisories and production problems. Intermedics, on the other hand, was quick to develop new concepts with few problems, thereby showing great flexibility in adjusting to continual innovations.

These performance profiles for each stage of the innovation process show how firms can vary from stage to stage. Effective performance at each stage is essential to bring about successful, competitive innovations. Within each stage of the innovation process, key roles and policies account for the differences in performance. The key roles that must be filled are shown in Figure 13.2. These roles are arranged according to the stage of the innovation process.[3] Unfortunately, a product advisory can also change a firm's relative market position. Here the U.S. Food and Drug Administration requires that companies make an announcement to confirm a suspected defect in a cardiac-pacing device.

Innovation: Roles, Policies, and Issues

Roles

Discovery requires an inventor. It also requires a champion to bring the concept to the point of formal review by management. Decision requires qualified people filling the roles of decision makers and sponsors who will stand up within top management and assume responsibility for the new-venture decision. The champion must continue to muscle the idea through the management hierarchy during the decision stage. Finally, in development, a program manager implements the concept. The sponsor is especially critical at this stage to ensure continuing support from the organization.

Policies

Filling key roles is not enough to foster innovation. Important as people are, management must also provide an environment conducive to innovation. The policies that create this environment are crucial, and management must have control over each one of them. However, the nature of the policies may vary with the stage of the innovation process. Management cannot just use rules of thumb for each policy area, but must tailor the policies to match each stage of the innovation process.

Issues

The three stages of the innovation process, coupled with the roles and policies for each stage, form an innovation-process matrix (see Figure 13.3). This matrix forms the structure to analyze the key issues in the innovation process. The two kinds of innovation issues that this matrix suggests are:

1. What roles should executives in an organization take during each of the three stages to facilitate innovation? In particular, what should be the role of top management, and how does one person's performing multiple roles assist innovation?
2. What policies should the firm use in each of the three stages to facilitate innovation? In particular, what are the most salient policies at each stage?

These issues are actually problems that must be resolved in order for a successful innovation to occur. Only then can a firm, an industry, or the nation enhance and maintain its market position. In discussing the lithium pacemaker, we will illustrate the stages, roles, and policies of the innovation process and begin to address the issues of innovation.

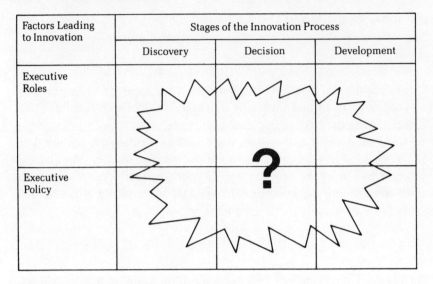

Factors Leading to Innovation	Stages of the Innovation Process		
	Discovery	Decision	Development
Executive Roles			
Executive Policy		?	

Figure 13.3   Innovation Process Matrix

A Major Innovation: The Lithium Pacemaker

The lithium battery is an advanced technology that replaced the older mercury-zinc technology. This innovation, which more than doubles the life of a pacemaker implanted in a patient, means that less frequent operations have to be performed on the patient to replace the pacemaker. Lithium-powered pacemakers are also more reliable and allow for better packaging of the entire pacemaker. All but a few of the executives interviewed agreed that this is the most significant innovation developed over the last decade, and that it accounts for the majority of the shifts in market share among pacemaker manufacturers. Figure 13.4 shows other innovations that had varying degrees of impact on the relative market shares of the five firms.

Five Cardiac-Pacing Firms

Cardiac Pacemakers

Although the new lithium-battery technology was developed by an independent entrepreneur, it was made available to anyone. However, none of the existing firms were interested in this unproven technology as they preferred to stay with the old one. Nevertheless, several former Medtronic employees saw the opportunity and seized upon it: they formed Cardiac Pacemakers (CPI) and, together with the inventor of the new battery, developed the new pacemaker.

The first president of CPI revealed in the interview that he got enjoyment out of "doing the things people say cannot be done." The existing firms were saying lithium-powered pacemakers were too risky, but CPI bet against the odds. Discovery began with an independent entrepreneur and former engineering associate of Medtronic who developed the lithium battery for pacemakers. The CPI founders trusted this person enough to leave their jobs at Medtronic. No formal marketing research was conducted: Only informal discussions with potential customers took place. As the founders really knew the customers through extensive past interactions, they could see matching a new technology with some identified consumer needs.

The basic decision to start CPI and develop the lithium pacemaker was made by the new president, investors, and the management team, with the president playing the key leadership role through the decision stage. Subsequent innovations at CPI utilized more formal group decision making, eventually allowing for a vote to complete a decision. As is the case with most innovations, formal studies played no significant role with the lithium pacemaker. Generally, early innovation decisions at CPI took only a few months before development began. But the decision makers were well qualified to do their own analyses; they were all experienced in the business and had successfully started other businesses.

Development took place quickly: It took CPI only one year from the time it sought capital until its first pacemaker was implanted. During that same period, other pacing companies were having trouble simply upgrading their products for each new model year. CPI was effective at development, because the entire company was essentially a cohesive venture team. The team had to be cohesive, since the original lithium pacemaker could not sell itself: The executives were the key salespeople who had to overcome buyer resistance. Consumers would ask, "If it's so great, why doesn't Medtronic have it?"

CPI soon became an industry force. It continued to innovate as the company grew, becoming so attractive that Eli Lilly bought it in 1978. Soon after, however, CPI's performance began to suffer. Figure 13.4 shows that product problems and decreasing innovative performance led to the erosion of CPI's market share over the last several years. Related to this decline were the exodus of key personnel, including several entrepreneurial executives who pursued other new ventures, and an R&D budget that did not match that of other industry leaders. Part of the erosion may also have been due to a rebirth of Medtronic's innovative thrust.

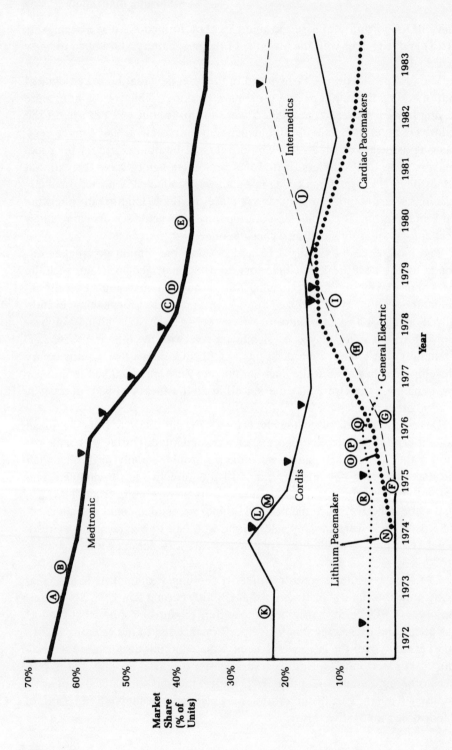

Cardiac Pacemakers

Medtronic

Medtronic, the reigning industry leader, followed a classic decline in market position. As Figure 13.4 shows, Medtronic, which once had nearly 70 percent of the market, dropped to about 40 percent. Although Medtronic produced several innovations during the decade, it lost its foothold because of growing competition, a series of product problems, and such missed key innovation opportunities as the lithium pacemaker. Thus, its competitors achieved their market-share successes by being first with something new and by avoiding serious technical problems in the form of product advisories. Yet, Medtronic has shown relative stability in the early 1980s. The "40 percent and beginning to fight" pattern is common for industry leaders in a maturing market, as Buzzell and Wiersema found using the PIMS database.[4]

Cordis

Formerly number two—and now trying to regain this position after Intermedics' inroads—Cordis illustrates the good and bad of the innovation process. In 1973, Cordis introduced the first effective, remotely programmable pacemaker. Several points of market share were quickly won. But subsequent product problems and disagreements over good manufacturing practices with the Food and Drug Administration canceled the gains. For the next several years, Cordis struggled to improve its development process, which the executives admitted was their weak stage in the innovation process. The result was a

---

Figure 13.4 (left) U.S. Market Shares of Five Major Cardiac Pacemaker Producers

Key:
○ = Innovation
▼ = Product Advisory
A = Isotope-powered Pacemaker
B = Satellite Assembly Plants
C = Lithium-powered Pacemaker
D = Lifetime Warranty on Pacemaker
E = Small, Programmable Pacemaker
F = CMOS Technology Pacemaker
G = Small, Lithium-powered Pacemaker
H = Color Ads in Medical Journals

I = Programmable Pacemaker with Telemetry
J = Dual-chamber Pacemaker
K = First Programmable Pacemaker
L = Improved Electrode (ball tip)
M = Improved Electrode (porous tip)
N = First Lithium-powered Pacemaker
O = Small, Lithium-powered Pacemaker
P = Programmable, Lithium-powered Pacemaker
Q = Price Based on Longevity of Pacemaker
R = Advanced Mercury-Zinc-powered Pacemaker

Sources:
R.B. Emmitt, *Pacemakers: Industry and Company Prospects* (New York: F. Eberstadt & Co., March 1978); J. France, *Cardiac Pacemaker Industry: A Basic Study* (Minneapolis: Smith Barney, Harris Upham & Co., April 1983); L.A. Sanders and K.S. Abramowitz, *Cardiac Pacing Industry* New York: Sanford C. Berstein & Co., August 1978); A.H. Snider, *Medical Devices Industry* (Minneapolis: Kidder, Peabody & Co., January 1981).

late entry with the lithium pacemaker. However, a change in management led to improved development performance, as shown by its increasing market share in 1982. Now new concepts can be implemented successfully at Cordis.

General Electric

In spite of a decreasing commitment to pacing products, General Electric introduced a pacemaker with an improved mercury-zinc battery in 1975. The pacemaker division was profitable until 1976. As shown in Figure 13.4, the company gained a few points of market share and probably would have gained even more had CPI not introduced the lithium pacemaker, which outperformed even GE's advanced mercury-zinc technology. Then in 1976, product problems began to tarnish GE's overall corporate image, especially after Paul Harvey delivered a radio commentary on problems with GE's cardiac-pacing products. According to the former General Electric managers interviewed, this unfavorable publicity reduced sales not only of GE's pacing products but also of its other consumer products like light bulbs and appliances. These factors, coupled with a poor showing of pacing products in GE's corporate portfolio analysis, led to the divestiture of its pacing department in 1977.

Intermedics

Starting up in late 1974 with a very small pacemaker that utilized the then new CMOS (complementary metal-oxide-semiconductor) electronics technology, Intermedics was more successful than the founding president expected it to be. Led by a former Medtronic salesman, Intermedics, in fact, was a dramatic success. For most of the decade, the company continued to innovate and was quick to adopt the lithium battery after CPI introduced it to the market. Occasional product problems were overshadowed with more innovations. Nonetheless, the pace was hectic; growth pains finally caught up with Intermedics about 1982 when its market share leveled off, perhaps because of its multiple forays into unrelated product lines.

Perhaps the problem with Intermedics was its overeagerness to innovate, not only in developing new pacing products but in trying to start up and innovate within other product lines. As a result of inadequate resources, Intermedics has recently begun to divest some of its ventures in an effort to stem corporate losses. Here is a case where pursuing too many innovations at once led to failure. Keeping this in mind, the following advice should be heeded: As innovation requires resources, management should focus on a few good prospects.[5]

The market-share performance of these pacing companies shows the possible impact of innovations in a competitive industry. Although the initial gains in market share are sometimes offset by product problems and insufficient resources, industry innovation, as suggested by the cardiac-pacing industry, is necessary for a firm just to maintain its market share (see Figure 13.4).

Required Key Roles for Innovation

The innovation process will never succeed unless the proper people fill the key roles at each stage (see Figure 13.2 and Table 13.1). Discovery requires an inventor and a champion to bring the new concept to management's attention. Appropriate strategic decisions must then be made at the decision stage by qualified decision makers and sponsors within top management. The champion must remain active at this stage. Finally, at the development stage, a program manager and sponsor must work together to bring about the successful implementation of an innovation.

It is not clearly recognized that multiple roles can be filled by the same person or people. For example, in a start-up company, the founding entrepreneur can conceivably fill all the roles. In contrast, in a large, bureaucratic organization, the hierarchy may fill many of the roles—that is, multiple people in the chain of command may be involved in each stage of the innovation process. For the eighteen innovations in Table 13.1, one person typically filled the roles of inventor and champion and sometimes also served as the program manager. Only three innovations depended upon an outside inventor. This multiplicity of roles provides continuity during the program and should be encouraged.

Role of Top Management

The level of management involvement with innovative activities is strongly related to the innovativeness of the firm. For example, the circled inventors in Table 13.1 show that top management (presidents and vice-presidents) typically becomes involved with significant innovations—those that are medium or high in novelty or market-share impact, or both. The most innovative eras of Cordis, CPI, and Intermedics enjoyed top-management participation in the innovation process. Conversely, as each company began to lose its competitive vigor, the innovation process was delegated to a lower level of management.

The lesson for top management is clear: if you want significant innovation to occur in your company, get involved! Conservative professional management will not do the job. Entrepreneurship is required. At the very least, top management must champion and sponsor ideas. But even more critically, top

Table 13.1 People and Roles Required for Innovation

Innovation	Firm	Novelty	Market-Share Impact	Inventor	Champion	Decision Maker	Sponsor	Program Manager
							Person Filling Innovation Roles	
Isotope-powered Pacemaker	Medtronic	High	Low	O	(P)	(P)	(P)	S
Satellite Assembly Plants	Medtronic	Med	Low	(VP)	(VP)	H	H	M
Lithium-powered Pacemaker	Medtronic	Low	Low	S	S	H	H	S
Lifetime Warranty on Pacemaker	Medtronic	Med	Low	S	S	H	(P)	S
Small, Programmable Pacemaker	Medtronic	Low	Med	(P)	S	H	H	M
CMOS Technology Pacemaker	Intermedics	High	High	(P)	(P)	(P)	(P)	(P)
Small, Lithium-powered Pacemaker	Intermedics	Low	Med	(P)	(P)	(P)	(P)	(P)
Color Ads in Medical Journals	Intermedics	High	Med	(VP)	(VP)	(VP)	(VP)	S
Programmable Pacemaker with Telemetry	Intermedics	High	High	(P)	(P)	(P)	(P)	M
Dual-chamber Pacemaker	Intermedics	Med	High	(VP)	(VP)	(VP)	(VP)	M
First Programmable Pacemaker	Cordis	High	High	(P)	(P)	(P)	(P)	(VP)
Improved Electrode (ball tip)	Cordis	Med	Low	S	S	(P)	(P)	S
Improved Electrode (porous tip)	Cordis	Med	Low	O	S	(VP)	(VP)	S
First Lithium-powered Pacemaker	CPI	High	High	O	(P)	(P)	(P)	(VP)
Small, Lithium-powered Pacemaker	CPI	Low	Med	S	S	H	(VP)	S
Programmable, Lithium-powered Pacemaker	CPI	Med	Med	(VP)	(VP)	H	H	S
Price Based on Longevity of Pacemaker	CPI	Low	Low	H	H⁻	H	H	H
Advanced Mercury–Zinc-powered Pacemaker	GE	Low	Low	S	M	H	H	M

Key:
O = Outside
P = President
VP = Vice President
S = Specialist
H = Hierarchy
M = Manager
◯ = Top Level Management Involvement (president or vice president)

254

management, in the role of decision makers, must be willing to assume the risk of bad results in order to generate important successes. These three roles—champion, decision maker, and sponsor—can provide continuity and solid executive leadership throughout the innovation process.

The alternative, of course, is for top management to simply wait to hear what others come up with, evaluate the ideas with a conservative portfolio analysis (also conducted by someone else), delegate program leadership, and maintain minimal involvement in the innovation process. The end result, however, would very likely be minimal innovation.

Policies Observed in the Five Firms

A firm's key policy should be to have innovation as a stated organizational goal, often in the form of a market-share target. Several other policies should complement the clear goals to innovate. For example, marketing research, effective comunication between R&D and marketing, formal planning, appropriate risk levels in decision making, actual emphasis on quality R&D activities, and the form of program management are especially important policy areas that the executive seeking innovation must address.

1. Innovation as an Organizational Goal

The policies the executives of each firm employ help to explain the firms' innovations and resulting market performances. Most fundamental of these policies is whether a goal exists to innovate or not to innovate. The executives at CPI and Intermedics, for example, expressed a strong desire to gain market share, and they recognized that innovation was one way to do this. CPI had a goal to gain 10 percent of the market. Asked if there was a goal to gain market share, an executive at Intermedics summed up his firm's policy by saying "absolutely and overwhelmingly yes." In contrast, executives at Medtronic recalled a formally stated goal to gain market share toward the end of the decade, but they admitted that the goal was not taken very seriously. The policy was more defensive than offensive.

Without clear offensive goals that foster innovation, a defensive posture occurs by default. Moreover, the goals to innovate must be reinforced in each stage of the innovation process. In discovery, these goals can be reinforced by listening to new ideas and by keeping in touch with the creative people in the organization. During the decision stage, a "fair and speedy trial" of the concept will show people that the company is not dragging its feet.

If a champion must move the hierarchical corporate mountain to have an impact, the goals to innovate will be perceived as little more than corporate rhetoric. At the development stage, lack of support in the form of resources and choice of key people to fill the innovation roles is a signal to prospective program managers that management is only half-committed; therefore, they should not risk their own careers on the project.

2. Use of Marketing Research

Of the thirty-nine executives interviewed, only two executives—both at Intermedics—could cite exemples where marketing research actually led to new ideas. Almost 80 percent rated marketing research as marginal in the discovery of new ideas. The research approach that did pay off, however, was having company executives talk to customers. Two lessons can be learned from this: First, marketing research, as typically practiced, is not a source of new product concepts; second, having executives talk regularly with customers is![6]

In the decision stage, executives gave mixed reviews in rating the effectiveness of marketing research. Overall, its value appears to be borderline. The exception is Intermedics, where all the executives rated it as definitely effective. In the development stage, marketing research seems to play a consistently useful role in final concept definition and market testing. In short, the closer the concept is to commercial reality, the more effective marketing research becomes.

3. R&D and Marketing Communications

An in-depth study of those companies that introduced the most significant innovations reveals a picture of regular, effective discussions between R&D and marketing. In the early years of Intermedics and CPI, cohesive, yet confrontative, management teams and few levels of management enhanced communication. In contrast, marketing and R&D at Cordis and Medtronic were disjointed, until the late 1970s, to the point where they even had separate physical locations several miles apart. Indeed, part of the poor evaluation of marketing research within these firms may be due to the unwillingness of other corporate departments to review marketing-research results and take them seriously. Enhanced communication between R&D and marketing can improve results at each stage of the innovation process. But while it is important to encourage the sharing of ideas between these two departments, it is also important, at the discovery stage particularly, to maintain independent hot lines, as ideas are just as likely to occur in one area as the other.

At the decision stage also, the points of view of both marketing and R&D

are essential to formulate a solid business concept. Similarly, an effective development stage requires a synergistic combination of marketing and R&D perspectives that balances customer needs and technical feasibility.

4. Use of Formal Planning

As with marketing research, formal planning becomes more effective as the new concept approaches actual commercialization. Although all the firms had a formal planning process, only 30 percent of the executives rated it definitely effective or marginally effective. About 70 percent rated it ineffective for discovery of new concepts. In decision making, the formal planning process was rated definitely ineffective by 24 percent of the respondents. It was rated marginally effective by 33 percent of them, and definitely effective by 43 percent. The value of formal planning increases to the point of being considered essential at the development stage.

This dramatic increase in effectiveness of formal planning, as a new concept marches through the three stages, is a reflection of the degree of formality appropriate at each stage of the innovation process. Except for General Electric, the majority of executives in each company said that formal studies were not involved in the discovery of new product concepts. However, formal studies take on increasing value in the decision stage and even further value during the development stage. The innovation process requires a different level of formal planning in each stage.

5. Level of Risk at the Decision-Making Stage

Innovation is risky; therefore, to avoid short-run risks, avoid innovation. Figure 13.5 shows how executives rated their own firms on the following: (1) willingness to take risks during the decision stage; and (2) R&D capability at the development stage. The ratings were also consistent with how each competitor viewed the risk-taking level and R&D capability of the other firms. Intermedics and Cordis followed high-risk policies, while Medtronic and General Electric were conservative. CPI was at an intermediate point because, although it was founded under high-risk conditions, it became more conservative over time.

The risk-level policy influences decision making at the development stage. Unfortunately, there is little room for risky decisions in development. The abundance of product advisories, indicated by the triangles in Figure 13.4, shows the results of taking excessive risks in development. Once a new concept is approved for development, effective R&D is essential, since risk can be reduced through technical competence and quality products.

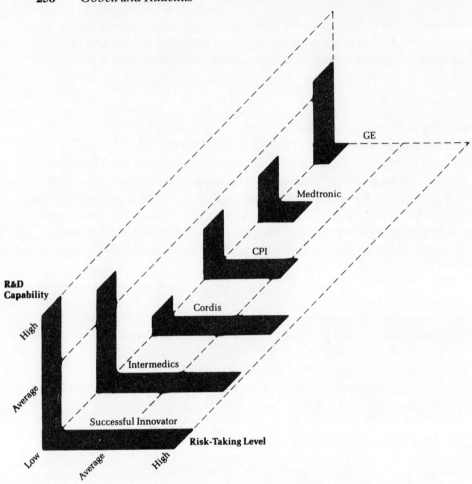

Figure 13.5 1981 Executive Ratings of Their Firms on Decision-Stage, Risk-Taking Level, and Development-Stage R&D Capability

6. R&D Capability at the Development Stage

Although they may appear to conflict, quality R&D must complement a willingness to take high risks. Figure 13.5 shows how the firms rated their own R&D capability. Intermedics felt it had a powerful combination of high-risk decisions and high-quality R&D. This is the profile of a successful innovator. On the other hand, Cordis showed, until recently, the profile of an unsuccessful innovator. Although Cordis was well respected for its eagerness to pursue new concepts, it was also well known for its inability to implement good ones.

Management and organization changes, however, have brought Cordis back to the posture of a successful innovator by improving its R&D capability.

Along with less willingness to take risks, CPI has shown a lower capability for development in the last several years. It has been a waning innovator, on the road to becoming a follower. Still, being second or third to introduce a new product technology can be effective, if the following can compensate with a quick and effective development process. Medtronic and General Electric both show the profile of a *strong* follower. These companies combined conservative decision making with solid development capability. They also had the resources for more aggressive production and marketing strategies to complete the strong follower profile. Yet, even though this profile is often equated with "excellence" and is frequently seen in American management, it does not foster significant innovation; rather, it depends upon others to lead the way and assume the risk of being first.

7. Form of Program Management

A policy that follows from capable R&D is the form of program management an organization chooses by design or default. One extreme is a functional organization with a coordinator who integrates activities across functions. This is appropriate only in a small company, such as Intermedics or CPI at their startup. Here the president or a vice-president personally serves as the program manager and the whole company is, in effect, a venture team focusing on a few key concepts.

The other extreme, appropriate in a larger organization, is a parallel organization composed of the existing formal organization and a venture team.[7] This allows the organization to pursue more routine activities and not interfere with the new program team. IBM used this approach with its personal computer program.[8] In effect, this parallel organization approach approximates the start-up company without attempting the hopeless task of reforming the entire organization.

Matrix management is the compromise. Most executives interviewed were generally disgusted with this form of management. Both CPI and Medtronic tried and abandoned it. Medtronic abandoned it when it fostered a problematic product, the Xytron pacemaker, which led to several product advisories. The confusion and lack of clear leadership led to great stress and turnover among program members. The entire company seemed to share the anxiety that resulted from an inappropriate application of matrix management.

Although matrix management has its place, it should not be used when pursuing significant innovations.[9] Its primary place is in product improvement or for multiple, similar product programs where resources must and can be effectively shared. Innovation requires the most effective project management possible; this requirement leaves little room for a compromise as difficult to implement as matrix management. If resources are so limited that key functional people are required to perform multiple roles, the company should consider dropping programs so a few key projects can be given priority and undivided attention. Innovation requires total commitment from the most qualified people in the organization: It is not an add-on task.

Conclusion: Lessons To Be Learned

The cardiac-pacing industry offers lessons and guidelines that apply to all high-technology industries where state-of-the-art breakthroughs must be discovered and converted quickly into marketable products. It is clear that the roles and policies change through the discovery, decision, and development phases of innovation. Organizations must recognize these changing roles and use this knowledge in placing people in key positions and establishing policies. Table 13.2 summarizes the roles and policies needed in each stage of the innovation process.

Good People in Key Roles

In order for effective innovation to occur, good people in key roles are essential. Ideally, top management should fill some of the key roles. Also, whenever possible, one person should fill multiple roles to provide continuity in the innovation process. Sometimes the CEO in a small firm can assume multiple roles such as creator, product champion, and actual program manager. And the more of these roles he or she is able to fill, the better the project integration is and the faster decisions are made. But when organizational size precludes the CEO championing the innovation throughout the innovation process, the CEO must, nonetheless, show continuing interest and support for important projects. This is necessary even though responsibility can be delegated to the inventor, a vice-president, or program manager who has clear personal ownership in the success of the innovation. Furthermore, key people who perform must continue on the program as it grows because of the personal loyalty, experience, and skills brought to the project.

Innovation involves great risk because of the potential cost of failure. But not innovating is even more dangerous. Innovation also involves great change to the jobs of people throughout an organization. So real innovation requires a strong, committed leader who is actively involved and highly visible in the innovation process. In the pacing industry, several breakthrough innovations

Table 13.2 Key Innovation Lessons

Factors Leading to Innovation	Nature of Lesson	Stage of the Innovation Process		
		Discovery	Decision	Development
Executive Roles	Inventor	Find new concepts by talking to customer		
	Champion	Promote major innovations	Continue promotion	
	Decision Maker		Assume responsibility for new concept choice	
	Sponsor		Be a visible advocate of the concept	Shepherd the program through development
	Program Manager			Major innovations require top executive involvement
Executive Policy	Goal Setting	Goals to innovate must be communicated	Goals must be reinforced through timely decisions	Goals must be supported with adequate resources
	R&D/Marketing Communication	Require communication between two units	Insist that two units prepare joint proposals	Both must be solidly represented on the venture team
	Use of Marketing Research (MR)	Do not depend on normal MR techniques	MR will tend not to support innovation	MR is useful for testing and refining concepts
	Use of Formal Planning (FP)	FP is of little value in finding new concepts	Excessive FP can paralyze decisions	Good FP is essential
	Level of Risk-Taking		Some risk is unavoidable	Risk can be reduced with limited exposure
	R&D Capability			Capable R&D is required for innovation
	Form of Program Management			Use a venture team; avoid matrix management

were both created and championed by the CEO—often at great organizational and career risk. Organizational "sacred cows" are antithetical to innovation, so the environment requires an open, confrontative interaction between all contributors—a hard-to-achieve goal.

Effective Policies

Policies impact innovation, and there are some policy lessons to be learned from the cardiac-pacing industry. Goals to innovate must be clear, supported by top management, and understood by those involved in the innovation process. While the focus shifts from concepts to marketing as the innovation process moves from discovery to decision to development, the goals to innovate need support at each stage. Communication between R&D and marketing departments—true combatants in many technical firms—must be encouraged and, if necessary, forced. The value of both marketing research and formal planning becomes greater in the two later phases of innovation: Both activities have minor significance at the discovery stage.

The organizational environment must foster a flexible, can-do attitude among people responsible for innovation. There must also be a sense of urgency similar to the one present in the Lockheed "Skunk Works" that produced the U-2 and SR-71 aircraft designs, or Seymour Cray's supercomputer lab in remote Chippewa Falls, Wisconsin, that designed the Cray-1.[10] Such an environment promotes a willingness of top management to take high risks at the discovery and decision stages of innovation and to reduce these risks through excellent R&D at the development stage.

Structurally, once a concept has survived the discovery stage, a venture team should be formed to bring it through the decision and development stages. But top management alone must have the courage not only to champion ideas with great potential but also to shut down projects when their chances of success seem remote—a decision that is devastating to committed project team members.

Venture team membership from both R&D and marketing departments helps. Both IBM's personal computer and Apple's MacIntosh were developed by venture teams. The 3M Company sometimes encourages this communication by physically locating marketing personnel in R&D labs, a technique that helps informal as well as formal communication. And 3M also tries to have R&D people call on customers.[11]

All of the cardiac-pacing firms have managed part or all of the innovation process successfully at various times, and their shifting market-share performances indicate when each was most successful. This is a remarkably innovative industry. The smaller firms, such as Intermedics and CPI, closely approximated venture teams in the early part of the decade and were, as might be expected, especially innovative. However, the restraints of the larger organization (e.g., at GE), seem to inhibit the innovation process. Medtronic is working to overcome size and stimulate its effectiveness in the discovery and decision stages. Cordis has recently improved the development stage and is now introducing more new, successful products. CPI is working to improve its development stage to become more competitive. Each firm has the potential to be a successful innovator if it considers all the roles and policies required in each stage of the innovation process.

Innovation is essential if American firms are to compete and succeed in today's global markets. Experiences of American cardiac-pacing firms provide lessons about the roles and policies needed as innovation moves through the discovery, decision, and development stages. Firms in other American industries can tailor these management lessons from the cardiac-pacing industry to achieve more innovative organizations.

Notes and References

Introduction

W. J. Abernathy and B. S. Chakravarthy, "Government Intervention and Innovation in Industry: A Policy Framework", *Sloan Management Review*, Spring 1979.

T. J. Allen, "Performance of Information Channels in the Transfer of Technology," *Industrial Management Review*, Fall 1966.

T. J. Allen, *Managing the Flow of Technology* (Cambridge: MIT Press, 1977).

T. J. Allen, J. M. Utterback, M. S. Sirbu, N. A. Ashford, and J. H. Hollomon, "Government Influence on the Process of Innovation in Europe and Japan," *Research Policy*, April 1978.

F. M. Andrews, "Innovation in R&D Organizations: Some Relevant Concepts and Empirical Results," in E. B. Roberts et al., eds., *Biomedical Innovation* (Cambridge: MIT Press, 1981).

M. R. Baker and W. H. Pound, "Project Selection: Where We Stand," *IEEE Transactions on Engineering Management*, vol. EM-11, no. 4, December 1964.

R. A. Burgelman, "Managing the Internal Corporate Venturing Process," *Sloan Management Review*, Winter 1984.

W. M. Capron, ed., *Technological Change in Regulated Industries* (Washington, DC: The Brookings Institution, 1971).

H. Cohen, S. Keller, and D. Streeter, "The Transfer of Technology from Research to Development," *Research Management*, May 1979.

K. G. Cooper. "Naval Ship Production: A Claim Settled and a Framework Built," *Interfaces*, December 1980.

A. C. Cooper and D. Schendel, "Strategic Responses to Technological Threats," *Business Horizons*, February 1976.

C. M. Crawford, "Defining the Charter for Product Innovation," *Sloan Management Review*, Fall 1980.

G. F. Farris, "The Technological Supervisor: Beyond the Peter Principle," *Technology Review*, 1973.

N. D. Fast, "The Future of Industrial New Venture Departments," *Industrial Marketing Management*, 1979.

J. Friar and M. Horwitch, "The Emergence of Technology Strategy: A New Dimension of Strategic Management," *Technology in Society*, Winter 1985/1986.

G. F. Frontini and P. R. Richardson, "Design and Demonstration: The Key to Industrial Innovation," *Sloan Management Review*, Summer 1984.

A. R. Fusfeld, "How To Put Technology into Corporate Planning," *Technology Review*, May 1978.

A. R. Fusfeld and F. C. Spital, "Technology Forecasting and Planning in the Corporate Environment: Survey and Comment," in B. V. Dean and J. L. Goldhar, eds., *Management of Research and Innovation*. TIMS Studies in the Management Sciences, vol. 15 (North-Holland Publishing Co., 1980).

A. Gerstenfeld, "A Study of Successful Projects, Unsuccessful Projects, and Projects in Process in West Germany," *IEEE Transactions on Engineering Management*, vol. EM–23, no. 3, 1976.

A. Gerstenfeld and L. H. Wortzel, "Strategies for Innovation in Developing Countries," *Sloan Management Review*, vol. 19 (1977), no. 1.

D. H. Gobeli and W. Rudelius, "Managing Innovation: Lessons from the Cardiac-Pacing Industry," *Sloan Management Review,* Summer 1985.

O. Hauptman and E. B. Roberts, "The Impact of Regulatory Constraints on Formation and Growth of Biomedical and Pharmaceutical start-ups," MIT Sloan School of Management Working Paper No. 1651–85, May 1985.

T. Hirota, "Environment and Technology Strategy of Japanese Companies," MIT Sloan School of Management Working Paper No. 1671–85, June 1985.

M. Horwitch and C. K. Prahalad, "Managing Technological Innovation—Three Ideal Modes," *Sloan Management Review,* Winter 1976.

S. B. Johnson, "Comparing R&D Strategies of Japanese and U.S. Firms," *Sloan Management Review,* Spring 1984.

R. Katz, "Managing Careers: The Influence of Job and Group Longevities," in R. Katz, ed., *Career Issues in Human Resource Management* (Englewood Cliffs, NJ: Prentice-Hall, 1982).

R. Katz and T. J. Allen, "Investigating the Not Invented Here (NIH) Syndrome: A Look at the Performance, Tenure, and Communication Patterns of 50 R&D Project Groups," *R&D Management,* vol. 12 (1982), no. 1.

R. Katz and T. J. Allen, "Project Performance and the Locus of Influence in the R&D matrix," *Academy of Management Journal,* vol. 26, 1985.

T. S. Kuhn, *The Structure of Scientific Revolutions* (Chicago: University of Chicago Press, 1963).

J. Langrish, M. Gibbons, W. G. Evans, and F. R. Jevons, *Wealth from Knowledge* (London: Macmillan, 1972).

P. R. Lawrence and J. W. Lorsch, *Organization and Environments* (Boston: Harvard Business School, 1967).

M. A. Maidique, "Entrepreneurs, Champions, and Technological Innovation," *Sloan Management Review,* Winter 1980.

M. A. Maidique and R. H. Hayes, "The Art of High-Technology Management," *Sloan Management Review,* Winter 1984.

D. G. Marquis and I. M. Rubin, "Management Factors in Project Performance," MIT Sloan School of Management Working Paper, 1966.

D. G. Marquis and D. L. Straight, "Organizational Factors in Project Performance," MIT Sloan School of Management Working Paper No. 133–65, 1965.

J. P. Martino, *Technological Forecasting for Decision Making.* (New York: Elsevier, 1972).

J. A. Morton, *Organizing for Innovation* (New York: McGraw-Hill, 1971).

S. Myers and D. G. Marquis, *Successful Industrial Innovation* (Washington, DC: National Science Foundation, 1969).

T. O'Rourke, Presentation at Pugh-Roberts Associates, Inc., Workshop on Critical Issues in Technology Management, April 15, 1986.

D. Pelz and F. M. Andrews, *Scientists in Organizations,* rev. ed. (Ann Arbor, MI: University of Michigan Press, 1976).

D. Peters and E. B. Roberts, "Unutilized Ideas in University Laboratories," *Academy of Management Journal,* vol. 12 (June 1969), no. 2.

T. J. Peters and R. H. Waterman, *In Search of Excellence* (New York: Harper & Row, 1982).

M. E. Porter, *Competitive Advantage: Creating and Sustaining Superior Performance* (New York: Free Press, 1985).

J. B. Quinn, "Technological Innovation, Entrepreneurship, and Strategy," *Sloan Management Review,* Spring 1979.

E. B. Roberts, *The Dynamics of Research and Development* (New York: Harper & Row, 1964).

E. B. Roberts, "Entrepreneurship and Technology: A Basic Study of Innovators," *Research Management,* July 1968.

E. B. Roberts, "Exploratory and Normative Technological Forecasting: A Critical Appraisal," *Technological Forecasting,* Fall 1969.

E. B. Roberts, "Research and Development System Dynamics," in E. B. Roberts, ed. *Managerial Applications of System Dynamics* (Cambridge: MIT Press, 1978).

E. B. Roberts, "Stimulating Technological Innovation: Organizational Approaches," *Research Management,* November 1979.

E. B. Roberts, "New Ventures for Corporate Growth," *Harvard Business Review,* July-August 1980.

E. B. Roberts, "Strategic Management of Technology," in *Global Technological Change: Symposium Proceedings* (Cambridge: MIT Industrial Liaison Program, June 1983).

E. B. Roberts and C. A. Berry, "Entering New Businesses: Selecting Strategies for Success," *Sloan Management Review,* Spring 1985.

E. B. Roberts and A. Frohman, "Internal Entrepreneurship: Strategy for Growth," *The Business Quarterly,* Spring 1972.

E. B. Roberts and A. Frohman, "Strategies for Improving Research Utilization," *Technology Review,* March/April 1978.

E. B. Roberts and A. R. Fusfeld, "Staffing the Innovative Technology-Based Organization," *Sloan Management Review,* Spring 1981.

E. B. Roberts and D. Peters, "Commercial Innovation from University Faculty," *Research Policy,* April 1981.

R. Rothwell, C. Freeman, A. Horlsey, V. T. P. Jervis, A. B. Robertson, and J. Townsend, "SAPPHO Updated–Project SAPPHO Phase II," *Research Policy,* 1974.

J. J. Smith, J. E. McKeon, K. L. Hoy, R. L. Boysen, L. Shechter, and E. B. Roberts, "Lessons from 10 Case Studies in Innovation," *Research Management,* September-October 1984.

W. E. Souder, "Effectiveness of Product Development Methods," *Industrial Marketing Management,* 1978.

H. J. Thamhain and D. L. Wilemon, "Leadership, Conflict, and Program Management Effectiveness," *Sloan Management Review,* Fall 1977.

G. L. Urban, Presentation at MIT Summer Session Program on the Management of Research, Development, and Technology-Based Innovation, June 18, 1986.

G. L. Urban and J. R. Hauser, *Design and Marketing of New Products* (Englewood Cliffs, NJ: Prentice-Hall, 1980).

J. M. Utterback, "Innovation and the Diffusion of Technology," *Science,* February 15, 1974.

J. M. Utterback, "Systems of Innovation: Macro/Micro," in W. N. Smith and C. F. Larson, eds., *Innovation and U.S. Research* (Washington, DC: American Chemical Society, 1980).

J. M. Utterback and W. J. Abernathy, "A Dynamic Model of Product and Process Innovation," *Omega,* vol. 3 (1975), no. 6.

J. M. Utterback and L. Kim, "Invasion of a Stable Business by Radical Innovation," in P. R. Kleindorfer, ed., *The Management of Productivity and Technology in Manufacturing* (New York: Plenum Press, 1986).

J. M. Utterback and A. E. Murray, "The Influence of Defense Procurement and Sponsorship of Research and Development on the Development of the Civilian Electronics Industry," MIT Center for Policy Analysis Working Paper CPA-77-2, June 1977.

E. A. von Hippel, "Has a Customer Already Developed Your Next Product?" *Sloan Management Review,* Winter 1977.

E. A. von Hippel, "Lead users: A Source of Novel Product Concepts," *Management Science,* July 1986.

H. B. Weil, T. A. Bergan, and E. B. Roberts, "The Dynamics of R&D Strategy," in E. B. Roberts, ed., *Managerial Applications of System Dynamics* (Cambridge: MIT Press, 1978).

Chapter 1

This article is an abbreviated version of the authors' chapter, "Critical Functions: Needed Roles in the Innovation Process," which will appear in *Career Issues in Human Resource Management,* R. Katz, ed. (Englewood Cliffs, NJ: Prentice-Hall, forthcoming).

1. For a different and more intensive quantitative view of project life cycles, see E. B. Roberts, *The Dynamics of Research and Development* (New York: Harper & Row, 1964).
2. See E. von Hippel, "Users as Innovators," *Technology Review,* January 1978, pp. 30–39.
3. For issues that need to be highlighted in a competitive technical review, see A. R. Fusfeld, "How to Put Technology into Corporate Planning," *Technology Review,* 80.
4. For further perspectives on project transfer, see E. B. Roberts, "Stimulating Technological Innovation: Organizational Approaches," *Research Management,* November 1979, pp. 26–30.
5. See D. C. Pelz and F. M. Andrews, *Scientists in Organizations* (New York: John Wiley, 1966).
6. E. B. Roberts, "Entrepreneurship and Technology," *Research Management,* July 1968, pp. 249–266.
7. D. G. Marquis and I. M. Rubin, "Management Factors in Project Performance" (Cambridge, MA: MIT Sloan School of Management, Working Paper, 1966).
8. T. J. Allen, *Managing the Flow of Technology* (Cambridge, MA: The MIT Press, 1977); and R. G. Rhoades et al., "A Correlation of R&D Laboratory Performance with Critical Functions Analysis," *R&D Management,* October 1978, pp. 13–17. Our empirical studies have pointed out three different types of gatekeepers: (1) technical—relates well to the advancing world of science and technology; (2) marketing—senses and communicates information relating to customers, competitors, and environmental and regulatory changes affecting the marketplace; and (3) manufacturing—bridges the technical work with the special needs and conditions of the production organization. See Rhoades et al. (October 1978).
9. Roberts (July 1968): 252.
10. One role we have observed frequently is the "quality controller" who stresses high work standards in projects. Other critical roles relate more to organizational growth than to innovation, e.g., the "effective trainer" who could absorb new engineers productively into the company was seen as critical to one firm that was growing 30 percent per year.
11. One study that demonstrated this phenomenon is N. R. Baker et al., "The Effects of Perceived Needs and Means on the Generation of Ideas for Industrial Research and Development Projects," *IEEE Transactions on Engineering Management,* EM–14, 1967, pp. 156–165.
12. Section VI describes a methodology for collecting these data.
13. See Allen (1977).
14. See Roberts (July 1968).
15. See E. B. Roberts and D. H. Peters, "Commercial Innovations from University Faculty," *Research Policy,* in press.
16. One study showed that engineers who eventually became managers of large projects began supervisory experiences within an average of 4.5 years after receiving their B.S. degrees. See I. M. Rubin and W. Seelig, "Experience as a Factor in the Selection and Performance of Project Managers," *IEEE Transactions on Engineering Management,* EM–14, September 1967, pp. 131–135.
17. For further perspectives on the consequences of this short-run view by U.S. managers, see R. H. Hayes and W. J. Abernathy, "Managing Our Way to Economic Decline," *Harvard Business Review,* July–August 1980, pp. 67–77.
18. For a variety of industrial approaches to the dual ladder, see the special July 1977 issue of *Research Management* or, more recently, *Research Management,* November 1979, pp. 8–11.
19. In a more macroscopic way, March and Simon observed years ago that innovation could occur only in the presence of organizational slack. See J. G. March and H. A. Simon, *Organizations* (New York: John Wiley, 1958).
20. For more details on various job-design dimensions appropriate to the critical functions, see E. B. Roberts and A. R. Fusfeld, "Critical Functions: Needed Roles in the Innovation Process," in *Career Issues in Human Resource Management,* R. Katz, ed. (Englewood Cliffs, NJ: Prentice-Hall, forthcoming).
21. For samples of questionnaire items, more details on diagnostic uses of the resulting data, and numerical outputs from one company's assessment, see Roberts and Fusfeld (forthcoming).

Chapter 2

1. K. J. Arrow in *The Rational Direction of Inventive Activity: Economic and Social Factors,* R. Nelson, ed. (Princeton: Princeton University Press, 1962), p. 624.
2. E. B. Roberts, "Entrepreneurship and Technology," in *The Factors in the Transfer of Technology,* W. H. Gruber and D. G. Marquis, eds. (Cambridge, MA: MIT Press, 1969), p. 259.
3. I am indebted to Anil Gupta for first suggesting the use of the word *network* to describe this system of communication and political links.
4. The stages of corporate development used in this article follow the work of B. R. Scott. See, for instance, B. R. Scott, "The New Industrial State, Old Myths and New Realities," *Harvard Business Review,* March–April 1973, pp. 133–148; and B. R. Scott, "Stages of Corporate Development 1, 2" (Case Clearing House, Howard Business School, the President and Fellows of Harvard College, 1971).
5. For a definition, see Table 2.3.
6. These terms are defined later in this article.
7. J. A. Schumpeter, *History of Economic Analysis* (England: Oxford University Press, 1954), p. 554.
8. J. A. Schumpeter, *Capitalism, Socialism, and Democracy* (New York: Harper & Row, 1975), p. 132.
9. D. A. Schon, "Champions for Radical New Inventions," *Harvard Business Review,* March–April 1963, p. 84.
10. One of the first to suggest means of managing this resistance to change was P. R. Lawrence, "How to Deal with Resistance to Change," *Harvard Business Review,* January–February 1954. However, in 1969 in a disarmingly candid retrospective commentary on his *Harvard Business Review* classic, Professor Lawrence wrote, "There is . . . an implication in the article that the social and human costs of change can be largely avoided by thoughtful management effort. Today I am less sanguine about this."
11. R. Rothwell, C. Freeman, A. Horlsey, V. T. P. Jervis, A. B. Robertson, and J. Townsend, "SAPPHO Updated—Project SAPPHO Phase II," *Research Policy* 3 (1974), pp. 258–291.
12. E. B. Roberts and A. B. Frohman, "Internal Entrepreneurship: Strategy for Growth," *The Business Quarterly,* Spring 1972, pp. 71–78.
13. E. B. Roberts, "Generating Effective Corporate Innovation," *Technology Review,* October–November 1977, pp. 27–33.
14. L. Grossman, *The Change Agent* (New York: AMACOM, 1974).
15. J. A. Morton, *Organizing for Innovation* (New York: McGraw-Hill, 1971), p. 95.
16. L. Kusiatin, "The Process and Capacity for Diversification Through Internal Development" (DBA diss., Harvard Graduate School of Business Administration, April 1976).
17. O. Collins and D. G. Moore, *The Organization Makers* (New York: Appleton-Century-Croft, 1970).
18. *Ibid.*
19. O. F. Collins, D. G. Moore, and D. B. Umwalla, *The Enterprising Man* (Board of Trustees, Michigan State University, 1964).
20. T. D. Duchesneau and J. B. Lafond, "Characteristics of Users and Nonusers of an Innovation: The Role of Economical Organizational Factors" (Paper presented at the Annual Convention of the Eastern Economic Association, Hartford, Connecticut, April 1977). In addition, private correspondence of November 30, 1977, provided expanded details on research data.
21. R. P. Olsen, "Equipment Supplier—Producer Relationships and Process Innovation in the Textile Industry" (Harvard University Graduate School of Business Administration, November 17, 1975).
22. *Ibid.* Olsen's champions generally were each identified with a *series* of innovations.
23. Rothwell, Freeman, Horlsey, Jervis, Robertson, and Townsend (1974).

24. *Ibid.*

25. The five key areas identified by the SAPPHO group are all interdisciplinary in character. The first is at the boundary of research and development and organizational behavior; the fourth and fifth are at the boundary of research and development and administrative systems; the second and the third are at the interface between marketing and R&D. Two of these areas have been studied by MIT investigators, Allen (communications) and von Hippel (user needs), who have broadly confirmed and significantly extended the SAPPHO results. A substantial literature also exists in the area of marketing management and project management and related techniques for maximizing the efficiency of R&D. Managerial characteristics, particularly those of the technological entrepreneur, have been studied extensively by another MIT scholar, Roberts, whose conclusions regarding entrepreneurship are also broadly consistent with the SAPPHO group. See Roberts and Frohman (Spring 1972); Roberts (October–November 1977); T. A. Allen, *Managing the Flow of Technology: Technology Transfer and the Dissemination of Technological Information within the R&D Organization* (Cambridge, MA: MIT Press, 1977); R. S. Rosenbloom and F. W. Wolek, *Technology and Information Transfer* (Boston: Division of Research, Graduate School of Business Administration, Harvard University, 1977); and E. von Hippel, "The Dominant Role of Users in the Scientific Instrument Innovation Process," *Research Policy* 5 (1976), pp. 212–239.

26. J. L. Bower, *Managing the Resource Allocation Process* (Homewood, IL: Richard Irwin, 1972).

27. In this article the terms *sponsorship* and *business definition* will be used in preference to *impetus* and *context*. Bower's context also includes the administrative system, while business definition, as it is used here, is a narrower term that includes only the strategic part of the context.

28. Roberts (October–November 1977); "What Do We Really Know about Managing R&D" (A talk with Ed Roberts), *Research Management, TK,* November 1978; and R. Rhoades, E. B. Roberts, and A. R. Fusfeld, "A Correlation of R&D Laboratory Performance with Critical Function Analysis," *Research Management* 9, October 1978, pp. 13–17.

29. J. K. Galbraith, *The New Industrial State* (Boston: Houghton Mifflin, 1967).

30. A. D. Chandler, *Strategy and Structure* (Cambridge, MA: MIT Press, 1962); B. R. Scott, *An Open Model of the Firm* (DBA diss., Graduate School of Business Administration, Harvard University, 1962); J. H. McArthur and B. R. Scott, *Industrial Planning in France* (Boston: Division of Research, Harvard Business School, 1969); M. Salter, *Stages of Corporate Development: Implications for Management Control* (Mimeo, 1967); and L. Wrigley, *Diversification and Divisional Autonomy* (DBA diss., Graduate School of Business Administration, Harvard University, 1970).

31. Chandler (1962).

32. Scott (1971).

33. Wrigley (1970).

34. A single business is defined here as one that manufactures a single product, a line of products with variations in size and style, or a closely related set of products linked by technology or market structure.

35. W. J. Abernathy and J. Utterback, "A Dynamic Model of Process and Product Innovation," *Omega* 3 (1975), pp. 639–656.

36. W. J. Abernathy and P. L. Townsend, "Technology, Productivity, and Process Change," in *Technological Forecasting and Social Change* 7 (New York: American Elsevier Publishing, 1975), pp. 379–396.

37. S. Myers and D. G. Marquis, *Successful Technological Innovations* (Washington, DC: National Science Foundation, NSF 69–17).

38. Dr. James Utterback, personal communication.

39. T. Burns and G. M. Stalker, *The Management of Innovation* (London: Tavistock Publications, 1966).

40. Rimbruster Office Automation, Inc. (Intercollegiate Case Clearing House, 4-674-009, Rev. 10.76), p. 9. An updated case of this firm reveals that Rimbruster was a disguised name for Redactron (see Redactron Corporation, Intercollegiate Case Clearing House, 1-276-163) and Redactron's president, Evelyn Berezin.

41. *Ibid.*, p. 3.

42. *Ibid.*, p. 8.

43. For background information on Henry Kloss, see "Advent Corporation (C)" (Intercollegiate Case Clearing House, 9-674-027). The quotation is from "Advent Corporation (D)" (Intercollegiate Case Clearing House, 9-676-053), p. 3.

44. Sci-Tex (Intercollegiate Case Clearing House, 1-678-009), p. 10.

45. J. K. Galbraith, *The New Industrial State* (Boston: Houghton Mifflin, 1967), pp. 88–89.

46. G. Bylinsky, *The Innovation Millionaires* (New York: Charles Scribner's Sons, 1976), p. 161.

47. R. Adams, "Do You Sincerely Want to Be a Millionaire?" *Boston Magazine,* November 1972, p. 45.

48. J. S. Schwartz, "The Decision to Innovate" (DBA diss., Harvard University Graduate School of Business Administration, 1973), p. 107.

49. Interview with Digital Equipment Corporation executive.

50. Schwartz (1973); and J. W. Lorsch and P. J. Lawrence, "Organizing for Product Innovation," *Harvard Business Review,* January–February 1965.

51. Schwartz (1973), p. 111.

52. "Pilkington Float Glass (A)" (International Case Clearing House, Harvard Business School, 9-670-069).

53. Alistair Pilkington is now chairman of Pilkington Brothers, the first person outside the direct lineage of the founder to hold that position. See J. B. Quinn, "Technological Innovation, Entrepreneurship, and Strategy," *Sloan Management Review,* Spring 1979, pp. 19–30.

54. L. Wrigley, "Divisional Autonomy and Diversification" (DBA diss., Harvard Business School, 1970).

55. Bob Evans, as quoted by T. A. Wise, "IBM's $5,000,000,000 Gamble," *Fortune,* September 1966.

56. Interview with IBM executive.

57. Wise (September 1966); and T. A. Wise, "The Rocky Road to the Marketplace," *Fortune,* October 1966.

58. M. A. Maidique and J. Ince, " 'The Grumman Corporation' and 'Grumman Energy Systems' " (Intercollegiate Case Clearing House, 1979).

59. *Business Week,* June 27, 1977.

60. Shortly after his appointment as general manager, Peterson was promoted to president of Grumman Energy Systems, Inc., a wholly owned subsidiary of the Grumman Corporation.

61. Roberts (October–November 1977).

62. W. J. Abernathy and J. M. Utterback, "Innovation and the Evolving Structure of the Firm" (Harvard University Graduate School of Business Administration, Working Paper 75018, June 1975).

63. J. M. Utterback, "Management of Technology" (Center for Policy Alternatives, MIT, February 28, 1978).

64. W. J. Abernathy and J. M. Utterback, "Patterns of Industrial Innovation," *Technology Review,* June–July 1978.

65. A. C. Cooper and D. Schendel, "Strategic Responses to Technological Threats," *Business Horizons,* February 1976.

66. B. Uttal, "Gene Amdahl Takes Aim at IBM," *Fortune,* September 1977. For a case study of a data-processing center (Hughes) that saw performance/price ratio in favor of the Amdahl 470 over the IBM 370, see J. B. Woods, "Converting from 370 to 470," *Datamation,* July 1977. The sales rate information is from Amdahl 1978 quarterly reports.

67. Frank Cary, as quoted by Uttal (September 1977).

68. T. Levitt, *Marketing for Business Growth* (New York: McGraw-Hill, 1974), p. 148.

Chapter 3

Notes

1. For discussions on the development of project management, its various organizational types, and applications, see Killiam [17].
2. This observation is supported by several studies that analyzed the managerial style employed by project managers to elicit support and investigated the relationship of various styles to project performance. For specific results, see [3], [7], [9], [11], [12], [14], and [35].
3. Conflict is defined here as a disagreement between one party and another caused by technical issues, administrative-oriented issues, or personality differences. Conflict is detrimental if it impedes project objectives with no positive consequences. It can be beneficial if it results in the development of new information that enhances the decision-making process. For an informative discussion, see Pondy [21].
4. See [6], [21], and [26].
5. Several articles have been written on the authority problems of project managers, but the types of influence available to project leaders and the effectiveness of such tools are not so well documented. See [11] and [13].
6. French and Raven's original typology [9] of interpersonal influences has been modified by Gemmill and Thamhain [12] and used for various power style studies on project managers in situations similar to the current investigations. Also, see [11] and [27].
7. For a detailed discussion, see Walton and Dutton [31]; Walton, Dutton, and Cafferty [32], Pondy [22]; and Kelly [16].
8. The five methods of conflict resolution were originally defined by Blake and Mouton [1] and Burke [2]. The definitions are widely used in social-science research.
   The specific typology of aphorisms is based on the research of Lawrence and Lorsch [19], who developed various sets of aphorisms to describe methods of resolving conflict. These aphorisms have been used in other research of similar nature to avoid the potential bias that might be introduced otherwise by the use of social-science jargons. For further details, see Burke [3].
9. Nonparametric evaluation methods were used because the survey data contained only nominal or ordinal measurements. The theories, methodology, and specific techniques for applying nonparametric methods are discussed in detail in [5] and [25].
10. For a discussion on leadership style effectiveness in work environments with different degrees of task complexity, managerial position power, and quality of the organizational climate, see Thamhain and Wilemon [29].
11. Earlier studies by Gemmill and Thamhain [12] obtained similar results with a completely independent data sample.
12. Perhaps in the future, a more rigorous approach for measuring position power can be developed so that its effect on project-management performance and leadership style can be shown more explicitly.

References

[1] Blake, R. R., and Mouton, J. S., *The Managerial Grid* (Houston: Gulf Publishing Co., 1964).
[2] Burke, R. J., "Methods of Resolving Interpersonal Conflict," *Personnel Administration,* July–August 1969, pp. 48–55.
[3] Burke, R. J., "Methods of Managing Superior-Subordinate Conflict," *Canadian Journal of Behavioral Science* 2 (1970), pp. 124–135.
[4] Cleland, D. I., "The Deliberate Conflict," *Business Horizons,* February 1968, pp. 78–80.
[5] Conover, W. J., *Practical Nonparametric Statistics* (New York: Wiley, 1971).

[6] Evan, W. M., "Conflict and Performance in R&D Organizations," *Industrial Management Review,* Fall 1965, pp. 37–46.

[7] Evan, W. M., "Superior-Subordinate Conflict in Research Organizations," *Administrative Science Quarterly* 10 (1965), pp. 52–64.

[8] Eyring, H. B., "Some Sources of Uncertainty and Their Consequences in Engineering Design Projects," *IEEE Transactions on Engineering Management* 13 (1966), pp. 176–180.

[9] French, J. R. P., Jr., and Raven, B., "The Basis of Social Power," in *Studies in Social Power,* D. P. Cartwright, ed. (Ann Arbor: Research Center for Group Dynamics, University of Michigan, 1959).

[10] Fusfeld, A. R., and Foster, R. N., "The Delphi Technique: Survey and Comment," *Business Horizons,* June 1971, pp. 63–74.

[11] Gemmill, G. R., and Thamhain, H. J., "The Effectiveness of Different Power Styles of Project Managers in Gaining Project Support," *IEEE Transactions on Engineering Management* 20 (1973), pp. 38–43.

[12] Gemill, G. R., and Thamhain, H. J., "Influence Styles of Project Managers: Some Project Performance Correlates," *Academy of Management Journal* 17 (1974), pp. 216–224.

[13] Gemmill, G. R., and Wilemon, D. L., "The Power Spectrum in Project Management," *Sloan Management Review,* Fall 1970, pp. 15–25.

[14] Hollander, E. P., and Julian, J. W., "Contemporary Trends in the Analysis of Leadership Processes," *Psychological Bulletin* 71 (1969), pp. 387–397.

[15] Kahn, R. L., Wolfe, D. M., Quinn, R. P., Snoek, J. D., and Rosenthal, R. A., *Organizational Stress: Studies in Role Conflict and Ambiguity* (New York: Wiley, 1964).

[16] Kelly, J., "Make Conflict Work for You," *Harvard Business Review,* July–August 1970, pp. 103–113.

[17] Killiam, W. P., "Project Management: Future of Organizational Concepts," *Marquette Business Review,* Summer 1971.

[18] Lawrence, P. R., and Lorsch, J. W., "New Management Job: The Integrator," *Harvard Business Review,* November–December 1967, pp. 142–152.

[19] Lawrence, P. R., and Lorsch, J. W., *Organization and Environment* (Boston: Division of Research, Graduate School of Business Administration, Harvard University, 1967).

[20] Maier, N. R., and Hoffman, L. R., "Acceptance and Quality of Solutions as Related to Leaders' Attitudes Toward Disagreement in Group Problem Solving," *Journal of Applied Behavioral Science* 1 (1965), pp. 373–386.

[21] Pondy, L. R., "Organizational Conflict: Concepts and Models," *Administrative Science Quarterly* 12 (1967), pp. 296–320.

[22] Pondy, L. R., "A Systems Theory of Interdepartmental Conflict," *Academy of Management Journal* 9 (1966), pp. 246–256.

[23] Seiler, J. A., "Diagnosing Interdepartmental Conflict," *Harvard Business Review,* September–October 1963, pp. 121–132.

[24] Sheriff, M., "Superordinate Goals in the Reduction of Intergroup Conflict," *American Journal of Sociology* 63 (1958), pp. 349–356.

[25] Siegel, S., *Nonparametric Statistics for the Behavioral Sciences* (New York: McGraw-Hill, 1956).

[26] Thamhain, H. J., and Wilemon, D. L., "Conflict Management in Project Life Cycles," *Sloan Management Review,* Spring 1975, pp. 31–50.

[27] Thamhain, H. J., and Wilemon, D. L., "Conflict Management in Project-Oriented Work Environments," *Proceedings of the Sixth International Meeting of the Project Management Institute* (Washington, DC), September 18–21, 1974.

[28] Thamhain, H. J., and Wilemon, D. L., "The Effective Management of Conflict in Project-Oriented Work Environments," *Defense Management Journal,* July 1975, pp. 29–40.

[29] Thamhain, H. J., and Wilemon, D. L., "Leadership Effectiveness in Program Management," Eighth Annual International Symposium of the Project Management Institute (Montreal, Canada), October 1976.

[30] Thompson, J. D., *Organizations in Action* (New York: McGraw-Hill, 1967).
[31] Walton, R. E., and Dutton, J. M., "The Management of Interdepartmental Conflict: A Model and Review," *Administrative Science Quarterly* 14 (1969), pp. 73–84.
[32] Walton, R. E., Dutton, J. M., and Cafferty, T. P., "Organizational Context and Interdepartmental Conflict," *Administrative Science Quarterly* 14 (1969), pp. 522–542.
[33] Wilemon, D. L., "Project Management Conflict: A View from Apollo," *Proceedings of the Third Annual Symposium of the Project Management Institute* (Houston), October 1971.
[34] Wilemon, D. L., "Project Management and Its Conflicts: A View from Apollo," *Chemical Technology* 2 (1972), pp. 527–534.
[35] Wilemon, D. L., and Cicero, J. P., "The Project Manager: Anomalies and Ambiguities," *Academy of Management Journal* 13 (1970): pp. 269–282.

Chapter 4

Notes

Presented at the MIT Conference on Human Factors in the Transfer of Technology, May 19, 1966. The research reported in this article was initially supported by a grant from the National Aeronautics and Space Administration (NaNsg 235–62), and since November, 1963, by grants from the Office of Science Information Service, National Science Foundation (GN233 and GN353). The author gratefully acknowledges the aid of Maurice P. Andrien, Jr., Richard J. Bjelland, Stephen I. Cohen, Daniel S. Frischmuth, Richard H. Frank, Arthur Gerstenfeld, William D. Putt, and Peter G. Gerstberger, who participated as research assistants in various phases of the data collection, and expresses his appreciation to the companies, project managers, and engineers who must remain anonymous but without whose help the study could not have been conducted.

1. See, for example, the Weinberg Report [9], [4], [5], and [6]; for a dissenting voice, [2].
2. The term *research* will be used here in a generic sense, encompassing any and all activities from the basic to the developmental end of the R&D spectrum.
3. In other words, everything except analysis and experimentation, and personal experience, which can be considered to operate from within the project.
4. Two of the twenty-seven subproblems occurred in the single fundamental science project; the remainder are from the developmental projects. Since the results presented in this section are essentially the same for both of these subsamples, the data have been aggregated.
5. Yule's Q correlation for dichotomous data. No significance level is given.

References

[1] Allen, T. J., *The Utilization of Information Sources During R&D Proposal Preparation* (MIT Sloan School of Management Working Paper No. 97–64, 1964).
[2] Bar-Hillel, Yehoshua, "Is Information Retrieval Approaching a Crisis?" *Amer. Document., 14* (1963), pp. 95–98.
[3] Bennis, W. G., *Changing Organizations* (New York: McGraw-Hill, 1966).
[4] Faegri, Kurt, "Science Babel," *Nature, 177* (1956), pp. 343–344.
[5] Fozzy, Paula, "The Publication Explosion," *Bull. Atom. Scientists, 17* (1962), pp. 34–38.
[6] Glass, Bentley, "Information Crisis in Biology," *Bull. Atom. Scientists, 17* (1962), pp. 7–12.
[7] Katz, Daniel, and Kahn, R. L. *The Social Psychology of Organizations* (New York: John Wiley, 1966).
[8] Menzel, H., *Review of Studies in the Flow of Information Among Scientists* (New York: Columbia University, Bureau of Applied Social Research, New York, 1960).
[9] President's Science Advisory Committee, *Science, Government and Information: The Respon-*

sponsibilities of the Technical Community and Government in the Transfer of Information (Washington, DC, Govt. Printing Office, 1963).

[10] Shilling, C. W., and Bernard, Jessie, *Informal Communication Among Bioscientists* (Washington, DC: The George Washington University Biological Sciences Communication Project Report No. 16A, 1964).

Chapter 5

Notes

1. Our data base is derived primarily from innovations in the following fields: scientific instruments; process equipment used in the manufacture of (1) silicon-based semiconductors, (2) electronic subassemblies, and (3) corrugated cardboard; engineering polymers and additives for these; and construction equipment. Readers interested in a detailed discussion of our findings in some of these areas and in the research methodology used may wish to read von Hippel [1] and [2]. We gratefully acknowledge the support provided for this research by the Division of Policy Research and Analysis, National Science Foundation via Grant #DA–44366.

2. By innovative products, we mean those that offered users in their judgment a significant functional advantage over previously available products. "Me-too" products are excluded. See von Hippel [1] and [2] for a detailed discussion.

3. When making your estimates of ROII, note that "return" is whatever is important to the party involved. It may be monetary, as in dollars of product sold, or it may not be. (For example, instrument users are strongly motivated to develop scientific instruments by "return" measured in knowledge and peer approval.) Your knowledge of what is important to participants in your industry will help you see "return" as potential innovators would see it.

4. Very large companies may worry that examination of the products of small companies for new product ideas may seem predatory to antitrusters—even if the small company has not made much of a go of the product and you are gathering data on what *not* to do as well as what to do. If this seems to be a problem, you might consider studying where the smaller company gets the idea for its version of the product. Typically, its need information may also have more product design content than the consumer data you are otherwise forced to use.

References

[1] von Hippel, E. A., "The Dominant Role of Users in the Scientific Instrument Innovation Process," *Research Policy,* Vol. 5, No. 3 (July 1976), pp. 212–239.

[2] von Hippel, E. A., "The Dominant Role of the User in Semiconductor and Electronic Subassembly Process Innovation" (MIT Sloan School of Management Working Paper #853–76, April 1976); also, *IEEE Transactions on Engineering Management,* in press.

[3] Rosenberg, M., *The Logic of Survey Analysis* (New York: Basic Books, 1968).

[4] Corey, E. R., *The Development of Markets for New Materials* (Boston: Division of Research, Graduate School of Business Administration, Harvard University, 1956).

Chapter 6

This article was first presented as a speech before the Canadian Research Management Association in May 1978.

1. This projection assumes a population growth rate of 1.8 percent.

2. This projection assumes an energy growth rate of 4–5 percent.

3. This projection assumes world GNP growth at 4–5 percent.

4. E. Schumacher, *Small Is Beautiful* (New York: Harper & Row, 1973).

5. For some of the national policy issues that this article poses, see J. B. Quinn, "National Policies for Science and Technology: New Approaches for Public Needs," *Research Management,* November 1977, pp. 11–18. In this article I approach problems at the individual enterprise level.

6. J. Jewkes, D. Sawers, and R. Stillerman, *The Sources of Invention* (London: Macmillan, 1958); J. Schmookler, *Invention and Economic Growth* (Cambridge, MA: Harvard University Press, 1966); and E. Mansfield, *Industrial Research and Technological Innovation* (New York: Norton, 1968).

7. "Head Ski Company" (case study, President and Fellows of Harvard University, 1968); and *Wall Street Journal,* January 16, 1968, p. 1.

8. See J. Dessauer, *My Years with Xerox* (New York: Doubleday, 1971); J. Ermenc, "Interview with Chester Carlson, December 1965" (Hanover, NH: Thayer School of Engineering); and J. B. Quinn, "Xerox Corporation (A)" (secondary source case, Amos Tuck School, 1978).

9. See D. Schon, *Technology and Change* (New York: Delacorte, 1967).

10. For effects of risk perception by the financial community, see U.S. Department of Commerce, *Technological Innovation: Its Environment and Management,* 1967; and "The Consequences of a Worsening Shortage," *Business Week,* September 22, 1975, p. 62.

11. R. C. Dean, Jr., "The Temporal Mismatch—Innovation's Pace vs Management's Time Horizon," *Research Management,* May 1974, pp. 12–15.

12. J. A. Timmons, L. E. Smollen, and A. L. M. Dingee, Jr., *New Venture Creation: A Guide to Small Business Development* (Homewood, IL: Dow Jones-Irwin, 1977).

13. See Schon (1967); and G. Bylinsky, *The Innovation Millionaires* (New York: Scribner, 1976).

14. See Dean (May 1974).

15. See L. Beman, "Why Business Ran Out of Capacity," *Fortune,* May 1974, pp. 260–271; and "The Breakdown of U.S. Innovation," *Business Week,* February 16, 1976, pp. 56–68.

16. For further discussion of the second point, see M. Hanan, "Corporate Growth Through Venture Management," *Harvard Business Review,* January–February 1969, pp. 43–61; and K. H. Vesper and T. G. Holmdahl, "How Venture Management Fares in Innovative Companies," *Research Management,* May 1973, pp. 30–32.

17. T. A. Wise, "I.B.M.'s $5,000,000,000 Gamble," *Fortune,* September 1966, pp. 118–124; T. A. Wise, "The Rocky Road to the Marketplace (Part II: I.B.M.'s $5,000,000,000 Gamble)," *Fortune,* October 1966, pp. 138–152; and G. Bylinsky, "Vincent Learson Didn't Plan It That Way, But I.B.M.'s Toughest Competitor Is—I.B.M.," *Fortune,* March 1972, pp. 55–61.

18. See Quinn (November 1977).

19. L. A. B. Pilkington, "Review Lecture: The Float Glass Process" (London: The Royal Society, 1969); J. Ermenc, "Interview with Sir Alastair Pilkington, June 25, 1968" (Hanover, NH: Thayer School of Engineering); and J. B. Quinn, "Pilkington Brothers, Ltd." (unpublished case, Amos Tuck School, 1977).

20. E. Roberts, *The Dynamics of Research and Development* (New York: Harper & Row, 1964); E. Pessemier, *Managing Innovation and New Product Development* (Cambridge, MA: Marketing Science Institute, 1975); and J. B. Quinn, "Long-Range Planning of Industrial Research," *Harvard Business Review,* July–August 1961, pp. 81–102.

21. For a classic description of Oppenheimer as such a manager, see N. F. Davis, *Lawrence and Oppenheimer* (New York: Simon & Schuster, 1969).

22. See J. B. Quinn, "Strategic Goals: Process and Politics," *Sloan Management Review,* Fall 1977, pp. 21–37.

23. Quinn (July–August 1961); and J. B. Quinn and J. A. Mueller, "Transferring Research Results to Operations," *Harvard Business Review,* January–February 1963, pp. 49–66.

24. For an example, see D. J. Smalter and R. L. Ruggles, Jr., "Six Lessons from the Pentagon," *Harvard Business Review,* March–April 1966, pp. 64–75.

25. The OST system of Texas Instruments, Inc., contains many of the detailed characteristics. See Texas Instruments, Inc., 9–172–054, ICCH, Harvard University.

Chapter 7

Notes

1. See Kosann [11].
2. See *Photon* [12], *Crossfield and Zip* [6], and Du Bois [7].
3. See Zito [22].
4. For data on Advent see Zito [22], *Advent* [1], and Gumpter [8].
5. See *Strang Corporation* [18].
6. Not only is the U.S. industrial R&D expenditure concentrated in terms of size of corporation, it is also concentrated in terms of industry. In 1971, 81 percent of all U.S. industrial R&D was performed by five industries. The industries were: (1) aircraft and missiles, (2) electrical equipment and communication, (3) chemicals and allied products, (4) machinery, and (5) motor vehicles and other transportation equipment. See *Research and Development in Industry* [16].
7. See Prahalad [14].
8. "Piercing Future Fog in the Executive Suite" [13].
9. Wise [20] and [21].
10. *Texas Instruments Incorporated* [19].
11. Wise [20] and [21].
12. *Infotech Systems, Inc.* [10].
13. For information on the breeder reactor and the changing attitude toward its development see Cochoran [5], Bupp and Derian [3], and *Reference Note on Breeder Reactors* [15].
14. For information on opposition to the ABM, see Cahn [4].
15. Sigal [17].
16. Horwitch [9].
17. Bloom and Curhan [2].

References

[1] *Advent* (A&B) ICH 9–672–018, 019. (Boston, MA: Intercollegiate Case Clearing House, 1973).
[2] Bloom, G. F., and Curhan, R. C., "Technological Change in the Food Industry," *Technology Review,* December 1974, pp. 20–29.
[3] Bupp, I. C., and Derian, J., "The Breeder Reactor in the U.S.: A New Economic Analysis," *Technology Review,* July–August 1974, pp. 26–36.
[4] Cahn, A. *Eggheads and Warheads: Scientists on the ABM* (Cambridge, MA: Center For International Studies, MIT, 1971).
[5] Cochoran, T. B., *The Liquid Metal Fast Breeder Reactor: An Environmental Critique* (Washington, DC: Resources for the Future, 1974).
[6] *Crossfield and Zip* ICH 9–665–005 (Boston, MA: Intercollegiate Case Clearing House, 1964).
[7] Du Bois, P. C., "What Happened to Photon: Pioneering Technology Doesn't Always Pay Off," *Barrons,* September 17, 1973.
[8] Gumpter, D., "Does Anybody Want a TV Set That Has a 4-by-6 Foot Screen?" *Wall Street Journal,* June 11, 1974, pp. 1, 25.
[9] Horwitch, M., *Technological Evaluation and the Rise of a Societal Issue—A History of Sonic*

Boom Decision-Making in the US/SST Program: 1964–1969 (DBA thesis, Harvard University Graduate School of Business Administration).

[10] *Infotech Systems, Inc.* ICH 9–647–030 (Boston, MA: Intercollegiate Case Clearing House, 1973).

[11] Kosann, M., "Metpath, Inc." Presented at the Management of Technological Innovation Seminar, December 11, 1974, at Harvard University Graduate School of Business Administration.

[12] *Photon* (A–E) ICH 9–607–012 and 013, ICH 9–609–033, 034 and 035 (Boston, MA: Intercollegiate Case Clearing House, 1961, 1963).

[13] "Piercing Future Fog in the Executive Suite," *Business Week*, April 28, 1975, pp. 46–53.

[14] Prahalad, C. K., *The Strategic Process in a Multinational Corporation* (DBA thesis, Harvard University Graduate School of Business Administration).

[15] *Reference Note on Breeder Reactors* ICH 9–674–006 (Boston, MA: Intercollegiate Case Clearing House, 1974).

[16] *Research and Development in Industry,* 1971 NSF 73–305 (Washington, DC: National Science Foundation, 1973), pp. 2, 5, 8.

[17] Sigal, L. V., "Bureaucratic Objectives and Tactical Uses of the Press," *Public Administration Review,* July–August 1973, pp. 336–345.

[18] *Strang Corporation* ICH 6–371–283 (Boston, MA: Intercollegiate Case Clearing House, 1970).

[19] *Texas Instruments Incorporated* ICH 9–172–054 (Boston, MA: Intercollegiate Case Clearing House, 1972).

[20] Wise, T. A., "IBM's $5,000,000,000 Gamble," *Fortune,* September 1966, p. 118.

[21] Wise, T. A., "The Rocky Road to the Marketplace," *Fortune,* October 1966, p. 139.

[22] Zito, T., "The Big Picture," *Playboy,* November 1974, p. 106.

Chapter 8

1. J.-J. Servan-Schreiber, *The American Challenge* (New York: Atheneum, 1968).

2. S. Ramo, *America's Technology Slip* (New York: John Wiley, 1980).

3. R. Pascale and A. Athos, *The Art of Japanese Management* (New York: Simon & Schuster, 1981).

4. T. J. Peters and R. H. Waterman, Jr., *In Search of Excellence* (New York: Harper & Row, 1982). For purposes of this article, the high-technology industries are defined as those that spend more than 3 percent of sales on R&D. These industries, though otherwise quite different, are all characterized by a rapid rate of change in their products and technologies. Only five U.S. industries meet this criterion: chemicals and pharmaceuticals; machinery (especially computers and office machines); electrical equipment and communications; professional and scientific instruments; and aircraft and missiles. See National Science Foundation, *Science Resources Studies Highlights,* NSF81–331, December 31, 1981, p. 2.

5. W. Ouchi, *Theory Z: How American Management Can Meet the Japanese Challenge* (New York: John Wiley, 1980).

6. C. E. Makin, "Ranking Corporate Reputations," *Fortune,* January 10, 1983, pp. 34–44. Corporate reputation was subdivided into eight attributes: quality of management, quality of products and services, innovativeness, long-term investment value, financial soundness, ability to develop and help talented people, community and environmental responsibility, and use of corporate assets.

7. M. A. Maidique and B. J. Zirger, "Stanford Innovation Project: A Study of Successful and Unsuccessful Product Innovation in High-Technology Firms," *IEEE Transactions on Engineering Management,* in press. M. A. Maidique, "The Stanford Innovation Project: A Comparative Study of Success and Failure in High-Technology Product Innovation," *Management of Technological Innovation Conference Proceedings* (Worcester Polytechnic Institute, 1983).

8. A similar conclusion was reached by Romanelli and Tushman in their study of leadership in the minicomputer industry, which found that successful companies alternated long periods of continuity and inertia with rapid reorientations. See E. Romanelli and M. Tushman, "Executive Leadership and Organizational Outcomes: An Evolutionary Perspective," *Management of Technological Innovation Conference Proceedings* (Worcester Polytechnic Institute, 1983).

9. One of the authors in this article has employed this framework as a diagnostic tool in audits of high-technology firms. The firm is evaluated along these six dimensions on a 0–10 scale by members of corporate and divisional management, working individually. The results are then used as inputs for conducting a strategic review of the firm.

10. General Electric evidently has also recognized the value of such concentration. In 1979, Reginald Jones, then GE's CEO, broke up the firm into six independent sectors led by "sector executives." See R. Vancil and P. C. Browne, "General Electric Consumer Products and Services Sector" (Boston, MA: Harvard Business School Case Services 2–179–070).

11. Personal communication with David Packard, Stanford University, March 4, 1982.

12. After only eighteen months as Geneen's successor as president, Lyman Hamilton was summarily dismissed by Geneen for reversing Geneen's way of doing business. See G. Colvin, "The Re-Geneening of ITT," *Fortune,* January 11, 1982, pp. 34–39.

13. "RCA: Still Another Master," *Business Week,* August 17, 1981, pp. 80–86.

14. "R&D Scoreboard," *Business Week,* July 6, 1981, pp. 60–75.

15. R. Stata, Analog Devices *Quarterly Report,* 1st Quarter, 1981.

16. "Why They Are Jumping Ship at Intel," *Business Week,* February 14, 1983, p. 107; and M. Chase, "Problem-Plagued Intel Bets on New Products, IBM's Financial Help," *Wall Street Journal,* February 4, 1983.

17. These SAPPHO findings are generally consistent with the results of the Stanford Innovation Project, a major comparative study of U.S. high-technology innovation. See M. A. Maidique, "The Stanford Innovation Project: A Comparative Study of Success and Failure in High Technology Product Innovation," *Management of Technology Conference Proceedings* (Worcester Polytechnic Institute, 1983).

18. Maidique and Zirger (in press); several other authors have reached similar conclusions. See, for example, Peters and Waterman (1982).

19. Personal communication with Tom Jones, chairman of the board, Northrop Corporation, May 1982.

20. W. R. Thurston, "The Revitalization of GenRad," *Sloan Management Review,* Summer 1981, pp. 53–57.

21. T. Wise, "IBM's $5,000,000,000 Gamble," *Fortune,* September 1966; and "A Rocky Road to the Marketplace," *Fortune,* October 1966.

22. A. P. Sloan, *My Years with General Motors* (New York: Anchor Books, 1972), p. 401.

23. Personal communication with Ken Fisher, 1980. Mr. Fisher was president and CEO of Prime Computer from 1975 to 1981.

24. At Genentech, Cetus, Biogen, and Collaborative Research, four of the leading biotechnology firms, a top scientist is also a member of the board of directors.

25. See, for example, J. A. Morton, *Organizing for Innovation* (New York: McGraw-Hill, 1971).

26. Jimmy Treybig, president of Tandem Computer, Stanford Executive Institute Presentation, August 1982.

27. See D. A Schon, *Technology and Change* (New York: Dell, 1967), and Peters and Waterman (1982).

28. S. Myers and E. F. Sweezy, "Why Innovations Fail," *Technology Review,* March–April 1978, pp. 40–46.

29. *Texas Instruments* (A), 9–476–122, Harvard Business School case; *Texas Instruments Shows U.S. Business How to Survive in the 1980's,* 3–579–092, Harvard Business School case; *Texas Instruments "Speak and Spell Product,"* 9–679–089, revised 7/79, Harvard Business School case.

30. Arthur K. Watson, Address to the Eighth International Congress of Accountants, New York

City, September 24, 1962, as quoted by D. A. Schon, "Champions for Radical New Inventions," *Harvard Business Review,* March–April 1963, p. 85.

31. Personal communication with Tom Jones, chairman of the board, Northrop Corporation, May 1982.
32. Personal communication with Bob Hungate, general manager, Medical Supplies Division, Hewlett-Packard, 1980.
33. Personal communication with Richard Frankel, president, Kevex Corporation, April 1983.
34. Personal communication with Herb Dwight, president and CEO, Spectra-Physics, 1982.
35. Personal communication with Alexander d'Arbeloff, cofounder and president of Teradyne, 1983.
36. Personal communication with Ray Stata, president and CEO, Analog Devices, 1980.
37. Personal communication with Bernie Gordon, president and CEO, Analogic, 1982.
38. Personal communication with Paul Rizzo, 1980.
39. Personal communication with Tom McAvoy, president of Corning Glass, 1979.
40. Personal communication with Milt Greenberg, president of GCA, 1980.
41. Wise (September 1966).
42. L. R. Sayles and M. K. Chandler, *Managing Large Systems: Organizations for the Future* (New York: Harper & Row, 1971).
43. R. A. Burgelman, "A Model of the Interaction of Strategic Behavior, Corporate Context and the Concept of Corporate Strategy," *Academy of Management Review* (1983), pp. 61–70.
44. S. Zipper, "TI Unscrambling Matrix Management to Cope with Gridlock in Major Profit Centers," *Electronic News,* April 26, 1982, p. 1.
45. M. Barnfather, "Can 3M Find Happiness in the 1980's?" *Forbes,* March 11, 1982, pp. 113–116.
46. R. Hill, "Does a 'Hands Off' Company Now Need a 'Hands On' Style?" *International Management,* July 1983, p. 35.
47. Barnfather (March 11, 1982).
48. *Quotations from Chairman Mao Tse Tung,* S. R. Schram, ed. (Bantam Books, 1967), p. 174.
49. D. G. Marquis, "Ways of Organizing Projects," *Innovation,* August 1969, pp. 26–33; and T. Levitt, *Marketing for Business Growth* (New York: McGraw-Hill, 1974), in particular, ch. 7.
50. Charles Ames, former CEO of Reliance Electric, as quoted in "Exxon's $600-million Mistake," *Fortune,* October 19, 1981.
51. See, for example, W. J. Abernathy and J. M. Utterback, "Patterns of Industrial Innovation," *Technology Review,* June–July 1978, pp. 40–47.
52. T. Kuhn, *The Structure of Scientific Revolutions,* 2d ed. (Chicago, IL: University of Chicago Press, 1967).
53. After reviewing an early draft of this article, Ray Stata wrote, "The articulation of dynamic balance, of yin and yang . . . served as a reminder to me that there isn't one way forever, but a constant adaption to the needs and circumstances of the moment." Ray Stata, president, Analog Devices, letter of November 29, 1982.
54. Quoted in "Some Contributions of James E. Webb to the Theory and Practice of Management," a presentation by Elmer B. Staats before the annual meeting of the Academy of Management on August 11, 1978.
55. Romanelli and Tushman (1983).

Chapter 9

1. The literature on strategic planning is rapidly mounting and is impossible to cite in total. However, several of the better sources are D. F. Abell, "Using PIMS and Portfolio Analysis in Strategic Market Planning" (Paper presented at the XXIII International Meeting of The Institute of Management Science, Athens, Greece, July 1977); G. S. Day, "Diagnosing the Product Portfolio," *Journal of Marketing,* April 1977, pp. 29–38; B. Hendley, "A Fundamental

Approach to Strategy Development," *Long Range Planning,* December 1976, pp. 2–11; B. Hendley, "Strategy and the Business Portfolio," *Long Range Planning,* February 1977, pp. 9–15; M. Laric and C. Jain Subhash, eds. *Strategic Planning for Growth Management* (Proceedings of the American Marketing Association and University of Connecticut Conference, March 14, 1978); W. Rothschild, *Putting It All Together* (New York: AMACOM, 1976), chs. 3–7; M. Hanan, "Reorganize Your Company Around Its Market," *Harvard Business Review,* November–December 1974; and D. J. Luck and O. C. Ferrell, *Marketing Strategy and Plans* (Englewood Cliffs, NJ: Prentice-Hall, 1979), ch. 2.

For an excellent summary of the literature on strategic planning, which includes the most complete bibliography, see H. W. Boyd, Jr., and J. Larreche, "The Foundations of Marketing Strategy," in *Review of Marketing,* G. Zaltman and T. V. Bonoma, eds. (Chicago: American Marketing Association, 1978), pp. 41–72.

2. Several researchers have begun to address the subject of new product strategy in a serious way. Their thinking helped stimulate the current research paper.

See B. Andrews, *Creative Product Development* (New York: Longman, 1975), chs. 4 and 8 in particular; C. Freeman, *The Economics of Industrial Innovation* (Harmondsworth, England: Penguin, 1974), ch. 8; D. S. Hopkins, *Business Strategies for Problem Products* (The Conference Board, 1977); H. Nystrom, "Company Strategies for Research and Development," *Proceedings* (Strathclyde, NY, Macmillan Co. International Symposium on Industrial Innovation, 1978); L. W. Steele, *Innovation in Big Business* (New York: Elsevier, North-Holland Publishing, 1975), ch. 6 in particular; B. Twiss, *Managing Technical Innovation* (New York: Longman, 1974), ch. 2 in particular; and R. C. Bennett and R. G. Cooper, "Beyond the Marketing Concept," *Business Horizons,* June 1979, pp. 76–83.

3. For good examples, see P. H. Engel, "The Rubenstein Religion," *Across the Board,* October 1977, pp. 79–87; "Loctite: Ready To Fend off a Flock of New Competitors," *Business Week,* June 19, 1978, pp. 116–118; P. Berman, "With Fashion Coming In, Can Levi Strauss Branch Out?" *Forbes,* August 21, 1978, pp. 41–45; and "Hallmark Now Stands for a Lot More than Cards," *Business Week,* May 29, 1978, pp. 57–58. Though business press reports are customarily scanty, the ones used for this study were surprisingly complete.

4. The proper manner of defining business targets has been the subject of considerable debate, though most of the controversy concerns the portfolio of *present* products. For a good discussion of the problem, see Abell (July 1977); and Boyd and Larreche (1978), pp. 46–60.

5. Again, the literature on market-share strategy is extensive. See Boyd and Larreche (1978); R. D. Buzzell, B. T. Gale, and R. G. M. Sultan, "Market Share—A Key to Profitability," *Harvard Business Review,* January–February 1975, pp. 97–106; P. N. Bloom and P. Kotler, "Strategies for High Market Share Companies," *Harvard Business Review,* November–December 1975, pp. 63–72; and *Perspectives on Experience* (Boston: Boston Consulting Group, Inc., 1972).

6. H. I. Ansoff and J. M. Stewart, "Strategies for a Technology-Based Business," *Harvard Business Review,* November–December 1967, pp. 71–83. Others have also offered paradigms in this area. See Twiss (1974), and Steele (1975).

7. Hopkins (1977). In addition, see B. Merrifield, "Industrial Project Selection and Management," *Industrial Marketing Management* (1978), pp. 324–330. The author offers a checklist that he recommends be used somewhat as a limited version of this article's Product Innovation Charter.

8. "Texas Instruments Shows U.S. Business How to Survive in the 1980s," *Business Week,* September 18, 1978, pp. 86–92.

9. "New Leaders in Semiconductors," *Business Week,* March 1, 1976, pp. 40–46. A very similar comparison of Digital Equipment Corporation and Data General can be found in B. Uttal, "The Gentleman and the Upstarts Meet in a Great Mini Battle," *Fortune,* April 23, 1979, pp. 98–108.

10. "Innovators in the Salted Snacks Market," *Business Week,* October 30, 1978, pp. 73–74.

11. "Why the Firearms Business Has Tired Blood," *Business Week,* November 27, 1978, pp. 107–112.

Chapter 10

The authors express their deep appreciation to an anonymous reviewer who assisted in clarifying a number of aspects of this article.

1. E. B. Roberts, "New Ventures for Corporate Growth," *Harvard Business Review,* July–August 1980, pp. 134–142.
2. R. P. Rumelt, *Strategy, Structure and Economic Performance* (Harvard Business School, Division of Research, 1974).
3. R. P. Rumelt, "Diversification Strategy and Profitability," *Strategic Management Journal* 3, 1982, pp. 359–369.
4. H. R. Christensen and C. A. Montgomery, "Corporate Economic Performance: Diversification Strategy versus Market Structure," *Strategic Management Journal* 2, 1981, pp. 327–344.
5. R. A. Bettis and W. K. Hall, "Risks and Industry Effects in Large Diversified Firms," *Academy of Management Proceedings* '81, pp. 17–20.
6. O. J. Holzmann, R. M. Copeland, and J. Hayya, "Income Measures of Conglomerate Performance," *Quarterly Review of Economics and Business* 15, 1975, pp. 67–77.
7. T. Peters, "Putting Excellence into Management," *Business Week,* July 21, 1980, pp. 196–205.
8. T. J. Peters and R. H. Waterman, *In Search of Excellence* (New York: Harper & Row, 1982).
9. M. H. Meyer and E. B. Roberts, "New Product Strategy in Small High Technology Firms: A Pilot Study" (MIT Sloan School of Management Working Paper #1428–1–84, May 1984).
10. H. R. Biggadike, "The Risky Business of Diversification," *Harvard Business Review,* May–June 1979, pp. 103–111.
11. L. A. Weiss, "Start-Up Businesses: A Comparison of Performances," *Sloan Management Review,* Fall 1981, pp. 37–53.
12. S. S. Miller, *The Management Problems of Diversification* (New York: John Wiley, 1963).
13. J. S. Gilmore and D. C. Coddington, "Diversification Guides for Defense Firms," *Harvard Business Review,* May–June 1966, pp. 133–159.
14. M. S. Salter and W. A. Weinhold, "Diversification via Acquisition: Creating Value," *Harvard Business Review,* July–August 1978, pp. 166–176.
15. Miller (1963).
16. J. P. Killing, "Diversification Through Licensing," *R&D Management,* June 1978, pp. 159–163.
17. Roberts (1980).
18. R. A. Burgelman, "Managing the Internal Corporate Venturing Process," *Sloan Management Review,* Winter 1984, pp. 33–48.
19. A. D. Chandler, *Strategy and Structure* (Cambridge, MA: MIT Press, 1962).
20. J. D. W. Morecroft, "The Feedback Viewpoint in Business Strategy for the 1980s" (MIT, Sloan School of Management, Systems Dynamics Memorandum D–3560, April 1984).
21. J. P. Killing, "How to Make a Global Joint Venture Work," *Harvard Business Review,* May–June 1982, pp. 120–127.
22. J. D. Hlavacek, B. H. Dovey, and J. J. Biondo, "Tie Small Business Technology to Marketing Power," *Harvard Business Review,* January–February 1977; and Roberts (1980).
23. "Acquiring the Expertise but Not the Company," *Business Week,* June 25, 1984, pp. 142B–142F; and "The Age of Alliances," *Inc.,* February 1984, pp. 68–69.
24. Roberts (1980).

25. R. P. Greenthal and J. A. Larson, "Venturing into Venture Capital," *Business Horizons,* September–October 1982, pp. 18–23.
26. G. F. Hardymon, M. J. Denvino, and M. S. Salter, "When Corporate Venture Capital Doesn't Work," *Harvard Business Review,* May–June 1983, pp. 114–120.
27. K. W. Rind, "The Role of Venture Capital in Corporate Development," *Strategic Management Journal* 2, 1981, pp. 169–180.
28. N. D. Fast, "Pitfalls of Corporate Venturing," *Research Management,* March 1981, pp. 21–24.
29. Procter & Gamble Company, *1983 Annual Report* (Cincinnati, OH: 1984), p. 5.
30. Miller (1963).
31. Gilmore and Coddington (1966).
32. W. L. Shanklin, "Strategic Business Planning: Yesterday, Today and Tomorrow," *Business Horizons,* October 1979, pp. 7–14.
33. *Business Week* (June 25, 1984); Hlavacek, Dovey, and Biondo (1977); and *Inc.* (February 1984).
34. C. A. Berry, "New Business Development in a Diversified Technological Corporation" (MIT Sloan School of Management/Engineering School Master of Science Thesis, 1983).
35. Salter and Weinhold (July–August 1978).

Chapter 11

The author gratefully acknowledges the support received from the Strategic Management Program of Stanford University's Graduate School of Business and the helpful comments made by Leonard R. Sayles, Steven C. Wheelwright, and an anonymous reviewer on an earlier version of this article. Parts of the article were presented at the Third Strategic Management Society Conference in Paris in October, 1983.

1. "DuPont: Seeking a Future in Biosciences," *Business Week,* November 24, 1980, pp. 86–98; and "General Electric: The Financial Wizards Switch Back to Technology," *Business Week,* March 16, 1981, pp. 110–114.
2. "Meet the New Lean, Mean IBM," *Fortune,* June 13, 1983, pp. 68–82.
3. "Allied after Bendix: R&D Is the Key," *Business Week,* December 12, 1983, pp. 76–86.
4. R. Biggadike, "The Risky Business of Diversification," *Harvard Business Review,* May–June 1979, p. 111.
5. N. D. Fast, "The Future of Industrial New Venture Departments," *Industrial Marketing Management* (1979), pp. 264–273.
6. E. von Hippel, "Successful and Failing Internal Corporate Ventures: An Empirical Analysis," *Industrial Marketing Management* (1977), pp. 163–174. Some of the diversity found by von Hippel, however, may be due to a somewhat unclear distinction between new product development and new business development.
7. J. R. Galbraith, "The Stages of Growth," *Journal of Business Strategy* 4 (1983), pp. 70–79.
8. J. L. Bower, *Managing the Resource Allocation Process* (Boston: Graduate School of Business Administration, Harvard University, 1970).
9. R. A. Burgelman, "Managing Innovating Systems: A Study of the Process of Internal Corporate Venturing" (unpublished doctoral dissertation, Columbia University, 1980); and R. A. Burgelman, "A Process Model of Internal Corporate Venturing in the Diversified Major Firm," *Administrative Science Quarterly,* June 1983, pp. 223–244.
10. D. A. Schon, "Champions for Radical New Inventions," *Harvard Business Review,* March–April 1963, pp. 77–86; and E. B. Roberts, "Generating Effective Corporate Innovation," *Technology Review,* October–November 1977, pp. 27–33.
11. One of the key problems encountered by Exxon Enterprises was precisely the existence of these new product development problems in the entrepreneurial ventures (Qyx, Quip, and

Vydec) it had acquired and was trying to integrate. See "What's Wrong at Exxon Enterprises," *Business Week,* August 24, 1981, p. 87.

12. The need for strategic forcing is consistent with findings suggesting that attaining large market share fast at the cost of early profitability is critical for venture survival. See Biggadike (May–June 1979).

13. Entrepreneurial activity used as insurance against environmental turbulence was first documented by R. A. Peterson and D. G. Berger, "Entrepreneurship in Organizations: Evidence from the Popular Music Industry," *Administrative Science Quarterly* 16 (1971), pp. 97–106; and R. A. Burgelman, "Corporate Entrepreneurship and Strategic Management: Insights from a Process Study," *Management Science* 29 (1983), pp. 1649–1664.

14. The importance of the middle-level manager in ICV was recognized by E. von Hippel (1977). The role of a "manager champion" or "executive champion" has also been discussed by I. Kusiatin, "The Process and Capacity for Diversification Through Internal Development" (unpublished doctoral dissertation, Harvard University, 1976); and M. A. Maidique, "Entrepreneurs, Champions, and Technological Innovation," *Sloan Management Review,* Winter 1980, pp. 59–76.

15. Biggadike (May–June 1979).

16. Fast (1979).

17. These frictions are discussed in more detail in R. A. Burgelman, "Managing the New Venture Division: Research Findings and the Implications for Strategic Management," *Strategic Management Journal,* in press.

18. An overview of different forms of corporate venturing is provided in E. B. Roberts, "New Ventures for Corporate Growth," *Harvard Business Review,* July–August 1980, pp. 132–142. A design framework is suggested in R. A. Burgelman, "Designs for Corporate Entrepreneurship in Established Firms," *California Management Review,* in press.

19. Some firms seem to have developed the position of corporate historian. See "Historians Discover the Pitfalls of Doing the Story of a Firm," *Wall Street Journal,* December 27, 1983. Without underestimating the difficulties such a position is likely to hold, one can imagine the possibility of structuring it in such a way that the relevant data would be recorded. Another instance, possibly a board-appointed committee, could periodically interpret these data along the lines suggested.

20. Some companies have developed innovative types of arrangements to structure their relationships with internal entrepreneurs. Other companies have established procedures to help would-be entrepreneurs with their decision to stay with the company or to spin off. Control Data Corporation, for example, has established an Employee Entrepreneurial Advisory Office.

Chapter 12

This article is based in part on research carried out with support from the U.S. Department of Transportation under contract No. DOT–TSC 1355. It has benefited from the comments and advice of Drs. Richard John and Bruce Rubinger of the Transportation Systems Center, DOT. However, the authors are solely responsible for all views and conclusions expressed in the article.

1. "The Innovation Recession," *Time,* October 2, 1978, p. 57.

2. A. J. Large, "Carter Will Turn to Executives for Advice on Ways to Foster Innovation by Industry," *Wall Street Journal,* September 14, 1978, p. 12.

3. R. A. Leone, "The Real Costs of Regulation," *Harvard Business Review,* November–December 1977, p. 57.

4. W. M. Capron, ed., *Technological Change in Regulated Industries* (Washington, DC: The Brookings Institution, 1971).

5. *Science Indicators* (Report of the National Science Board, National Science Foundation, 1975).
6. Capron (1971).
7. *Ibid.,* p. 11.
8. *Ibid.,* p. 206.
9. *Ibid.,* p. 12.
10. The term *product* also includes services.
11. K. J. Arrow, "Economic Welfare and the Allocation of Resources for Invention," in *The Rate and Direction of Inventive Activity: Economic and Social Factors* (Princeton, NJ: Princeton University Press, 1962), pp. 609–626; and R. R. Nelson, "The Allocation of Research and Development Resources: Some Problems of Public Policy," in *Defense, Science, and Public Policy,* E. Mansfield, ed. (New York: Norton, 1968), pp. 192–209.
12. "Interactions of Science and Technology in the Innovative Process" (National Science Foundation Report NSF BCL–C–567–73, Battelle Institute, Columbus, Ohio, March 1973).
13. A. H. Rubenstein and J. E. Ettlie, "Analysis of Federal Stimuli to the Development of New Technology by Suppliers to Automobile Manufacturers" (Final Report to the U.S. Department of Transportation, March 1977).
14. J. Utterback and A. Murray, "The Influence of Defense Procurement and Sponsorship of R&D on the Development of the Civilian Electronics Industry" (MIT Center for Policy Alternatives Report D–5, June 1977).
15. W. S. Baer, L. L. Johnson, and E. W. Merrow, "Analysis of Federally Funded Demonstration Projects: Final Report" (RAND Corporation R–1926–DOC, April 1976).
16. Definition used in the RAND report, Volume 2, p. 30.
17. *Ibid.,* p. 27.
18. *Ibid.,* p. 28.
19. K. E. Knight, "A Study of Technological Innovation: The Evolution of Digital Computers" (Ph.D. diss., Carnegie Institute of Technology, 1963); R. Miller and D. Sawers, *The Technical Development of Modern Aviation* (New York: Praeger, 1970); and J. E. Tilton, *International Diffusion of Technology: The Case of Semiconductors* (Washington, DC: The Brookings Institution, 1971).
20. W. R. McLaurin, *Invention and Innovation in the Radio Industry* (New York: Macmillan, 1949).
21. W. J. Abernathy, *The Productivity Dilemma: Roadblock to Innovation in the Automobile Industry* (Baltimore, MD: Johns Hopkins University Press, 1978).
22. H. D. Jacoby, J. D. Steinbruner et al., *Clearing the Air: Federal Policy on Automotive Emissions Control* (Cambridge, MA: Ballinger Publishing, 1973).
23. Baer, Johnson, and Merrow (April 1976).

Chapter 13

1. See R. H. Hayes and W. J. Abernathy, "Managing Our Way to Economic Decline," *Harvard Business Review,* July–August 1980, pp. 67–77.
2. This model is similar to the approaches developed by V. A. Thompson, "Bureaucracy and Innovation," *Administrative Science Quarterly,* June 1965, pp. 1–20; J. Q. Wilson, "Innovation in Organizations: Notes toward a Theory," in *Approaches to Organizational Design,* J. D. Thompson, ed. (Pittsburgh: University of Pittsburgh Press, 1966); J. D. Hlavacek, "Toward More Successful Venture Management," *Journal of Marketing,* October 1974, pp. 56–60; and M. A. Maidique, "Entrepreneurs, Champions, and Technological Innovation," *Sloan Management Review,* Winter 1980, pp. 59–76.
3. For a more detailed discussion of roles, see D. A. Schon, "Champions for Radical New Inventions," *Harvard Business Review,* March–April 1963, pp. 77–86; E. G. Roberts and A. R.

Fusfeld, "Staffing the Innovative Technology-Based Organization," *Sloan Management Review,* Spring 1981, pp. 19–34; and Maidique (Winter 1980).

4. R. D. Buzzell and F. D. Wiersema, "Successful Share-Building Strategies," *Harvard Business Review,* January–February 1981, pp. 135–144.

5. M. A. Maidique and R. H. Hayes, "The Art of High-Technology Management," *Sloan Management Review,* Winter 1984, pp. 17–31.

6. C. M. Crawford, "Marketing Research and the New Product Failure Rate," *Journal of Marketing,* April 1977, pp. 51–61; B. Abrams, "Top Executives View Marketers as Myopic and Unimaginative," *Wall Street Journal,* October 9, 1980, p. 29; J. May, "Marketing Research: Illuminating Neglected Areas," *Journal of Market Research Society,* July 1981, pp. 127–136; and T. J. Peters and R. H. Waterman, Jr., *In Search of Excellence* (New York: Harper & Row, 1982), pp. 156–199.

7. Thompson (June 1965); R. M. Hill and J. D. Hlavacek, "The Venture Team: A New Concept in Marketing Organization," *Journal of Marketing,* July 1972, pp. 44–50; and E. B. Roberts, "New Ventures for Corporate Growth," *Harvard Business Review,* July–August 1980, pp. 134–142.

8. See J. Greenwald, "The Colossus That Works," *Time,* July 11, 1983, pp. 44–54.

9. Peters and Waterman (1982), pp. 306–316.

10. J. B. Quinn, "Technological Innovation, Entrepreneurship, and Strategy," *Sloan Management Review,* Spring 1979, pp. 19–30; and R. J. Harris, Jr., "The Skunk Works: Hush-Hush Projects Often Emerge There," *Wall Street Journal,* October 13, 1980, p. 1.

11. R. M. Adams, "How 3M Builds Idea-Nurturing Work-Climate," *Marketing Times,* March–April 1978, pp. 13–14.

Index